THE
ULTIMATE GUIDE TO
HOMEBREWING

Inspiring | Educating | Creating | Entertaining

Brimming with creative inspiration, how-to projects, and useful information to enrich your everyday life, Quarto Knows is a favorite destination for those pursuing their interests and passions. Visit our site and dig deeper with our books into your area of interest: Quarto Creates, Quarto Cooks, Quarto Homes, Quarto Lives, Quarto Drives, Quarto Explores, Quarto Gifts, or Quarto Kids.

© 2020 Quarto Publishing Group USA Inc.

First Published in 2020 by The Harvard Common Press, an imprint of The Quarto Group, 100 Cummings Center, Suite 265-D, Beverly, MA 01915, USA. T (978) 282-9590 F (978) 283-2742 QuartoKnows.com

The Harvard Common Press titles are also available at discount for retail, wholesale, promotional, and bulk purchase. For details, contact the Special Sales Manager by email at specialsales@quarto.com or by mail at The Quarto Group, Attn: Special Sales Manager, 100 Cummings Center, Suite 265-D, Beverly, MA 01915, USA.

23 22 21 20 19   1 2 3 4 5

ISBN: 978-1-55832-983-6

Digital edition published in 2020
eISBN: 978-1-55832-984-3

Library of Congress Cataloging-in-Publication Data available

The content in this book appeared in the previously published titles:
The Brewer's Apprentice (Quarry Books, 2011)
Craft Beer for the Homebrewer (Voyageur Press, 2014)
Extreme Brewing, A Deluxe Edition (Quarry Books, 2012)
The Home Brewer's Guide to Vintage Beer (Quarry Books, 2014)
Gardening for the Homebrewer (Voyageur Press, 2015)

Design: Burge Agency
Cover Image: Shutterstock

Printed in China

THE
ULTIMATE GUIDE TO
HOMEBREWING
TECHNIQUES AND RECIPES
TO GET BREWING TODAY

THE EDITORS OF
THE HARVARD COMMON PRESS

HARVARD
COMMON
PRESS

CONTENTS

CHAPTER 1
THE BASICS OF BREWING

Brewers use only four ingredients to make a basic beer: water, barley, hops, and yeast. Each part is irreplaceable and essential to the process, so understanding its role and what it brings teaches you how to modify, tweak, and use the ingredients to create nearly any beer, wild or mild, you can dream up.

INGREDIENTS

WATER

Water constitutes 90 to 95 percent of a beer, so always use a clean source for brewing. Most tap water is acceptable as long as it's run through a carbon filter prior to brewing. Advanced brewers learn to adjust their water to suit their beer.

MALT

Malted grains bring color, aroma, and flavor to a beer, but most importantly, they are the fuel for creating alcohol. Malt houses let grains such as barley and wheat germinate and begin to grow, creating starch. Then, they dry the grains and stop the process, leaving a large amount of starch. The majority of any beer will use a pale malt (called base malt). Darker beer adds "specialty grains" that are roasted to different temperatures and impart various flavors and color.

New brewers often use liquid or dried malt extract to simplify the brewing process. This provides the same maltose (sugar) grains impart for brewing. While extracts are just as fermentable, their flavors can be inconsistent and lack the subtlety and complexity of true barley or wheat.

HOPS

These dried green flowers contribute bitterness, aroma, and flavor to a beer. A 5-gallon (19 L) batch of homebrew might need only an ounce (28 g) of dried hop pellets to balance a sweeter amber ale, while a hop-centric India pale ale could use up to 8 ounces (225 g) or more.

YEAST

This microorganism is the engine behind beer. It consumes sugar derived from the malt starch to make alcohol. There are hundreds of different brewing yeast strains, each working at different temperatures and producing varying flavors. German wheat beers (hefeweizens), for example, owe much of their spicy character to their specialized yeast.

UNDERSTANDING GRAVITY, CALCULATING ABV

When the sugars from your mash dissolve into the hot water, the liquid (your wort) becomes denser. As yeast ferments that sugar out, converting it to alcohol, the beer becomes less dense. By subtracting the second, third, or final gravity reading from the first, and then accounting for the density of alcohol (multiply by 1.31), you can easily calculate a beer's alcohol content. Starting gravity—final gravity x 1.31 x 100 = alcohol by volume

SUPPLIES

These are the supplies necessary to brew beer from grain to glass like a pro. Beginners should feel no shame in skipping the mash and lauter by adding malt extract to the kettle, but these are the tools of the trade for homebrewers ready to emulate their favorite brewmasters.

MASH TUN

Your crushed grains and hot water are combined in the mash tun to produce sugar during the first step of homebrewing. The two most common options are insulated coolers and metal mash kettles. Coolers, like the ones in which you would store beer at a party, hold the mash at a constant temperature with minimal work, but it's difficult to raise the mash temperature if needed. Mash kettles are heavy-duty pots, usually fitted with a spigot and false bottom for lautering.

LAUTER TUN

Often the mash and lauter tun are the same thing. A lauter tun is a large container with a screen or false bottom under the grains that allows the wort to drain out.

BREW KETTLE

Any large metal stock pot will do—copper, stainless steel, or aluminum—as long as it's big enough. Your brew kettle should have 1 to 2 gallons (3.8 to 7.6 L) more capacity than the liquid in it. Extract brewers use 5-gallon (19 L) pots, and all-grain brewers use at least 7-gallon (26.7 L) pots.

A COMMERCIAL BREWERY BREW DECK MAY LOOK ENDLESSLY COMPLICATED BUT FOLLOWS NEARLY ALL THE SAME PROCESSES AS A 5-GALLON (19 L) HOMEBREWERY.

WORT CHILLERS

These copper or stainless coils have an inlet (and outlet) for tap water to run through the coil. When placed in hot wort, the water-cooled coil quickly drops the wort temperature.

FERMENTOR

Brewers need a primary fermentor, usually a food-grade plastic bucket, and then a secondary fermentor, typically a glass carboy for aging. The bucket is easy to use and clean, but it is also porous, letting small amounts of oxygen in, making it a bad candidate for aging beer.

BOTTLING BUCKET

This plastic bucket with a spigot allows you to mix your beer with priming sugar and then easily dispense into bottles.

CAPPER

This simple device crimps bottle caps and seals your beer.

AUTOSIPHON

It's not a necessity, but this makes transferring beer from one container to another a breeze.

HYDROMETER AND REFRACTOMETER

These devices will tell you how much sugar is in your beer, indicating how much can be fermented, and later, how much has been fermented out.

THE BREWING PROCESS: AN OVERVIEW

Brewing is a simple process that's easily complicated. And this book assumes a basic understanding of the principles that turn barley starch and hop flowers into pale ales and porters. These steps provide a basic reference for the steps to reach a finished (and delicious) beer, but for a more in-depth look at brewing fundamentals, read Charlie Papazian's *The Complete Joy of Homebrewing* and John Palmer's *How to Brew*.

1. MASH AND LAUTER THE GRAINS

The first step on the road to homebrewing is mashing the malted grains. You need sugar to ferment beer, and this is where you create it. The mash is a mixture of crushed grains and hot water that converts the starch in barley, wheat, or other grains into sugar (which yeast will turn into alcohol). Barley has two enzymes (proteins that encourage chemical reactions) that break starch down into sugar when they're within particular temperature ranges. Homebrewers typically mix their grains with hot water and hold their mash between 145°F and 158°F (63°C and 70°C) for at least 20 minutes.

2. LAUTER

Once enzymes have converted most of the starch to sugar, drain the liquid out in a process called "lautering." Add additional hot water (around 170°F [77°C]) to help flush out the sugar. The first couple gallons (liters) of liquid drained out should be gently poured back over the grains. Water clarity should improve, and small bits of husk will stop coming out. This recirculation creates a filter to keep grain out of the wort. In total, you should have 5.5 to 6 gallons (20.9 to 22.7 L) of wort to create a 5-gallon (19 L) batch of beer.

3. BOIL

Boiling wort sanitizes the liquid and absorbs bitter acids from the hops. The longer hops are boiled, the more bitterness they add. The later the hops are added, the more flavor and aroma they infuse. After 60 minutes, cool the wort as quickly as possible to prevent infection by wild bacteria. Homebrew stores sell wort chillers that cool batches to room temperature in 20 minutes or less, but placing the kettle in an ice bath for 30 to 60 minutes also works.

4. INOCULATION

When the wort is at least below 100°F (38°C), and ideally around 80°F (27°C), you'll mix in oxygen and add the yeast (higher temperatures kill brewing yeast). The easiest way to aerate and add oxygen is by using an aeration stone. Another method is to pour the wort back and forth between the fermentor and kettle until there's a tall head of foam. You can also transfer the wort to the fermentor, seal the top, and shake it for 45 seconds. Before you add the yeast and seal the fermentor, measure the gravity (density) of your beer with a hydrometer or refractometer. This tells you how much sugar is in the wort. For reference, a beer that is aiming to hit 5 percent alcohol by volume (ABV) will have a starting gravity around 1.052. Finally, add the yeast and close the top of the fermentor. Use an airlock to allow CO_2, a byproduct of fermentation, to escape. Always use a fermentor that can accommodate your batch size plus some space for foaming during fermentation.

5. FERMENTATION

Every yeast has a particular temperature range for its ideal fermentation, but most beers ferment well at room temperature, which is around 70°F (21°C). After ten days, most of the sugar will have been converted into alcohol. You can take a second gravity reading to see how much sugar has fermented. Beer yeast leaves about a quarter of the total sugar behind (unlike a dry wine, for example). A common beer will have a final gravity around 1.012 to 1.016.

6. CONDITION

Conditioning acts like a filter. After the first (primary) fermentation, almost all the alcohol has been created, but letting the beer sit for at least two weeks will allow the yeast to stay active and literally clean itself up. With a siphon, transfer the beer to a conditioning fermentor, leaving the layer of yeast behind in the bottom of the primary. Tiny hops, barley, and yeast particles will also slowly sink to the bottom of the conditioning fermentor, clarifying the appearance and further improving the flavor.

7. BOTTLING

After your beer is fermented, conditioned, and tasting satisfactory (that one's up to you), the final step is to bottle. By adding a little (about 1 ounce per gallon [7 g per liter]) sugar to your beer and sealing it, the yeast will create both a small amount of alcohol and enough CO_2 to carbonate the brew. Five gallons (19 L) of beer needs about two cases of bottles, plus a six-pack (54 total), but don't be surprised if you lose beer along the way when transferring from the kettle and then again to the conditioning fermentor. To bottle, boil the priming sugar in a cup (240 ml) of water for 15 minutes to sanitize it and then cool the liquid and add it to the beer. Then, transfer to a bottling bucket with a spigot near the bottom, add the priming sugar, and siphon each beer individually into bottles. Cap the beer, let it sit at room temperature for 2 weeks, and then enjoy. Congratulations, you've made beer.

BARLEY TO BEER, SIMPLIFIED

Select your grains and crush them (most homebrew shops will do this for you).

For every pound (455 g) of grain, mix in 1 to 2 quarts (946 ml to 1.9 L) of hot water, creating the mash.

Hold the mash at a temperature between 145°F and 158°F (63°C and 70°C) for 30 to 60 minutes.

Add sparge water and drain out the liquid (now called the wort).

Heat the wort to a boil and hold there for 60 minutes.

Add hops: 1) at the start of the boil for bitterness, or 2) within the final 30 minutes for aroma and flavor.

Cool the wort to below 80°F (27°C) and transfer to the fermentor.

Shake the closed fermentor vigorously and then add yeast. Ferment the wort for 10 days as it becomes beer.

Siphon the beer to a second fermentor and age it for at least 2 weeks.

Add priming sugar (0.5 to 1 ounce per gallon [4 to 7 grams per liter]) and then bottle the beer.

Let the beer carbonate for 2 weeks and then enjoy.

RECIPE STANDARDS

RECIPE STANDARDIZATION

Batch size: 5 gallons (19 L)

Extract efficiency: 65% (One pound [455 g] of two-row malt with a potential extract value of 1.037 in 1 gallon [3.8 L] of water yields wort of 1.024.). In chapter 4, extract efficiency is 72%.

Extract values for malt extract:

LME (liquid malt extract) = 1.033 to 1.037
- -
DME (dry malt extract) = 1.045

Potential extract for grains:

Two-row base malt = 1.037 to 1.038
- -
Six-row base malt = 1.035
- -
Wheat malt = 1.037
- -
Munich malt = 1.035
- -
Vienna malt = 1.035
- -
Crystal malt = 1.033 to 1.035
- -
Chocolate malt = 1.034
- -
Dark-roasted grains = 1.024 to 1.026
- -
Flaked corn and rice = 1.037 to 1.038

Hops: The IBU (international bitterness units) is calculated on 25% utilization for a one-hour boil of hop pellets at SG of 1.050.

Process: The majority of the recipes in this book are extract recipes, which means they are brewed with malt extract as a base malt versus mashing and converting fermentable sugar from grains. This process generally takes 2 to 3 hours to perform (whereas an all-grain brew can take 4 to 6). The majority of the extract recipes in this book call for steeping crushed specialty grains in heated water, then adding malt extract, performing a partial boil, and then topping up to 5 gallons (19 L) in the fermentor with cold water. The term "extract efficiency" pertains to all-grain brewing as it depends on the mash and lautering conditions in your homebrewery. Each homebrewery will have a unique efficiency. The term refers to the value you would get from a mash if all conditions were perfect and 100% of the starch from the grains was converted into sugar.

All-grain recipes assume a 60-minute, single-infusion mash, sparge at 170°F (77 °C), a 60-minute or 90-minute boil (as indicated in each recipe), and then primary fermentation until final gravity is reached, followed by a 1-week conditioning period in a separate vessel. Deviations from this process, such as stepped mash, are indicated in the recipe instructions. Please note that the extract efficiency for the recipes in chapter 4 are calculated for 72%.

An all-grain mash separates the novices from expert homebrewers. Yes, malt extract is a good start for small kitchens and simple brewing, but once you're mashing, you're playing on the same field as professionals.

MASHING AND LAUTERING

The basic process is simple enough: Add hot water to grain, wait while the malt starch converts to sugar, and drain out the newly created sugar water to boil. Aside from being a necessary brewing step, it's an opportunity to shape and mold your beer. By adjusting the water temperature, you can make beer with the feel of a featherweight Belgian or the viscous body of a sticky imperial stout.

INTRODUCTION TO MASHING

Mashing is the first big step on the trip from grain to glass. By turning the barley starch into sugar, you've created not only fuel for your yeast to create alcohol but the base of your flavor. Here are the basic steps:

1: SELECT AND GRIND BREWING GRAINS: While malted barley is the most commonly used grain, portions of wheat, oats, and rye can be added to create different tastes and mouthfeels. Most homebrewing shops will be happy to grind your brewing grains.

2: MASH IN: Most simple beers need only a single infusion of hot water for the grains. By soaking the grains and holding them at around 153°F (67°C), enzymes in the barley will break starch down into sugar.

3: LAUTER: After most of the starch has converted, lauter, or drain, the grains from the sugar solution.

4: SPARGE: To assist the lautering, additional hot water (around 170°F [77°C]) is added to help rinse out the sugar and reach the desired brewing volume.

"Perhaps a bit of the magic of beer is that it transforms itself before our eyes. And the ultimate sleight of hand on the road to beer happens in the mash tun. Microscopic enzymes attack the barley's starch, converting it into sugars that will eventually become alcohol."

GRIST

The grind of your grain and the amount of water in the mash can further complicate your mash. Keeping a consistent grind and water-to-grain ratio will save you considerable headaches. If you mill your grain at home, know that too coarse of a grind will prevent the starch from getting wet while also insulating it from the hot mash water. If you grind too fine and have a mix of dust in your grist, you risk clogging your mash and extracting tannins from the grain.

For your water-to-grain ratio, 1 quart (946 ml) to 1 pound (455 g) of grain is considered thick and 2 quarts (1.9 L) to 1 pound (455 g) is thin. A thicker mash protects those enzymes from degrading, allowing them to work longer. If you use a thinner mash, your extract is more soluble and washes out of the grain better. A ratio of 1.25 quarts (1.2 L) per 1 pound (455 g) is considered a safe, efficient middle-ground ratio.

MASHING STEPS

Your average homebrewed beer gets all the diastolic conversion power (enzyme activity) it needs from an hour-long mash somewhere between 146°F and 158°F (63°C and 70°C). For a thinner beer, such as a Belgian ale, aim for the lower end of the scale. For a chewy beer with less fermentable sugar, mash hotter, and for something like an everyday pale ale, shoot for 153°F or 154°F (67°C or 68°C). Brewing tradition calls for additional steps to lower pH, increase starch solubility, and break down proteins and beta-glucan. However, today's base malt is packed full of enzymes and bred for lower protein levels. Furthermore, not being constrained within the restraints of Reinheitsgebot, Germany's restrictive brewing purity law, lowering the mash pH is as easy as dropping a teaspoon of lactic acid into the mash tun. If you feel like going the extra mile for the sake of tradition, look at the table (opposite).

NOTE: For most brewing purposes, the only additional step worth noting is the beta-glucan rest at 98°F to 113°F (37°C to 45°C) for 20 minutes. If you're using large amounts of rye, oatmeal, or unmalted grains, this rest breaks down the gummy beta-glucan molecules that would otherwise create a stuck mash.

MASH AND LAUTER TUNS

Professional brewers use insulated copper and stainless steel vessels, complete with stirring rakes and steam heat. Homebrew mash tuns, while decidedly less glamorous, are just as effective. The most common option for homebrewers is an insulated cooler with a false bottom or screen filter to drain out the wort. This cooler works as a combination mash and lauter tun, saving you the hassle and mess of transferring the hot, sticky grains to a second vessel to sparge.

When you mash in a cooler, your only challenge is hitting the mash temperature. You can preheat your cooler with a quart (946 ml) of hot water, but because your grains are at room temperature, they'll lower your strike water temperature as much as 20°F (11°C) depending on how much water you add. A thick mash on a cold day will need that extra 20°F (11°C), but a thin mash might only need an extra 10°F (6°C). Typically, though, a thick mash needs about 16°F (9°C) from the strike water.

Brewing software, such as BeerSmith and many online calculators, can give you a better estimate of strike water temperatures to begin, but it is best to take notes on how your mash tun reacts so you can calibrate future batches. Should you miss your target mash temperature, don't fret. Adding cold water to the tun or leaving the tun lid open will drop the temperature, while adding a quart (946 ml) of boiling water will raise it. Monitor the mash temperature closely with an instant-read thermometer.

LAUTER AND SPARGE

Lautering is the process of removing liquid from the grains. The sparge is a step in lautering that flushes converted sugars out of the grains and into the brew kettle. Further, you don't mash with the final amount of water that you'll boil. The sparge water will fill the gap to reach your desired batch size (usually 5 gallons, or 19 L). Preheat your sparge water to 168°F to 180°F (76°C to 82°C) to stop the diastolic conversion of your mash and optimize wort flow without extracting astringent tannins from the grain husks. Plan to use a lower temperature, however, if you want to continue the starch conversion throughout the lautering. Stop once you've hit your boil volume or a specific gravity of 1.012 (3 Plato) with your runoff.

ADDITIONAL REST STEPS

REST	TEMPERATURE	TIME (MINUTES)	BENEFIT
Dough In	95°F to 113°F (35°C to 45°C)	20	This initial step mixes the starches, enzymes, and water. It raises efficiency by a few points. To lower the pH, extend this rest to at least 2 hours.
Protein	113°F to 131°F (45°C to 55°C)	20 to 30	If you have poorly modified malt or a large share of unmalted grain, this will break down protein that would otherwise add a haze and additional body to the beer.
Beta-Glucan	95°F to 113°F (35°C to 45°C)	15 to 20	This breaks down the sticky beta-glucans that come with rye, oatmeal, and unmalted grains.
Beta-Amylase	131°F to 150°F (55°C to 66°C)	15 to 60	Beta-amylase produces maltose and is the main contributor in starch conversion.
Alpha-Amylase	154°F to 162°F (68°C to 72°C)	20 to 30	Some maltose is created, but so are unfermentable sugars.
Mash Out	170°F to 175°F (77°C to 79°C)	5 to 20	This final step ends the enzymatic activity.

A MASH FOR THE AGES: DECOCTION

If you want to make a truly old-school brew, start with a decoction mash. This age-old European brewing technique predates thermometers yet achieves the same processes of a modern multiple-step mash. Instead of adding hot water or heating the entire mash up to the next rest, brewers pull off and boil up to a third of the mash in a second vessel. Boiling aided with starch breakdown, and when the boiled mash was returned to the main vessel, it raised the overall temperature to the next rest.

The boiling caramelizes sugars and combines sugars and amino acids to create sweet melanoidins, flavors lost with a step mash. For this reason, many German brewers still swear by a full four-step triple decoction. Fortunately, you can get similar results at home from a single decoction.

MASH: Begin with a standard mash at 148°F to 158°F (64°C to 70°C) to convert your starch for at least 30 minutes.

PULL: Remove a third of the mash to a pot and gradually heat to a boilover 10 to 15 minutes.

STIR: As you reach a boil, stir the mash often and don't leave it unattended. You need to keep the decoction at a boil, but not scorch grains on the bottom of the pot.

MASH OUT: After boiling for 15 to 30 minutes, return the decoction to the mash. It should raise the temperature to about 167°F (75°C) and end the enzymatic activity.

BREWING TERM: *REINHEITSGEBOT*

In 1516, the Bavarian government created strict standards for brewing beer to maintain quality, as well as protect wheat and rye demand for bakers. The *Reinheitsgebot* famously limited beer to three ingredients—water, the barley, and hops (yeast was centuries away from being identified). The law was later adopted by all of Germany. It is still followed by brewers today. Some see it as a statement of purity; adventurous brewers see it as an archaic and unnecessary restriction.

BREWING TERM: PHENOL

Phenol is a flavor and aroma compound created by yeast from the ferulic acid in malt and, to a small extent, from hops. Most yeast strains are bred to avoid phenol production, but wheat beer and some Belgian strains create it on purpose. When phenol unexpectedly occurs in beer, it can be a sign of wild yeast contamination.

BITTERING HOPS

INTRODUCTION TO HOPS

After mashing, lautering, and sparging, brewers heat up their kettles of wort. Once the wort reaches a boil, they add hops to create bitterness in a beer. The longer hops are boiled, the more bitterness is added. Hops boiled for more than 30 minutes will contribute little flavor or aroma; however, the variety of hops used for bittering can change how the bitterness feels and how much is contributed. Just like some apples are more tart, with higher acid levels, hops with higher levels of bittering acids provide more kick.

A BRIEF HISTORY OF HOPS

The green, sticky harbingers of bitterness are a relatively recent addition to beer when you consider the beverage dates back to the dawn of civilization. The first records of hops cultivation come from Germany's Hallertau region in the year 736. Monastery (where else?) statutes from the eighth century appear to be the first records of using hops for beer. Until hops were adopted worldwide in the nineteenth century, brewers often used a mix of bitter herbs, such as bog myrtle, ground ivy, mugwort, and yarrow—called gruit—to balance the malt sweetness. Not only did most drinkers prefer the taste of hops, but the antibacterial nature of hops helped brewers ward off beer spoilage.

Like most agricultural commodities, today's hops have been bred and farmed to the point where they barely resemble those used even a century ago. The alpha acid contents of even the weakest hops today are many times more potent than both their wild and farmed ancestors. The last several decades have seen an explosion in the number of hop varieties thanks in large part to university research farms. So now whether you're a megabrewer looking for an efficient, super high-alpha acid hop or a homebrewer in search of a spicy, fruity American-European hybrid, there's a hop for you.

ALPHA ACIDS AND UTILIZATION

Within the hop flower (technically called a catkin) are small yellow sacks of oils. Much like barley has starch hidden within the husk, hops have alpha acids. In short, this is the good stuff.

The amount of these bitter acids you can extract from hops is a balance of boil time and wort sugar content. The greater the gravity of your wort, the less alpha acid in your beer. And the longer you boil, the more acids pull out. The alpha acids in hops isomerize during the boil, meaning the molecular shape changes, and they become water-soluble, sticking to your wort.

HOPS AWAITING THE FALL HARVEST.

Your average beer (specific gravity [SG] 1.040 to 1.060) will be able to utilize between 20 and 25 percent of the alpha acids over a 60-minute boil. Bumping up to 90 minutes will increase the utilization by only a point or two. Using hop plug or whole-leaf hops in place of the standard pelletized hops will also lower your overall utilization by about 10 percent due to the decreased surface area compared to a dissolved pellet.

COHUMULONE

There are three different alpha acids in hops: humulone, adhumulone, and cohumulone. It's unclear what humulone and adhumulone contribute beyond bitterness, but cohumulone levels control the type of bitterness. A beer hopped with low cohumulone-level hops will have a clean bitterness, while hops with a high level have harsher, biting bitterness.

KNOW YOUR BITTERING HOPS

Creating a beer with low or high IBUs and smooth or harsh bitterness comes down to the type of hops you use. Keep in mind that hops experience some variation every year based on growing conditions. Use these tables as a guide when formulating a recipe and then find out the precise numbers from your homebrew supply store.

CLEAN BITTERING HOPS	ALPHA ACIDS (%)	COHUMULONE (% OF AA)
U.S. Horizon	11 to 13	16 to 19
U.S. Simcoe	12 to 14	15 to 20
UK Challenger	6.5 to 8.5	20 to 25
Amarillo	8 to 11	21 to 24
U.S. Crystal	3.5 to 5.5	20 to 26
U.S. Glacier	5.5	11 to 13
U.S. Golding	4 to 5	20 to 25
U.S. Hallertau	3.5 to 5.5	18 to 24
U.S. Mt. Hood	5 to 8	22 to 23
U.S. Northern Brewer	8 to 10	20 to 30
U.S. Nugget	12 to 14	20 to 30
U.S. Santiam	5 to 7	22 to 24
U.S. Tettnang	4 to 5	20 to 25
U.S. Vanguard	5.5 to 6	14 to 16
German Hallertau	3.5 to 5.5	17 to 24
German Hersbrucker	3 to 5.5	19 to 25
German Magnum	12 to 14	24 to 25
German Select	4 to 6	21 to 25
UK Kent Golding	4 to 5.5	20 to 25

MEDIUM BITTERING HOPS	ALPHA ACIDS (%)	COHUMULONE (% OF AA)
U.S. Ahtanum	5.7 to 6.3	30 to 35
U.S. Centennial	9.5 to 11.5	29 to 30
U.S. Chinook	12 to 14	29 to 34
U.S. Columbus	14 to 16	30 to 35
U.S. Fuggle	4 to 5.5	25 to 32
U.S. Liberty	3 to 5	24 to 30
U.S. Magnum	12 to 14	24 to 28
U.S. Millennium	15.5	30
U.S. Perle	7 to 9.5	27 to 32
U.S./Czech Saaz	3 to 4.5	24 to 28
U.S. Sterling	6 to 9	22 to 28
U.S. Warrior	15 to 17	24
U.S. Willamette	4 to 6	30 to 35
French Strisselspalt	3 to 5	20 to 25
German Northern Brewer	7 to 10	28 to 33
German Perle	6 to 8	25 to 32
German Spalt	4 to 5	23 to 28
German Tettnang	3.5 to 5.5	23 to 29
German Tradition	5 to 7	26 to 29
Styrian Golding	4.5 to 6	25 to 30
UK First Gold	6.5 to 8.5	31 to 36
UK Fuggle	4 to 5.5	23 to 30
UK Northdown	7.5 to 9.5	24 to 30
UK Progress	5 to 7	25 to 30
UK Target	9.5 to 12.5	29 to 35

HARSH BITTERING HOPS	ALPHA ACIDS (%)	COHUMULONE (% OF AA)
U.S. Brewer's Gold	8 to 10	40 to 48
U.S. Cascade	4.5 to 7	33 to 40
U.S. Cluster	5.5 to 8.5	36 to 42
U.S. Galena	12 to 14	38 to 42
U.S. Newport	13.5 to 17	36 to 38
German Brewer's Gold	5.5 to 6.5	40 to 48
NZ Hallertau	7 to 9	35
NZ Pacific Gem	14 to 16	39
AU Pride of Ringwood	7 to 10	33 to 39

Hops are the balancing weights in beer. Unlike cider, mead, or wine, ales and lagers don't ferment dry. The residual sugar left behind would turn every pint into a sweet, malty dessert without the addition of bittering hops for balance.

IBU LEVELS FOR POPULAR STYLES OF BEER PER THE BEER JUDGE CERTIFICATION PROGRAM STYLE GUIDELINES

Add as much or as littler bitterness as you please—it's your beer after all—but knowing the bitterness ranges for classic beer styles can help you connect what you're tasting in your beer aisle to your homebrewery.

Style	IBU
Light American Lager	8 to 12
Classic Bohemian Pilsner	35 to 45
German Weissbier	8 to 15
English Pale Ale	30 to 50
American IPA	40 to 70+
Belgian Tripel	20 to 40
German Bock	20 to 27
American Stout	35 to 75
American Double IPA	70 to 100+

HOP BINES FRESH FROM THE FIELD IN YAKIMA VALLEY, WASHINGTON.

When picking hops, look beyond the alpha acids percentage when considering the bitterness of your final product. If you want a tongue-ripping bitterness in your pale ale, pick bittering hops with at least a 30 percent cohumulone share of the alpha acids.

INTERNATIONAL BITTERING UNITS

IBUs represent the proportion of iso-alpha acids in a beer. In a lab, a single IBU equals 1 milligram of isomerized alpha acid in 1 liter of wort. A high IBU number, however, does not guarantee a bitter beer. The perceived bitterness is a result of the balance between residual (unfermented) sugar and hops. Big, thick beers, including stouts and barleywines, require a high IBU level simply to achieve a level of balance.

At the same time, a drier pale ale with the same IBU level would feel more bitter simply because there's less sweet barley sugar to begin with.

FIRST WORT HOPPING

If you're curious enough to try something different, use first wort hopping on your next batch of hoppy beer. This old, German technique calls for an addition of hops while the wort collects in the kettle. The results of scientific studies on first wort hopping found slight increases in IBUs and flavor and aroma, with the theory that different chemical reactions happen to the hops as they steep in the roughly 140°F to 160°F (60°C to 71°C) wort. If you want to try this on your next pale ale, they recommend adding at least 30 percent of your hops to the first wort addition to notice a difference.

A DIGITAL KITCHEN SCALE IS PERFECT FOR PARSING YOUR HOP ADDITIONS.

INTERVIEW WITH
VINNIE CILURZO
OWNER, RUSSIAN RIVER BREWING CO., SANTA ROSA, CALIFORNIA, U.S.

Hopheads and IPA lovers can thank Vinnie for not only brewing the world's first double India Pale Ale, but also simply producing big, hoppy beer whether people wanted it or not. Created back when your average pale ale was still too bitter for craft beer lovers, Vinnie's Russian River Brewing Company celebrates his devotion to hops and now produces several of the world's most-sought-after IPAs.

YOUR FAMILY HAS A HISTORY IN THE BUSINESS OF FERMENTATION, BUT WITH WINE. WHY BEER?

After high school, I moved to San Diego and started homebrewing with my roommates. Even though the first batch was terrible, probably near undrinkable, I knew I wanted to continue on. And I liked the idea of being able to turn a batch in, say, 3 weeks instead of wine, which can take a year or two or even more. I loved that if you didn't get it quite right, you had another opportunity to brew and knock out another batch. Things weren't being dictated by season.

Eventually, I moved back to the winery and started working, and that's when I really got into homebrewing, in 1989. Down in the basement of the winery was where I did most of my early experimentation that still carried on into what we do today.

SO THAT LED TO OPENING YOUR OWN BREWERY, THE BLIND PIG.

Yes, that was in 1994. I had two other business partners, but I was the brewing side. I was there 3 years, then ducked out. They kept going a couple more years before they shut it down.

In 1997, [my wife] Natalie and I came up to Santa Rosa. Neither of us had jobs or a place to stay. We had a couple of leads and that was it. We got hired by Korbel to start Russian River Brewery in 1997. In 2003, they decided to get out of the beer business, so we bought the name and the brewery, closed for a year, and then reopened as a brewpub.

YOU MAY HAVE BREWED THE FIRST DOUBLE IPA ON THE PLANET.

The Blind Pig IPA was definitely a straight-up IPA and there weren't a lot of IPAs being made at the time, particularly in bottles. Rubicon was making one at their pub. Vince and Gina Marsaglia were making their first IPA at their Pizza Port brewpub.

THE SWAMIS IPA.

Yeah, and as a bright-eyed, fell-off-the-turnip-truck homebrewer turning pro, I didn't know how to bump a recipe up or take a homebrew from a 5-gallon (19 L) batch and turn it into seven barrels. I still remember Vince just giving me their entire recipe for the Swamis to use as a reference.

BUT YOU BREWED THE FIRST DOUBLE IPA AT BLIND PIG.

It was the first beer we made at Blind Pig, called Inaugural Ale. We took what was going to be our regular IPA recipe and literally doubled the hops on it and brought the alcohol up a little bit. Everything was all-malt at the time—we didn't use any sugar—which is something we use a lot of now in our double IPAs.

We actually let it dry-hop for a year and then released it. Our second year, we started brewing it on the spot. Back then, those beers were way more bitter than they are now, comparing what I remember the anniversary beers to be, compared to our Pliny the Elder beer. It's got more roundness to it, more malt foundation, a little more balance.

THE PIZZA PORT STILL SERVES UP ITS INFLUENTIAL SWAMIS IPA.

THE ANNIVERSARY IPA HAD SOME HARSHER BITTERNESS.

As someone put it, it was like licking the rust off a tin can. That definitely was very true of those beers. One of these days, I'm going to have to break out the recipes and rebrew it. I think a part of those beers at Blind Pig can never be re-created because of the equipment we were using.

YEAH, YOU HAVE TO GET YOURSELF SOME PLASTIC FERMENTORS.

Well, that too, but the kettle was so inefficient, and then the utilization was so poor, that you'd have to pour gobs of hops in to achieve any sort of bitterness. When you did that, you were obviously also extracting all sorts of flavor from the hops.

THERE HAD TO BE MORE TO THE VISION THAN SEEING VINCE'S SWAMIS RECIPE. WHAT ON EARTH CAUSED YOU TO MAKE A BEER THAT IS JUST SO HUGELY BITTER?

I was homebrewing our Blind Pig IPA recipe for a long time, taking it to the homebrew club in Temecula and the SoCal Homebrewers Festival. I was getting a lot of great remarks for it. When we looked at the market, there were pale ales, but we kind of wanted to do something different and the IPA was the flavor we liked. For the anniversary beer, the double IPA—that was purely because we thought the equipment and the plastic fermentors might not yield something that was sellable on the first batch. So I thought we should take our regular IPA recipe, double the hops on it, and the idea was not only would we get this super, over-the-top hoppy beer, but also that hops act as a natural preservative. Really, I didn't know any better, but that's still how we all operate.

BREWING LEGEND: PIZZA PORT

In 1987, siblings Vince and Gina Marsaglia bought up a struggling restaurant outside San Diego called Pizza Port. Vince began homebrewing in their extra storage space and began commercially brewing in 1992. With a passion for hops long before consumers would catch on, Vince helped define Southern California as the home of American IPA. The brewpub has since expanded to three additional locations along with purchasing Stone Brewing's original facility, allowing Port to launch its Lost Abbey family of Belgian-style beers.

You can no more blame craft beer drinkers for raising the IPA above all others than you can blame hops for tasting and smelling tenaciously good. When the carbonation and essential hop oils are just right, a beer's aroma can burst forth upon hitting your glass, only further whetting your appetite. You might even say that a fine hoppy beer is a tease.

MASTER OF THE HOPS
VINNIE CILURZO

TALKING ABOUT BITTERING HOPS, HOW LONG OF A BOIL DO YOU RECOMMEND?

I know a lot of brewers will cut to a 60-minute boil, but we use a 90-minute boil for blowing off all the dimethyl sulfide (DMS) that might be there in the malt. We typically have three hop additions, sometimes four. Now that we're all-steam at both our breweries, we're getting a ripping boil. The efficiencies are much higher. I know Blind Pig IPA was somewhere around 92 IBUs. Compared to how many hops it takes now on a per-barrel basis, we were probably using one and a half times as many hops back then, but in doing so we captured just a ton of hop flavor.

WHEN YOU CONSIDER YOUR BITTERING HOPS, DO YOU LOOK AT THEIR COHUMULONE CONTENT?

When I started, I didn't really think about cohumulone. A textbook will tell you that you have to use a low-cohumulone hop or you'll get a harsh bitterness. I think an IPA or double IPA benefits from a hop like Chinook, which we use as the bittering hop in Blind Pig, and the Columbus/Tomahawk/Zeus (CTZ), also used as bittering hops. These aren't low-cohumulone hops, and I like them because they add a bit of an edge to a beer and a little more personality, as opposed to only using a hop like Magnum, Warrior, or Horizon, which have a superlow cohumulone and translate to a really nice, clean bitterness.

"I thought we should take our regular IPA recipe, double the hops on it, and the idea was not only would we get this super, over-the-top hoppy beer, but also that hops act as a natural preservative. Really, I didn't know any better, but that's still how we all operate."

ARE THERE ANY NEW HOP VARIETIES YOU'RE EXCITED ABOUT?

I travel to Yakima once a year and often I'll be fortunate enough to rub some new varieties that are in their experimental phase. The hop growers, through a couple of different research groups, are always looking to breed new varieties. But, it takes about 10 years for a hop variety to go from its first planting to commercial availability. In most cases, each year each hop breeding program will start with at least 20,000 plants, but most often they will only have less than a dozen that might have a chance of making it.

DO YOU THINK THERE'S A LIMIT TO HOW MUCH BITTERNESS WE CAN PERCEIVE? AS IN, IS THERE A RELATIVE LEVEL OF IBU AFTER WHICH YOU'RE WASTING HOPS?

Yes, there is a point where you can't taste the bitterness and it becomes unpleasant. We have this thing at our brewery that we call the Lupulin Threshold Shift. This is the idea that as a person drinks more and more hoppy beers, their palate craves more hop flavor and more hop bitterness. So someone who started out drinking a pale ale might eventually move to an IPA and eventually move to a double IPA, and so on.

A BEACON TO HOPHEADS, VINNIE AND NATALIE'S RUSSIAN RIVER BREWING COMPANY.

INDIA PALE ALE

No style has captured the taste and excitement of American craft beer like the American IPA (and American Double IPA). At its essence, it's a beer overloaded with hops and propped with more malts than usual. A great IPA requires proper bittering and aroma hops.

"We have this thing at our brewery that we call the Lupulin Threshold Shift. This is the idea that as a person drinks more and more hoppy beers, their palate craves more hop flavor and more hop bitterness."

AROMA HOPS

INTRODUCTION TO AROMA HOPS

Aroma hops are added to the boil after bittering hops. Despite the name, they contribute both aroma and flavor. By adding them later in the boil, the aroma and flavor compounds are retained. The closer to the end of the boil the hops are added, the brighter and more crisp they'll be while also contributing more to aroma. Any hop variety can be used for aroma and bittering, but certain types have been bred for one or the other.

WEYERBACHER BREWING'S DOUBLE SIMCOE IPA IS ONE OF FEW SINGLE-HOP DOUBLE IPAS.

SUGGESTED HOP BLENDS

For lesser-known hops, most postharvest descriptions from distributors leave much to be desired. How helpful is it to know a new variety's aroma is "mild and pleasant?" To help supplement your own batch-to-batch hopping experiments, try some of these hop mixes for flavor and aroma.

VARIETIES	BLEND RATIO	CHARACTER
Amarillo and Simcoe	1:1	Tropical fruit and pine
Crystal (or Mt. Hood) and Simcoe	3:1	Pine with herbal and floral hints
Amarillo and Centennial	1:1	Tropical fruit, lemon, grapefruit, and mango
Centennial, Amarillo, and Simcoe	1:1:1	Fruity, pine, and citrus
Goldings and Target	4:1	For English ales; earthy and spicy with hints of tangerine
Saaz and Hallertau	3:1	Pepper and floral
Strisselspalt and Crystal (or Mt. Hood)	1:1	Floral and citrus

FARMERS IN TETTNANG, GERMANY, CELEBRATE THEIR HARVEST WITH A HOPS QUEEN.

AMERICAN HOPS

American pale ales owe their hoppy beginnings to Cascade, which in 1972 became the first widely accepted American aroma hop. Innovation was slow for that generation of homebrewers, as most modern varieties didn't appear until the 1990s.

Today, about thirty American varieties are available with aromas ranging from pungent citrus to delicate floral spice. Hops defy concrete characterization and, to a degree, are like grapes with good and bad years. However, the more established a variety, the steadier it becomes year after year. Reliable standbys, such as Cascade and Centennial hops, are bedrocks of consistent brewing.

EUROPEAN HOPS

The classic hop fields in Kent, England, and Hallertau, Germany, grow beautiful, wonderfully subtle hops. Where American hops tend toward the big and bold citrus flavor, many German and English hops hold a more delicate spicy character. If blending both types of hops, and you should try it at some point, be wary of overpowering the milder hops.

If you're re-creating classic European styles, strictly traditional hops aren't always necessary. Going back more than 100 years, British brewers were known to employ American hops when the prices were right. Today, German brewers import about a third of their hops from the United States.

HOP TERRIOR

Hop distributors largely sell hop varieties as a commodity, with only a country of origin to distinguish them. Just like vintners might have a favorite hillside of grapes, brewers make appointments with growers to find the perfect crop and place orders for the year. Homebrewers can't always have the luxury of rubbing fresh cones between their fingers, but smaller independent growers may sell direct to brewers online in small quantities for homebrewing. Each farm's soil, climate, and tending bring a slight, but unique, character to hops.

HOP BURSTING

Hoppy doesn't always equate to bitter beer. In fact, by pulling your IBUs from aroma and flavor additions (the final 30 minutes of a boil), you can create a smoother bitterness that lets the malt stand up for itself in the final beer character.

The name "hop bursting" is a technique that calls for adding a charge of hops near the end of the boil. Some brewers prefer to distribute the hops over the final half hour their wort is on the heat. Others drop their hops in for the final 5 minutes. The essential rule to follow is that at least half of the IBUs should be drawn from the aroma and flavor additions.

POSTBOIL ADDITIONS

Once the heat is off, there are a few ways to boost the hop aroma. In each method, about 2 ounces (55 g) of hops will have a noticeable effect in a 5-gallon (19 L) batch of IPA.

HOPBACK

Immediately out of the kettle, before the wort even cools, brewers pump the hot liquid through a hopback. Think of it as adding back hop aromas and oil lost to the boil. The device goes back at least a couple hundred years in brewing history and is essentially a sealed container with a filter that allows wort to pass through the hops, absorbing the fragrant oils. The wort is then cooled, retaining the aromatic compounds. Some hopback advocates claim exposing the hops to hop wort is more sanitary, but hops have their own aseptic properties and infection through hops is rarely, if ever, an issue.

DRY-HOPPING

This simple, but slow, process can potentially add a crisper, more pungent hop aroma than a hopback. Brewers typically add the hops for the last 5 to 14 days of conditioning, but if that's all the time your beer will mature, rack the batch onto the hops. Unless added to a sterile, weighted hop bag, your addition may float on top of the beer, not maximizing contact area. This is more a problem for whole-leaf hops.

For an extra hop punch, try the technique of double dry-hopping. Split your dry hops into two equal charges. Then if, for example, you're dry-hopping for 10 days, add the first charge with 10 days remaining and the second with 5 days remaining. The two levels of dry-hopping will add depth to your aroma.

WHIRLPOOL HOPPING, HOP STANDS, AND HOP BURSTING

Each of these techniques involves adding hops to the wort in the kettle after the boil and before chilling. Whirlpool hopping and a hop stand are essentially the same thing. The only difference is that pro brewers, who work with much larger-volume batches of beer than homebrewers, create a whirlpool either in the brew kettle or in a separate vessel after the boil, creating a vortex that concentrates the hop material into the center of the kettle. A homebrewer making a 5-gallon (19-L) batch of beer doesn't necessarily need to do this, as the hops don't need to be in motion for the technique to work with a small volume; thus, homebrewers often refer to this technique as a hop stand (instead of whirlpool hopping). Hop bursting, on the other hand, is a technique where all of the boil hop additions including the bittering hops are added after the boil but before chilling. The idea behind all of these methods is to minimize vaporizing the essential oils in the hops. All of these additions can be employed from anywhere from 10 to 90 minutes, depending on the beer style.

THE FALL HOP HARVEST IN WASHINGTON STATE'S YAKIMA VALLEY, THE LARGEST HOP-GROWING REGION IN THE UNITED STATES.

HOP PELLETS SPILL OVER THE TOP OF A CONTAINER DURING A DRY-HOP ADDITION

HOP CHEMISTRY

Homebrewers can create more interesting beer if they understand the roles of the chemicals that make up those delicious alpha acids.

MYRCENE

Alpha acids and cohumulone help us understand bitterness (see page 17 for more), but myrcene is an easy indicator of pungent citrus and pine character. It's one of four essential oils that contribute to flavor and aroma. Hop distributors will list the share of myrcene just like alpha acids. The classic noble hops of Europe are low in myrcene (about 20 percent of the oils), while stereotypically rich American hops, such as Amarillo, Simcoe, and Cascade, are higher in myrcene (about 60 percent).

HUMULENE

Humulene represents a spicy, herbal central European character. Hops that are particularly strong in this sense, such as Fuggle, Saaz, and Hallertau, will have one to two times more humulene than myrcene.

SPOTLIGHT: HOW NEW HOPS ARE BORN

Every year, one or, if we're lucky, two new hops varieties are planted en masse and make their way to your local homebrew store. These low numbers aren't for a lack of effort. Every spring in the largest hop-growing region in the United States, the Yakima Valley, about 100,000 new varieties are bred through cross-pollination and planted with the hope that in 10 years one of these plants will produce strong, pleasing, and consistent hops.

Over the first year, about half the breeds will simply die, while others are quickly eliminated for reasons such as poor disease resistance, weak cone structure, and bad yield. The following year, about 100 potential varieties remain and the planting expands so farmers can begin to predict how they'll act if widely planted. Some will develop strong onion or garlic aromas while others lack consistency. After 5 or 6 years, growers begin letting brewers experiment. If the feedback is positive, the next Simcoe or Amarillo may be born.

NICK FLOYD

**THREE FLOYDS BREWING CO.,
MUNSTER, INDIANA, U.S.**

Known as the "Alpha King," Nick and his mastery of hops started at an unlikely brewery. But he has developed a cult following for beers that are almost bawdy in their hoppiness.

WHAT WAS YOUR FIRST BREWING JOB?

The first job I could get was in Auburndale, Florida, alligator country, at the Florida Brewery, which made Falstaff, Gator Lager, Malta, and even Hatuey, the Cuban brand.

WHAT TURNED YOU ON TO HOPPY BEER?

I had a Sierra Nevada in Tampa and I was amazed, and then I started liking fresh German hoppy stuff.

IT SOUNDS LIKE IT GOT YOUR ATTENTION AND IMAGINATION. THEN WHAT?

This uptight German dude in Chicago had a job available at the Weinkeller Brewery. I'm like, you have all stainless equipment and I can make whatever I want? Ja.

I started bringing in all the Cascade, Centennial, or whatever freak-show new American hops we could get our hands on. But the German guy was so tightly wound he must have fired half of Chicago, and the place didn't last long.

LET'S SAY YOU'VE GOT A HANDFUL OF HOPS, BUT THEY DON'T NECESSARILY SMELL LIKE WHAT THEY'LL BRING TO THE BEER . . .

They don't, but for us, when we smell the hops, we can visualize it. Any hint of dirt, onions, or bad aromas will be picked up later if you dry-hop. Not so much with kettle hops. The way we do it is hand to nose to kettle.

DO YOU HAVE CURRENT FAVORITE HOP VARIETIES AND OLD STANDBYS?

Our big three are Centennial, Cascade, and Warrior. We mix different high-alpha American hops to emulate what we want, basically.

ISOMETRIZED HOP EXTRACT: WHERE DOES THAT FIT IN?

You might look at it as an abomination by big breweries, 'cause they use gallons of that. But I think it's a secret weapon for making double IPAs and giant IBUs without having the vegetable matter you'd otherwise need. It has its benefits.

All our double IPAs [use it]. I think they have a place, but it's an art to using them. I say why not try it out for anything over 80 IBUs.

IS THERE A LIMIT TO HOP AROMA? CAN YOU OVER-DRY-HOP?

Not to me. Yeah, I'm sure when you spend a lot of money making four kegs of beer, that might be a limit. It tastes the same as XYZ IPA, but you can brag about it on your menu and charge more at bars. The hop aroma wars are like World War II tanks: The Germans came out with a new Panzer, and then suddenly the Russians have their new tank. I think the war's ended, but some brewers are still going. I guess we've been there, done that, and know where our limit is.

WHAT DO YOU THINK ABOUT IDEAL WINDOWS FOR IPA OR PALE ALE, ABOUT HOW FAST HOPS DETERIORATE?

It's a big issue for double IPAs. All these beer geeks want to drink it at 2 weeks old and say it's garbage at 5 weeks. It kills me because real IPAs took 3 or 4 months to get to India and then they were mellow and rounded.

YOU DON'T MIND A LITTLE TIME ON YOUR BEERS?

I like Alpha King when it's 3 months old, but to the new extreme geeks, that's past its prime. They're not looking for any other nuances besides getting kicked in the nostril by a pinecone. Even our double IPA at 8 months, people say it's crap. Me personally, I like stuff that's aged a bit more.

SO WHERE DO YOU PUT AGING LIMITS?

I'd go by IBUs. A day for every IBU, if it's bottled clean to begin with.

IS THERE A THRESHOLD AFTER THAT?

I think anything over 90 IBUs you can give at least half a year or a year. And don't call it a drain-pour, just 'cause hops have mellowed a bit; it's still a good, clean, bitter, bright IPA. Look for the other nuances in the beer.

THREE FLOYDS' GUMBALLHEAD BROKE GROUND AS ONE OF THE FIRST HOPPY WHEAT BEERS THANKS TO ITS USE OF AMARILLOS.

IT'S NO SURPRISE THAT THE THREE FLOYDS BREWPUB IS SWATHED IN HOP PLANTS.

DO YOU HAVE A PREFERENCE BETWEEN WHOLE-LEAF HOPS AND PELLETS?

We choose pellets for their stability. If we were closer to growers, we might favor whole leaf. But for shipping and storing, pellets make more sense. Some of the greatest microbreweries out there use pelletized hops, so I don't think there's a disadvantage.

YOU'RE KNOWN MORE FOR NEW AMERICAN HOP VARIETIES THAN TRADITIONAL EUROPEANS. CAN EUROPEAN VARIETIES BE USED IN NONTRADITIONAL WAYS?

Oh yeah. We make Blackheart, an English version of Dreadnaught Imperial IPA, with Styrian Golding and East Kent Golding hops.

WHAT'S A BLEND OF AMERICAN AND EUROPEAN HOPS YOU ENJOY?

I'd use a small amount of Warrior for bitterness and then large amounts of English aroma varieties.

BARREL AGING

In the stainless, sanitary world of brewing, wood-aged beer stands out as a place where science must give way to the art of brewing.

Barrel- and wood-aged beer are the beacons of extreme brewing and push the boundaries and flavor of beer. Barrels are a devil to control, and brewers are often at the mercy of their barrels, which can bring an amazingly complex new character to old recipes, or destine a batch for a drain-pour. And, ironically, barrel conditioning is a throwback to the days before copper and stainless brewing vessels.

The two main options for barrels (and thus wood additives) are American and French oak. Both impart vanilla, but American oak has a more aggressive character with lower tannins. Technically, American oak can come from anywhere within the United States, which does not guarantee a consistent flavor, so check with your cooperage (barrel maker) for the origin. The white oak from Oregon, for example, is a different species that has more in common with European oaks.

FRENCH COOPER ALAIN NUNES HANDCRAFTS THREE BARRELS A DAY FOR THE CHÂTEAU MARGAUX WINE ESTATE.

French oak, the more traditional barrel wood for wine, imparts a subtler, spicy character with high tannin levels. The wood has a tighter grain, meaning it releases flavor more slowly and there's less oxygenation. French oak proponents claim the slower extraction produces a more complex character. New French barrels typically run double the price of American oak, but Hungarian oak has a history as being the less-expensive substitute.

TOASTED WOOD

Just like specialty grains, wood is dried and toasted to varying degrees to achieve particular flavor profiles. Most brewers use a medium or medium-plus toasted oak; however, bourbon barrels are also charred to create a charcoal layer over the toasted oak. Naturally, toast levels vary by cooperage, but some basic profiles hold:

Lighter toasts are more subtle with fresh fruit flavors.

Medium toasts project more vanilla and spice.

Heavy toasts show more caramelized and roasted notes and need the shortest maturation time.

EVERY BARREL HAS A UNIQUE CHARACTER. BREWERS AT AVERY BREWING SAMPLE BARRELS FOR FUTURE BLENDING.

WOOD AND TEMPERATURE

Just like yeast, wood also responds to temperature changes. A temperature rise will draw your brew into the wood, while a drop pushes it back out. A mildly unstable temperature may not actually be a bad thing if you're looking to speed your infusion process.

BARREL SIZE

It's easy to talk about barrels and wood in terms of weight or capacity, but surface area determines the rate of flavor extraction. The smaller the barrel, the greater the ratio of surface area to liquid. Although a professional brewer might leave his ale in a 60-gallon (227 L) barrel for 6 months, a homebrew-scale 5-gallon (19 L) barrel can work its magic in a mere 2 weeks. The same theory works for other forms of oak. Oak powder works quicker than thin-cut chips, which then are still faster than cubes and spirals.

BEYOND THE BARREL

Wood additives are largely produced to help vintners supplement a barrel's character when they become neutral and lose their flavor. In the hands of inventive brewers, they can infuse wonderful character into any beer style and fairly accurately re-create a bourbon barrel at a fraction of the cost and headache. However, additives cannot perfectly mimic the barrel-aging process—the porous structure of wood allows for slight oxidation. Like most flavor additions to beer, oak and other wood additives should be added to the conditioning tank as beer ages.

EIGHT-INCH (20 CM) OAK INFUSION SPIRALS OFFER AN IDEAL COMPROMISE FOR HOMEBREWERS SEEKING AN AUTHENTIC BARREL CHARACTER WITHOUT COMMITTING TO AN ACTUAL (AND EXPENSIVE) BARREL. MOST 5-GALLON (19 L) BATCHES REQUIRE ONLY ONE OR TWO SPIRALS.

OAK ESSENCE

Available in liquid or powder, this is the fastest way to add oak character, but it is considered the least consistent. Dosage runs from 1 to 4 ounces per 5 gallons (1.5 to 6 g per liter). The liquid is instant, and the powder needs no more than 1 week. Expect a lightly toasted oak character and be careful to filter out the powder; otherwise, your beer will have a distinct sawdust taste.

OAK CHIPS

These roughly cut wood chips release their flavor in as little as 1 week. They're generally regarded as a more aggressive method and character, but have proved to be a great addition to hoppy beers.

They are also the easiest way to simulate a bourbon barrel. Here's how:

Soak the chips (or any of the other solid options) in your favorite bourbon overnight.

Drain or include the liquid depending on the desired intensity.

Add the chips to the beer for only 1 to 4 weeks. You can always just add sanitized (steamed for 15 minutes) chips and bourbon separately.

Typically, 2 ounces (55 g) of chips will make a noticeable impact after 1 week in a 5-gallon (19 L) batch.

"In the hands of inventive brewers, wood additives can infuse wonderful character into any beer style and fairly accurately recreate a bourbon barrel at a fraction of the cost and headache."

SPIRALS

American and French oak spirals minimize mess and claim to do 8 months of maturation in 6 weeks. Although professionals use 4-foot (1.2 m) segments in their tanks, one or two 8-inch (20 cm) spirals will do for most 5-gallon (19 L) batches.

BEANS AND CUBES

Beans and cubes are designed to release flavor at the same rate as traditional barrels, and the producers claim the slower extraction creates a smoother, more complex character. They need at least 2 months of aging (6 months is ideal), but they can also mature and be reused for up to 1 year of total contact time. Use 2 to 3 ounces per 5 gallons (1.5 to 4.5 g per liter).

ADDING SPIRITS

Numerous laws (which vary by locale) prevent commercial brewers from adding straight liquor to beer, even if it's just flavoring. Homebrewers, however, are safe from these regulations. One cup (240 ml) of spirits for 5 gallons (19 L) generally provides balanced flavors. Adding 1.5 ounces per gallon (11 g per liter) will bring a noticeable aroma, flavor, and lighter mouthfeel.

FIRESTONE WALKER BREWING CONDITIONS A PORTION OF EVERY PALE ALE BATCH IN OAK WITH THEIR PATENTED FIRESTONE UNION OAK BARREL BREWING SYSTEM.

PREPARE YOUR BARREL

If you dive in and either buy a small wine barrel or organize a group brewing session to fill a larger bourbon barrel, prep your barrel to make sure your beer doesn't go to waste.

INSPECT FOR INFECTION

Your first step is to check for infection. Stick your nose in the bunghole and take a big whiff. If there are any signs of acetic acid (smells like vinegar), nothing good can come from the barrel. If the barrel is used, pour out and collect any remaining liquid. It'll give you a taste of what you can expect from the aging. New barrels should have a sweet oak smell.

HOT WATER SWELL AND CLEANING

The repeated rinses from swelling a new barrel (sealing the cracks) should be all the cleaning needed. If you have a used barrel, wash out any deposits with hot water. To swell, fill the barrel one-tenth full with hot water. Put the bung in place and slosh the barrel to coat the inside with water. Let it stand for 30 minutes on its head, then repeat on the other side. Drain and refill all the way to test for any seepage.

TASTING AND EVALUATING YOUR BEER

A DOUBLE FLIGHT OF BEERS FROM HOWE SOUND BREWING IN SQUAMISH, BRITISH COLUMBIA, CANADA.

INTRODUCTION TO EVALUATING BEER

In the stainless, sanitary world of brewing, wood-aged beer stands out as a place where science must give way to the art of brewing. Barrel—and wood-aged beer stand as one of the beacons of extreme brewing by pushing the boundaries and flavor of beer. Barrels are a devil to control, and brewers are often at their mercy, which can bring an amazingly complex new character to old recipes, or destine a batch for a drain-pour. Ironically, barrel conditioning is a throwback to the days before copper and stainless brewing vessels.

Then, somewhere down the road, often years later, comes the good beer. Beer that not only tastes great, but is so wonderful you actually want to taste it, not chug it, for a change. Forget searching for cheap beers with no aftertaste—you want all the flavor you can get. Drinking beer for its character, not its alcohol content and availability, is what craft beer, homebrewing, and beer appreciation is all about.

Whether you want to fine-tune your homebrew or your tongue, learning to taste and evaluate beer will lead you to better beverages all around.

Everyone has an opinion on beer, but thoughtful evaluation requires more than a thumbs up or down. Judging a beer requires that you taste and enjoy a beer for what it is, regardless of personal preference. Most IPAs rate higher than light lagers, but a true taster also has to consider which is a better representation of their style. More important, judging beer identifies imperfection and room for improvement so that a brewer can learn their mistakes and make better beer.

THE PROPER POUR

Before you can really taste or even admire a beer, you need to give it a proper pour. There are unending variations of what should be a simple task. There's the classic no-foam pour where you let beer sneak down the side until your glass is filled. You can squeeze a few more ounces (grams) into your cup, but this mutes the aroma. There's the showier pour straight to the bottom. This does a fine job of releasing aroma but leaves a huge head between you and the liquid you're dying to sip.

Instead, hold your glass at a 45-degree angle and pour the beer onto the middle of the wall. About halfway through the pour, turn the glass upright and pour the rest straight down to create a 1- to 2-inch (2.5 to 5 cm) head. For more effervescent beers, wait longer to turn the glass; for low carbonation, pour straight down earlier. It's a bit of an art, but it's a skill you won't mind practicing.

APPEARANCE

You can't judge a beer by its label and packaging, but a quick inspection can tell you what flavor is in store. Dusty bottles on the store shelves, for instance, may indicate a beer is well past its prime. For homebrewed beer, hold your bottle up to light to look for a ring around the inside of the neck—this indicates an infection. Infections often lead to overcarbonation, so open any ringed bottles over a sink.

COLOR

A beer's color gives only a small indication of flavor. Two identical-looking red ales could have completely different characters: An all-Munich malt beer will have a sweet caramel and bready taste, while adding just a few ounces (grams) of black patent barley to Pilsner malt during brewing will create the same appearance with none of the flavor.

Still, every beer style has an appropriate range of color defined by its SRM (Standard Reference Method). This scale runs from 0 to about 70 with light lagers registering a 2, imperial stouts pulling 50 to 70, and an amber ale in the neighborhood of 20. Good homebrewing software will calculate your SRM along with original gravity so you can check against your style's guidelines.

A BELGIAN SERVER FINISHES WITH AN EXTRA TALL POUR TO CREATE A PROPER HEAD.

CLARITY

Hazy beer is appropriate and preferred for some styles, such as German and Belgian wheat beers (hefeweizens and witbiers) as well as "New England-Style" IPAs. In brewing competition, some haze is acceptable for India Pale Ales due to chill haze. Clear, clean beer typically results from good sanitation, and using a bit of Irish moss at the end of a boil draws out tannins and proteins. Properly maturing your beer in the secondary fermentor also creates clear beer; as a beer ages, yeast and other particles fall out of suspension.

AROMA

The only thing that could be simpler than drinking is sniffing, right? There's a lot you can learn by smelling your beer. Aroma is the gateway to flavor.

Beer is a complex but delicate drink, and the pour releases volatile notes that disappear within minutes, if not seconds. The second you set your beer down, dive in nose first. Take several short sniffs and focus on both the upfront character and then the background.

If you stop to take notes or ponder the beer, an occasional swirl of the glass will help raise the head and release a new burst of aroma. You can also let the aroma build by placing a coaster or your hand over the glass during and after the swirl.

TASTE

It should go without saying that you can't properly taste beer out of a bottle or can. But for anyone who needs reminding, there are two problems with trying to taste this way.

■ First, you can't smell the beer. The majority of our perceived taste comes from aroma, and you might notice food tastes more dull when you have a snuffed-up nose.

■ Second, the small opening on cans and bottles forces you to pour faster, accelerating the beer onto your tongue and releasing more carbonation, which in turn clouds the flavor.

To properly taste beer:

Step 1: With your beer poured, the color examined, and the aroma suitably sniffed, take a sip and swirl it around your mouth to coat your tongue.

Step 2: Swallow and then exhale through your nose to bring the flavor back.

Step 3: For all the various flavors and notes, pick them out one at a time and examine whether you like them and then whether they're appropriate for the intended style.

TO TASTE BETTER, YOU NEED TO BUY FRESH BEER. SO EXERCISE CAUTION BUYING A BEER THAT...

Has exposure to sunlight from the shelf. UV rays create the skunky beer phenomena.

Is leaking. Always check the tops of corked bottles. If the cork is partially pushed out or there's residue around the edge, back away.

Has grown dusty. Not all beer is dated, but all beer can collect dust.

Is on clearance sale or deep discount. This may indicate the beer has been hanging around too long.

Is out of season. Pumpkin beer isn't meant for March, and summer beers are typically stale by mid-fall.

In formal homebrew tasting, there are rarely wrong answers, just ill-informed ones. A written description from judging and style guidelines can help only so much to understand how a style should taste. You need to try commercial examples to understand how similar beers stack up. To be a better taster, yes, you need to drink more beer, albeit thoughtfully. Take notes and keep tasting logs; this is likely to be the most enjoyable research and study you can find. Through sampling the standards and quintessential beers of a style, you begin to develop a library of potential flavors.

KNOW YOUR LIMITS

Beyond learning the notes and characteristics of a beer, you also need to know your limits. Everyone's palate reacts differently to certain chemicals and a good judge understands their strengths and weaknesses. Again, hone this by drinking more beer and also discussing it with friends to hear what they can taste and you can't.

JUDGES ELIMINATE CANDIDATES FROM THE BEST IN SHOW ROUND AT THE DRUNK MONK CHALLENGE HOMEBREW COMPETITION.

MOUTHFEEL

The feel of a beer is the final sense to evaluate and can be the most ambiguous. Light American lagers (such as Bud or Miller Lite) feel light and refreshing because they can have about the same weight and density as water. Bigger beers, with more unfermented sugar (such as Aventinus Weizenbock or Old Rasputin Imperial Stout), are thicker with a high density. Carbonation also forms our perception of mouthfeel. Some people falsely assume Guinness Draught is a big and alcoholic beer because it feels thick on their tongue. It's actually no stronger than a light beer. The difference comes from its nitrogen carbonation, which has smaller bubbles and makes it feel heavier, but also smoother.

TROUBLESHOOTING OFF FLAVORS

When good beer goes bad, there's a group of usual suspects to round up.

YOU TASTE	DIAGNOSIS
Sour, puckering mouthfeel; tastes and feels like a dirty lemon or grapefruit; beer may have a film on top.	You have a wild yeast infection most likely due to unsanitary equipment or conditions. Keep your brewery clean and your beer sealed from the world.
Plastic bandages, cough medicine, plastic, chlorine, or assorted medical supplies.	You're most likely tasting chlorophenol, a chemical created through the bonding of chlorine from your brewing water or cleaner with normally tasty phenols created by your yeast. It may also be wild yeast contamination. Either way, check your water and sanitizer.
Alcohol, as in bottom-shelf spirits or cleaning solvent.	If your beer is stronger than about 7 percent, continue aging. Otherwise, these fusel alcohols come from fermenting too warm and/or with poor aeration.
Wet cardboard in dark beer and paper in lighter beers, or if you're lucky, sherry.	Oxidation. Oxygen is one of beer's mortal enemies, and exposure during conditioning and bottling will make your beer taste like the sports section.
Astringent, dry, chalky bitterness like grape skins.	It could be an infection, but it is likely tannins from the malt. Mashing grains too hot, sparging for too long, or grinding them too fine will unleash this unpleasant aftertaste.
Butterscotch or movie theater popcorn butter.	Diacetyl. This fermentation by-product is appropriate and desirable in some English ales, but otherwise it indicates the beer was taken from primary fermentation too soon or wasn't adequately aerated.
Boiled or canned vegetables, commonly corn.	DMS, or dimethyl sulfide, can be an infection, but often results from a poorly vented brew kettle. Keep your equipment clean and pot uncovered to let the DMS boil off.
Fruit punch, berry flavors when there should be none.	While perfectly normal in Belgian ales, it's a mark of too-hot fermentation in cleaner beer styles like a pale ale or Pilsner.
Fresh, green apples.	Acetaldehyde. This is another sign of young beer. Adequate primary and secondary fermentation will clean this flaw out.
Apple cider.	Blame your sugars. You either have old, stale malt extract, or you added too much sugar.

THE PERFECTLY CLOUDY OMMEGANG WITTE TOPPED OFF WITH A VERTICAL POUR.

CHAPTER 2

CRAFT BREWER RECIPES

SMOKE
SURLY BREWING COMPANY, MINNEAPOLIS, MINNESOTA

The big-bottle, specialty releases are among the most sought-after brews from Minnesota's Surly Brewing Company. Smoke is an early-winter offering that makes a great sipper as the nights grow longer. This ebony-black and silky-smooth Baltic porter gets an aromatic boost from generous use of German smoked malt. Dark malt flavors meld with notes of raisins, plums, and licorice to create a beautifully complex sipper. Note that this recipe must be made as either partial-mash or all-grain. It is also fermented with lager yeast, so the ability to carefully control fermentation temperature is required to achieve proper results.

INGREDIENTS

5 pounds (2.3 kg) Weyermann Smoked malt

12 ounces (340 g) Belgian aromatic malt

8 ounces (225 g) English black malt

8 ounces (225 g) Weyermann Carafa II

4 ounces (115 g) English chocolate malt

3.15 pounds (1.4 kg) light liquid malt extract

3.5 pounds (1.6 kg) light dry malt extract

0.85 ounces (24 g) Warrior hop pellets (16% AA) (60 minutes)

Wyeast 2124 Bohemian Lager

2 ounces (55 g) oak cubes (sanitize by steaming for 10 minutes or soaking in a neutral spirit)

5 ounces (140 g) corn sugar

1 Heat 2.5 gallons (9.5 L) of water to 163°F (73°C).

2 Crush the Weyermann Smoked, Belgian aromatic, English black, Weyermann Carafa II, and English chocolate malts and put into a nylon mesh brewing bag. Add the bag to the heated water. Temperature should be within a degree or two of 148°F (64°C). Maintain that temperature and steep for 60 minutes.

3 While the mash rests, heat 1.5 (5.7 L) gallons of water to 168°F (76°C) in a separate pot. When the mash is finished, return the pot to the heat and slowly raise the temperature to 168°F (76°C). Strain the grain into your brewpot and sparge with the water from the second pot.

4 Bring the wort to a boil, remove from the heat, and add the liquid and dry malt extracts. Stir well until the extract is completely dissolved.

Starting gravity:	Final gravity:	Final target alcohol by volume (ABV):	IBU:	SRM:
1.087	1.025	8.3%	50	45

5 Add water as needed to bring the total volume to 4 gallons (15.1 L), adding the hops as indicated in the ingredients list.

6 Chill the wort as quickly as possible to 58°F (14°C) using an ice bath or wort chiller. Transfer the wort to the fermentor and add cold water to bring the total volume to 5 gallons (19 L). Aerate the wort. Add the yeast.

7 Ferment at 51°F (11°C) until final gravity is achieved. Perform a diacetyl rest by raising the temperature to 65°F (18°C) for 5 days. Siphon to a secondary fermentor and slowly lower the temperature to 33°F (1°C).

8 After 3 weeks, add the oak cubes to the secondary. Sanitize them by steaming for 10 minutes or soaking in a neutral spirit.

9 Allow the beer to condition for 5 weeks. When fermentation is complete, bottle with the corn sugar.

ALL-GRAIN INSTRUCTIONS

Replace the malt extract with 10 pounds (4.5 kg) Canada Malting Pale Ale malt. Increase the amount of Weyermann smoked malt to 6.75 pounds (3 kg). Crush the grains and mash at 148°F (64°C) for 60 minutes. Sparge with 168°F (76°C) water until you reach a total volume of 6 gallons (22.7 L) in the brewpot. Reduce the 60-minute Warrior hop addition to 0.75 ounce (21 g).

SURLY BREWING COMPANY, MINNEAPOLIS, MINNESOTA

Since it opened in 2006, the Surly Brewing Company has made quite a sud-soaked splash in the Twin Cities of Minnesota. Today, Surly continues to brew and distribute high-quality beer in cans and on tap all around Minnesota and the greater Midwest and has even played a critical role in changing the liquor laws of Minnesota.

But before all that, Surly was the dream of collegiate homebrewer Omar Ansari, a hop-happy brewer who'd been concocting a wide variety of tongue-tingling libations since 1994. Once Ansari decided it was brewing or bust, he apprenticed at New Holland Brewing Company in Michigan and later enlisted Todd Haug of Rock Bottom Brewery (Minneapolis) to help set up the company, and Surly poured its first beers soon after.

Since then, the popularity of Surly has grown. Fueled by a love of community, aggressive marketing, and a bold approach to flavor and style, Surly is now one of the most recognized beer brands in the Midwest.

Early in 2011, Surly announced its intentions of opening a beer garden and restaurant on its grounds and increasing its brewing capacity to 100,000 barrels. Minnesota's convoluted liquor laws, however, prevented that from happening. But Surly Nation (Surly's not-so-silent majority of devoted consumers) did not relent, and several members of the Minnesota Legislature were moved to amend the law, which would allow breweries to distribute and sell their beer on brewery premises. The amendment—loosely regarded as the "Surly Bill"—passed and was signed into law by Governor Mark Dayton on May 25, 2011.

Furious, Bender, CynicAle, Darkness, Smoke, and Abrasive—Surly's beers are as bold as they sound. Featuring a bevy of traditional, seasonal, and specialty brews, Surly has made its name on these tasty beers. Furious, the flagship brew, is made with "a dazzling blend of American hops and Scottish malt . . . with waves of citrus, pine, and caramel-toffee." Darkness is one of Surly's most popular seasonal brews, featuring decadent flavors that delight the devil inside the palate: chocolate, cherries, raisins, coffee, toffee, and hops. No matter how you choose to be Surly, prepare yourself: It's rare for any of Surly's beers to rate beneath 5 percent ABV. Each 16-ounce (455 ml) can packs a wallop.

SNOWSTORM 2009 BALTIC PORTER

AUGUST SCHELL BREWING COMPANY, NEW ULM, MINNESOTA

S nowstorm is the August Schell Brewing Company's annual holiday-season special release. It's brewed to a different style every year, leading beer drinkers across the state of Minnesota to eagerly anticipate each new version. Some of the Snowstorm brews have become such fan favorites that they are now part of the brewery's regular lineup. The 2009 Baltic Porter was particularly popular. It's on the low end of the scale in terms of strength, but that doesn't mean the flavor is lacking. Notes of cocoa, molasses, and brown sugar carry through from sniff to swallow.

INGREDIENTS

8 ounces (225 g) chocolate malt

6.5 ounces (184 g) Victory malt

6 ounces (170 g) Briess Extra Special malt

3.5 ounces (99 g) Crystal 20L malt

3.5 ounces (99 g) Crystal 60L malt

2.5 ounces (71 g) Crystal 120L malt

12 pounds (5.4 kg) Munich liquid malt extract

12 ounces (340 g) light dry malt extract

0.85 ounce (24 g) Tettnang hop pellets (4.5% AA) *(60 minutes)*

1 ounce (28 g) Liberty hop pellets (4% AA) *(60 minutes)*

0.55 ounce (15.6 g) Tettnang hop pellets (4.5% AA) *(20 minutes)*

Wyeast 2000 Budvar Lager

6 ounces (170 g) corn sugar

1 Crush all the grains and steep in in 2 gallons (7.5 L) of water at 160°F (71°C) for 30 minutes.

2 Strain the grain into your brewpot and sparge with 0.5 gallon (2 L) of water at 160°F (71°C). Bring to a boil, remove from the heat, and add the liquid and dry malt extracts. Stir well until the extract is completely dissolved.

3 Add water to bring the total volume to 3 gallons (11.3 L). Bring the wort to a rolling boil. Boil for 60 minutes. Add the hops at the times indicated in the ingredients list.

4 Remove from the heat and chill the wort as quickly as possible to below 80°F (27°C) using an ice bath or wort chiller. Transfer the wort to the fermentor and add cold water to bring the total volume to 5 gallons (19 L). Aerate the wort. Add the yeast.

Starting gravity:	Final gravity:	Final target alcohol by volume (ABV):	IBU:	SRM:
1.072	1.027	6%	31	29

5 Ferment at 50°F (10°C) until final gravity is achieved. Siphon to a secondary fermentor and allow the beer to condition for 5 weeks at 33°F (1°C). When fermentation is complete, bottle with the corn sugar.

ALL-GRAIN INSTRUCTIONS

Replace the malt extract with 13 pounds (5.9 kg) of Munich malt. Crush the grains and mash at 147°F (64°C) for 15 minutes. Raise the temperature to 167°F (75°C) and rest for 20 minutes. Raise the temperature to 170°F (79°C). Sparge with 170°F (79°C) water until you reach a total volume of 6 gallons (22.7 L) in the brewpot. Reduce the 60-minute Tettnang hop addition to 0.7 ounce (20 g). Reduce the 60-minute Liberty hop addition to 0.8 ounce (23 g). Reduce the 20-minute Tettnang hop addition to 0.45 ounce (13 g).

AUGUST SCHELL BREWING COMPANY, NEW ULM, MINNESOTA

August Schell was born in 1828 in Durbach, Germany, in the Black Forest region. At twenty years old, Schell left Germany for the United States, making his way north from New Orleans to Cincinnati and, later, with his wife and daughters to Minnesota as part of the Cincinnati Turner Society, a group of northbound German immigrants. When they merged with another group of Germans, the southern Minnesota prairie town of New Ulm was born.

Schell immediately recognized Minnesota's lack of good German lager. He soon erected a small brewing company with partner Jacob Bernhardt, and the legend grew from there. Schell lived a good life, and upon his death at the age of sixty-three, the brewing company passed down to his sons. Over the next several decades, the August Schell Brewing Company changed hands several times, and though the owners' names haven't ended in Schell in more than 100 years, the Marti family is related through marriage to August.

Prohibition shut down more than 1,500 breweries around the country and only about 600 reopened after repeal. Schell's was one of them, and though times had been tough, the Marti family had recognized the value of nonalcoholic drinks as well, and now Schell's 1919 Classic American Draft Root Beer is almost as famous as the beer brand itself.

Today, the brewery counts more than thirty beers to its name, including Grain Belt, which Schell's bought in 2002 to save another legendary Minnesota beer from disappearing. Schell's remains the largest and oldest brewery in Minnesota, and as its 160th anniversary approaches, the future is bright for this historic brand.

Schell's bottles and distributes more than a dozen year-round and seasonal original and craft beers, as well as three Grain Belt–brand styles (Premium, Premium Light, and Nordeast). But it's one of the first beers of Schell's late 20th-century revival that really turned heads—the Pils.

Schell's Pils was first brewed in 1984 under the watchful (and successful) eye of owner Warren Marti. Brewed with 100 percent barley malt, Schell's cites Pils as boasting a "rich malt body, accented by a large hop/malt aroma, and a refreshing hop tang."

BITTERSWEET LENNY'S R.I.P.A

SHMALTZ BREWING, CLIFTON PARK, NEW YORK

S hmaltz Brewing also brews under the He'Brew banner under which they brew the "Chosen Beers," a lineup of extreme beers. Included in that lineup is Bittersweet Lenny's R.I.P.A, a rye-based double IPA. Coming in at an astounding original gravity of 1.096 and 10 percent ABV, R.I.P.A not only provides a wonderfully complex hop profile (weaving in no less than seven different hops!), it has a malt backbone to support them. Such a complex beer cannot be brewed with extract alone, and accordingly you will need to perform at least a partial mash. That said, your hard work will be rewarded.

INGREDIENTS

4 pounds (1.8 kg) two-row malt

1.9 pounds (0.86 kg) rye malt

9 ounces (255 g) flaked rye

4.6 ounces (130 g) wheat malt

9.15 pounds (4.15 kg) Pilsner liquid extract

1.1 ounces (31 g) Warrior hop pellets (16% AA) *(60 minutes)*

0.45 ounce (13 g) Cascade hop pellets (6% AA) *(20 minutes)*

0.45 ounce (13 g) Simcoe hop pellets (13% AA) *(20 minutes)*

0.45 ounce (13 g) Warrior hop pellets (16% AA) *(20 minutes)*

0.45 ounce (13 g) Cascade hop pellets (6% AA) *(10 minutes)*

0.45 ounce (13 g) Chinook hop pellets (13% AA) *(10 minutes)*

0.45 ounce (13 g) Crystal hop pellets (4.5% AA) *(10 minutes)*

0.3 ounce (8.5 g) Amarillo hop pellets (9.5% AA) *(5 minutes)*

0.3 ounce (8.5 g) Cascade hop pellets (6% AA) *(5 minutes)*

0.3 ounce (8.5 g) Simcoe hop pellets (13% AA) *(5 minutes)*

0.14 ounce (4 g) ground caraway seeds *(5 minutes)*

0.56 ounce (16 g) Centennial hop pellets (10.5% AA) *(end of boil)*

1 ounce (28 g) Amarillo hop pellets (9.5% AA) *(dry hop, 7 days)*

Wyeast 1056 American Ale, White Labs WLP001 California Ale, or Safale US-05

5 ounces (140 g) corn sugar

1 Crush all the grains and steep in 2 gallons (7.57 L) of water at 155°F (68°C) in order to reach a mash temperature of 144°F (62°C).

2 Rest for 45 minutes and apply heat to slowly raise the temperature to 152°F (67°C). Rest for 15 minutes.

3 Strain the grain into your brewpot and sparge with 3 gallons (11.35 L) of water at 168°F (76°C). Add water as needed to bring the total volume to 4.25 gallons (16 L).

4 Bring the water to a boil, remove from the heat, and add the liquid malt extract. Bring to a boil. Boil for 60 minutes. Add the hops as indicated in the ingredients list.

5 Chill the wort as quickly as possible to below 80°F (27°C), using an ice bath or wort chiller. Transfer the wort to the fermentor and add cold water to bring the total volume to 5 gallons (19 L). Aerate the wort. Add the yeast.

6 Ferment at 62°F (17°C) until final gravity is achieved. Siphon to a secondary fermentor and add the dry hop addition.

Starting gravity:	Final gravity:	Final target alcohol by volume (ABV):	IBU:	SRM:
1.096	1.010	10%	95–100	8.2

7 Allow the beer to condition on the dry hops for 7 days. When fermentation is complete, bottle with the corn sugar.

ALL-GRAIN INSTRUCTIONS

Replace the preceding grain bill with the following and mash at 144°F (62°C) for 45 minutes.

16.75 pounds (7.7 kg) two-row malt

2.25 pounds (1 kg) rye malt

11 ounces (312 g) flaked rye

5.5 ounces (156 g) wheat malt

4 ounces (113 g) amber malt

2.7 ounces (77 g) Caramunich malt

1.3 ounces (37 g) Crystal rye

1.3 ounces (37 g) Crystal 60L malt

Slowly raise the temperature to 152°F (67°C) and rest for 15 minutes. Sparge with 170°F (79°C) water until you reach a total volume of 6 gallons (22.7 L) in the brewpot. Reduce the 60-minute Warrior hop addition to 0.97 ounce (27.5 g).

SHMALTZ BREWING, UPSTATE NEW YORK

L'HAIM! For Gentile readers, *l'haim* is a traditional Jewish toast that means "to life." If there's one thing Shmaltz does well, it's celebrating its own good fortune and rejoicing in quality beer. Shmaltz was founded as "American Jewish Celebration Beer" and began, like many craft breweries, as an experiment. In 1996 during Chanukah, Jeremy Cowan and some friends decided to explore the world of homebrewing and mixed one of their first batches with hand-squeezed pomegranate juice. They called it "He'Brew Beer" and delivered it around the San Francisco Bay Area in Cowan's grandmother's beat-up Volvo.

Thus began the legend of He'Brew Beer and the Shmaltz Brewing Company. In 1997, Anderson Valley Brewing Company (Boonville, California) began distributing He'Brew Beer to wholesalers, and Cowan began his tenure as a full-time brewer. By 2003, Cowan found himself in New York, brewing and distributing beer through the Mendocino Brewing Company in Saratoga Springs. There are now six regular beers included in the He'Brew series: Origin Pomegranate Strong Ale, Messiah Bold, Bittersweet Lenny's R.I.P.A., Genesis Ale, Jewbelation, and Rejewvenator.

In 2008, Shmaltz grew again with the launch of the Coney Island Craft Lagers series of beers. Partnering with Coney Island USA—a certified 501(c)(3) nonprofit organization—a small portion of every sale was donated back to the nonprofit. The nano-batches of beer being produced, headed by Coney Island Lager and other experimental lagers, were attractive enough that a subsidiary of Boston Beer Company purchased the brand from Shmaltz in 2013.

Thanks to that sale, Cowan was able to build a 30,000-barrel capacity brewing facility in Clifton Park, New York. Quickly, regional sales of Shmaltz beers tripled. After five years in the facility, which boasted a tasting room, tours, and more, Shmaltz was pumping out 26,000 barrels annually. But in spring 2018, Cowan struck a deal with SingleCut Beersmiths, selling the facility and its assets in order to go back to contract brewing. Cowan retained ownership of all of the Shmaltz brands.

The Shmaltz Brewing Company is not shy about its products or its heritage. Every line and bottle features striking artwork and imagery related to the faith-inspired names of its products, and the company is widely recognized for its tongue-in-cheek yet serious examination of the Jewish world and history and its intersection with popular pop culture. For example, the tagline for Messiah Bold lager is "the beer you've been waiting for," alluding to the Jewish belief that the Messiah is yet to come. Bittersweet Lenny's R.I.P.A. is a tribute and homage to late comedian Lenny Bruce, and the beer is brewed with an "obscene" amount of hops. In 2010, the barrel-aged edition of R.I.P.A. garnered the silver medal in the Wood- and Barrel-Aged Strong Beer category at the Great American Beer Festival.

Shmaltz beers can be found in over twenty-five states around the nation, both in liquor stores and directly from wholesalers. Though the brewery may have closed down at the end of 2018, true believers in the company can still make a pilgrimage to New York to experience the full pantheon of Shmaltz's many offerings at tasting rooms in Troy and Saratoga Springs.

RUGBROD
THE BRUERY, PLACENTIA, CALIFORNIA

Rugbrød" is Danish for "rye bread." That dark and earthy Scandinavian staple provided the inspiration for this dark brown beer, which is loosely based on the traditional Scandinavian Christmas beer "Julebryg." Three types of rye give it an earthy, spicy bite that is enhanced by just a hint of roast. Add a side of bready, nutty barley malt and Belgian yeast, and you've got a festive brew that's appropriate for any time of year.

INGREDIENTS

1.06 pounds (481 g) Great Western caramel 60 malt

9.6 ounces (272 g) Bairds Brown malt

9.6 ounces (272 g) Simpsons Crystal Rye malt

4.8 ounces (136 g) chocolate rye malt

8.5 pounds (3.9 kg) rye liquid malt extract

0.5 ounce (15 g) Warrior hop pellets (16% AA) *(60 minutes)*

WLP570 Belgian Golden Ale

6 ounces (170 g) corn sugar

1 Crush all the grains and steep in 2.5 gallons (9.5 L) of water at 160°F (71°C) for 30 minutes.

2 Strain the grain into your brewpot and sparge with 0.5 gallon (1.9 L) of water at 160°F (71°C).

3 Bring the wort to a boil, remove from the heat, and add the rye liquid malt extract. Stir well until the extract is completely dissolved. Add water as needed to bring the total volume to 3 gallons (11.4 L). Bring to a boil. Boil for 60 minutes. Add the hops as indicated in the ingredients list.

4 Chill the wort as quickly as possible to below 80°F (27°C) using an ice bath or wort chiller. Transfer the wort to the fermentor and add cold water to bring the total volume to 5 gallons (19 L). Aerate the wort. Add the yeast.

Starting gravity:	Final gravity:	Final target alcohol by volume (ABV):	IBU:	SRM:
1.070	1.008	8%	30	27

5 Ferment at 74°F (23°C) until final gravity is achieved. Siphon to a secondary fermentor and allow the beer to condition for 5 to 7 days. When fermentation is complete, bottle with the corn sugar.

ALL-GRAIN INSTRUCTIONS

Replace malt extract with 9.5 pounds (4.3 kg) Great Western two-row pale malt and 3.6 pounds (1.6 kg) Weyermann rye malt. Crush the grains and mash at 155°F (68°C) for 60 minutes. Sparge with 170°F (77°C) water until you reach a total volume of 6 gallons (22.7 L) in the brewpot. Reduce the Warrior hop addition to 0.45 ounces (13 g).

THE BRUERY, PLACENTIA, CALIFORNIA

Since it opened in 2006, the Bruery of Orange County, California, has turned heads and tempted palates of adventurous bastions of beer far and wide. Formed by brothers Patrick and Chris Rue, the Bruery—a portmanteau of the word *brewery* and the name *Rue*—has garnered quite a reputation for its nontraditional beer flavors and Old World brewing methods. What began as a diversion from law school for Patrick grew into an obsession and finally blossomed into a business for the brothers Rue.

Many of the beers are brewed in the Belgian tradition, meaning none of them are filtered or pasteurized. Most of the carbonation in the bottled beers derives from bottle conditioning and a secondary bottle fermentation process. The Bruery prides itself on crafting "complex flavors from simple ingredients" and is devoted to creating wholesome beers in wholesome ways.

One of the goals of the Bruery is to push the limits of what beer really *is*. First, its quaffs are *strong*—their bourbon-aged ales often range from 13 to 19 percent ABV. If that sounds a lot like wine, it's because, well, those flavors and styles are incorporated into the beer.

The Vitis series blends Syrah, Chardonnay, and Pinots into its concoctions. The Orchard White, for example, sounds a lot more like a wine than a beer. In the bottle, Orchard White is an unfiltered, bottle-conditioned Belgian-style witbier, golden in color and spiced with citrus peel, lavender, coriander, and more, and a fruity, yeasty strain adds complexity and subtle flavors to the end product.

The Bruery produces about 2,500 barrels of beer annually, which can be found in many parts of the United States, including southern California, the Pacific Northwest, many Midwest states, the upper East Coast, and Florida. The Bruery produces several seasonal and year round beers, including Saison Rue, a Belgian-style ale brewed with rye; Mischief, a hoppy Belgian-style golden; Loakal Red, an oak-aged American red ale; Humulus Lager, a strong Imperial Pale Lager; Rugbrød, a Danish-style rye; and Hottenroth, a German-style wheat beer. Many other seasonal and brewery-only special batches are available, and a comprehensive map of where to find their brews can be found on The Bruery's website.

SAISON RUE
THE BRUERY, PLACENTIA, CALIFORNIA

P atrick Rue (the "rue" in Bruery) started homebrewing as a diversion while attending law school. Over time his hobby grew. As his passion for beer-making waxed, his love of the law waned. In 2008, he left lawyering behind and opened the brewery. His mix of traditional and experimental Belgian-style beers caught on. The Bruery quickly gained a national reputation that far exceeded its diminutive size. The flagship Saison Rue well exemplifies what the Bruery does. The traditional Belgian/French farmhouse ale base is given an extra spicy kick from rye malt. Wild and funky Brettanomyces yeast added at bottling brings significant changes to the beer as it matures.

INGREDIENTS

6 ounces (170 g) Bairds Brown malt

0.65 ounces (18.4 g) Magnum hop pellets (14% AA) *(first wort hop)*

9.15 pounds (4.2 kg) rye liquid malt extract

0.15 ounces (4.3 g) spearmint *(20 minutes)*

9 ounces (255 g) corn sugar *(5 minutes)*

0.5 ounce (15 g) Sterling hop pellets (5.5% AA) *(end of boil)*

WLP570 Belgian Golden Ale

WLP650 Brettanomyces bruxellensis

6 ounces (170 g) corn sugar

1 Crush the Bairds Brown malt and steep in 0.5 gallon (1.9 L) of water at 160°F (71°C) for 30 minutes with the first addition of Magnum hop pellets.

2 Strain the grain into your brewpot and sparge with 0.5 gallon (1.9 L) of water at 160°F (71°C). Bring the wort to a boil, remove from the heat, and add the liquid malt extract.

3 Stir well until the extract is completely dissolved. Add water as needed to bring the total volume to 3 gallons (11.4 L). Bring the wort to a rolling boil. Boil for 60 minutes. Add the hops, spearmint, and 9 ounces (255 g) of corn sugar according to the time indicated in the ingredients list.

4 Remove from the heat. Chill the wort as quickly as possible to below 80°F (27°C) using an ice bath or wort chiller. Transfer the wort to the fermentor and add cold water to bring the total volume to 5 gallons (19 L). Stabilize the temperature at 65°F (18°C). Aerate the wort. Add the yeast.

Starting gravity:	Final gravity:	Final target alcohol by volume (ABV):	IBU:	SRM:
1.072	1.008	8.5%	30	10

5 Let the temperature slowly rise to 85°F (29°C) over the course of fermentation. When final gravity is achieved, siphon to a secondary fermentor and allow the beer to condition for 5 to 7 days. When fermentation is complete, bottle with the WLP650 Brettanomyces bruxellensis and the corn sugar.

ALL-GRAIN INSTRUCTIONS

Replace malt extract with 9.25 pounds (4.2 kg) Great Western two-row pale malt and 4.4 pounds (2 kg) Weyermann rye malt. Crush the grains and mash at 150°F (66°C) for 60 minutes. Sparge with 170°F (77°C) water until you reach a total volume of 6 gallons (22.7 L) in the brewpot. Reduce the Magnum hop addition to 0.55 ounces (15.5 g).

ALLAGASH BLACK

ALLAGASH BREWING COMPANY, PORTLAND, MAINE

F rom its founding in 1995 as a one-man operation, Allagash Brewing Company has grown into one of the most respected makers of Belgian-style ales in the United States. The brewery's lineup spans the range from a light and lively witbier to barrel-aged strong ales and spontaneously fermented sours. All bottled beers at Allagash are bottle conditioned. Allagash was one of the first in the country to use the traditional cork-and-cage closure.

Allagash Black is a complex Belgian-style stout that balances subdued, roasted-malt bitterness and dark chocolate flavors with the fruity and spicy character of Belgian yeast. Its silky-smooth texture is offset by a crisp, dry finish.

INGREDIENTS

12 ounces (340 g) flaked oats

4 ounces (115 g) wheat malt

12 ounces (340 g) chocolate malt

3.2 ounces (91 g) black malt

6.6 pounds (3 kg) Pilsner liquid malt extract

4 ounces (115 g) light dry malt extract

1.25 ounces (35.5 g) Perle hop pellets (9% AA)

2 pounds (900 g) dark candy sugar rocks

0.5 ounce (15 g) Fuggles hop pellets (4.8% AA)

Wyeast 3787 Trappist High Gravity, Wyeast 3864 Canadian/Belgian Ale, or WLP 500 Trappist Ale

6 ounces (170 g) corn sugar

1 Crush the grains and steep in 2 gallons (7.6 L) of water at 160°F (71°C) for 30 minutes.

2 Strain the grain into your brewpot and sparge with 0.5 gallon (1.9 L) 160°F (71°C) water. Add water as needed to bring the total volume to 2 gallons (7.6 L).

3 Bring the water to a boil, remove from the heat, and add the liquid and dry malt extracts. Stir well until the extract is completely dissolved. Add water to bring the total volume to 3 gallons (11.4 L). Bring the wort to a rolling boil. Boil for 60 minutes. Add the hops as indicated in the ingredients list.

4 Remove from the heat and chill the wort as quickly as possible to below 80°F (27°C) using an ice bath or wort chiller. Transfer the wort to the fermentor and add cold water to bring the total volume to 5 gallons (19 L). Aerate the wort. Add the yeast.

Starting gravity:	Final gravity:	Final target alcohol by volume (ABV):	IBU:	SRM:
1.072	1.015	7.5%	45	38 TO 40

5 Ferment at 65°F to 70°F (18°C to 21°C) until final gravity is achieved. Siphon to a secondary fermentor. Allow the beer to condition for 2 weeks. When fermentation is complete, bottle with the corn sugar.

ALL-GRAIN INSTRUCTIONS

Replace the malt extract with 9.75 pounds (4.4 kg) Pilsner malt. Crush the grains and mash at 154°F (68°C) for 60 minutes. Sparge with 170°F (77°C) water until you reach a total volume of 6.25 gallons. (23.7 L) in the brewpot. Reduce the 75-minute Perle hop addition to 1.05 ounces (29.8 g).

ALLAGASH WHITE WAS FIRST BREWED BY FOUNDER ROB TOD IN 1995.

ALLAGASH BREWING COMPANY, PORTLAND, MAINE

If there's one thing Allagash knows, it's award-winning beer, particularly Belgian-style ales. The Allagash Brewing Company of Portland, Maine, began as a dream to fill a void in the craft brewing movement. Founder Rob Tod had experience working in breweries, and he recognized that although British and German styles had found their footing in America, the lighter Belgian styles and flavors hadn't quite landed on most beer drinkers' palates this side of the pond. He decided to start a modest fifteen-barrel brewhouse, and after selling his first batch in 1995—Allagash White, Tod's version of a Belgian traditional white beer, resplendent with hints of wheat, Curacao orange peel, coriander, and more—Allagash has continued pushing the limits of what a Belgian-style beer can be.

Allagash White is still the flagship beer of the company—the first style most newcomers to the brewery try. White is available year-round, as are five other distinctive styles in red, golden, and dark Belgian styles. Allagash also counts more than three dozen specialty, Tribute Series, limited-edition, collaboration, and draft-only beers to its name, mostly found at the brewery and specialty beer stores in New England. Allagash beers are strong, often pushing 8 to 10 percent ABV, as many of the specialty and limited-edition beers spend more than 18 months fermenting. The Allagash Brewery tour has also been named one of the best in America.

ALLAGASH CURIEUX

ALLAGASH BREWING COMPANY, PORTLAND, MAINE

Curieux was the first beer in Allagash's now-extensive barrel-aging program. It's made by aging the company's Tripel Ale in Jim Beam barrels for 8 weeks. The aged beer is then blended with a portion of fresh tripel. The result is a beer of extraordinary depth. The cotton candy and black pepper flavors of the tripel merge seamlessly with darker notes of vanilla, bourbon, and oak. This one is truly world class.

INGREDIENTS

4 ounces (115 g) Weyermann acidulated malt

6 pounds (2.7 kg) Pilsner liquid malt extract

1.65 pounds (748 g) light dry malt extract

1 ounce (28 g) Northern Brewer hop pellets (8% AA) *(90 minutes)*

2 pounds (900 g) dark candy sugar rocks *(45 minutes)*

1.4 pounds (635 g) sucrose (table sugar) *(60 minutes)*

0.5 ounce (15 g) Tettnang hop pellets (4.5% AA) *(end of boil)*

Wyeast 3787 Trappist High Gravity or WLP 500 Trappist Ale

Oak spirals soaked in Jim Beam bourbon whiskey *(10 days)*

6 ounces (170 g) corn sugar

1 Crush the Weyermann acidulated malt Crush and steep in 0.5 gallon (1.9 L) of water at 160°F (71°C) for 30 minutes.

2 Strain the grain into your brewpot and sparge with 0.5 gallon (1.9 L) of water at 160°F (71°C). Add water as needed to bring the total volume to 1.5 gallons (5.7 L).

3 Bring the water to a boil, remove from the heat, and add the liquid and dry malt extracts. Stir well until the extract is completely dissolved. Add water to bring the total volume to 3 gallons (11.4 L). Bring the wort to a rolling boil. Boil for 90 minutes. Add the hops, dark candy sugar rocks, and sucrose according to the ingredients list.

4 Remove from the heat and chill the wort as quickly as possible to below 80°F (27°C) using an ice bath or wort chiller. Transfer the wort to the fermentor and add cold water to bring the total volume to 5 gallons (19 L). Aerate the wort. Add the yeast.

Starting gravity:	Final gravity:	Final target alcohol by volume (ABV):	IBU:	SRM:
1.072	1.008	9%	35	4.5 TO 5

5 Ferment at 65°F to 70°F (18°C to 21°C) until final gravity is achieved. Siphon to a secondary fermentor. Allow the beer to condition for 10 days at 40°F (4°C) and then add the oak spirals soaked in Jim Beam bourbon whiskey (10 days).

6 Allow the beer to condition for 6 weeks at 40°F (4°C). When fermentation is complete, bottle with the corn sugar.

ALL-GRAIN INSTRUCTIONS

Replace the malt extract with 12.5 pounds (5.7 kg) Pilsner malt. Crush the grains and mash at 152°F (67°C) for 60 minutes. Sparge with 170°F (77°C) water until you reach a total volume of 6.25 gallons (23.7 L) in the brewpot. Reduce the 75-minute Northern Brewer hop addition to 0.88 ounces (25 g).

SAISON
FUNKWERKS, FORT COLLINS, COLORADO

A trip to Fort Collins, Colorado, should be near the top of every beer fan's to-do list. The picturesque college town is home to several breweries and brewpubs, ranging from the huge (Anheuser-Busch and New Belgium) to the tiny (Pateros Creek). Any visit to Fort Collins should include a stop at Funkwerks. Brewer Gordon Schuck focuses entirely on Belgian and French farmhouse-style ales. A sampler flight offers a smorgasbord of yeasty funkiness. The flagship Saison is super-dry with sharp, peppery spice notes from both yeast and hops. Light fruits round out the profile.

INGREDIENTS

1.13 pounds (513 g) Gambrinus Munich 10L malt

1.13 pounds (513 g) Gambrinus Wheat malt

6 pounds (2.7 kg) Pilsner liquid malt extract

0.8 ounces (23 g) Opal hop pellets (5.8% AA) (60 minutes)

0.6 ounces (17 g) Opal hop pellets (5.8% AA) (15 minutes)

Wyeast 3711 French Saison

5 ounces (140 g) Opal hop pellets (5.8% AA)

6 ounces (170 g) corn sugar

1 Crush the Gambrinus malts and steep in 2.25 gallons (8.5 L) of water at 160°F (71°C) for 30 minutes.

2 Strain the grain into your brewpot and sparge with 0.5 gallon (1.9 L) of water at 160°F (71°C). Bring the wort to a boil, remove from the heat, and add the liquid malt extract.

3 Stir well until the extract is completely dissolved. Add water as needed to bring the total volume to 3 gallons (11.4 L). Bring the wort to a rolling boil. Boil for 60 minutes, adding the hops at the times indicated in the ingredients list.

4 Chill the wort as quickly as possible to below 80°F (27°C) using an ice bath or wort chiller. Transfer the wort to the fermentor and add cold water to bring the total volume to 5 gallons (19 L). Aerate the wort. Add the yeast.

Starting gravity:	Final gravity:	Final target alcohol by volume (ABV):	IBU:	SRM:
1.055	1.005	6.8%	23	4.2

5 Ferment at 70 to 72°F (21 to 22°C) until final gravity is achieved. Siphon to a secondary fermentor and add the dry hops.

6 Allow the beer to condition for 7 days. When fermentation is complete, bottle with the corn sugar.

ALL-GRAIN INSTRUCTIONS

Replace the malt extract with 9 pounds (4 kg) of Gambrinus Pilsner malt. Crush the grains and mash in at 90°F (32°C). Raise the temperature to 145°F (63°F) and rest for 10 minutes. Raise the temperature to 158°F (70°C) and rest for 20 minutes. Mash out at 170°F (77°C). Sparge with 170°F (77°C) water until you reach a total volume of 6 gallons (22.7 L) in the brewpot. Reduce the 60-minute Opal hop addition to 0.7 ounces (20 g). Reduce the 15-minute Opal hop addition to 0.5 ounce (15 g).

FUNKWERKS, FORT COLLINS, COLORADO

Within just a few years of selling its first batch, Funkwerks carved out a niche for itself among Belgian-style aficionados, particularly those who love a spicy saison. Indeed, Funkwerks's Saison won silver in 2011 and gold in 2012 at the Great American Beer Festival in the French- and Belgian-style Saison category.

Not every brewery can claim top finishes within its first few years, but Funkwerks can, led by its flagship Funkwerks Saison.

But let's slow down a bit. What's a saison? Many people know what they like to drink without actually knowing what it is. Saison is a style of beer that originated in southern Belgium in the 1800s. Meaning "season" in French, saisons were typically brewed during the cold winter months and given to farmers during the hot summer season, when drinking water was questionable at best. The hops and spices in a good saison are bacteria-resistant and over time provide a wide variety of differentiation in color, texture, and flavor—just one of many reasons why saison-style beers are experiencing a comeback in America. No doubt part of that charge can be attributed to Funkwerks.

Funkwerks began with a one-barrel brewing system, but in 2012, the brewery has added additional fermentors to its operation, doubling brewing capacity. The brewery sports an additional taproom, where other year-round beers and a few specialty beers can be sampled.

The Saison is described as "a tawny, orange-hued beer," with aromas of tangerine, passion fruit, and black pepper (pepper is a common flavor in many saisons). On the palate, flavors of orange, ginger, and lemon verbena explode, and the ale finishes with a "dry, lingering bitterness" that encourages another sip. Other Funkwerks-brand beers include Deceit, which also won gold in the 2012 GABF for Belgian-style Strong Specialty Ale; Tropic King Imperial Saison, with hints of mango, peach, and passion fruit; Dark Prophet, a dark, barrel-aged Belgian composed of vanilla, cocoa, caramel, and more, perfect for those cold Colorado nights; and Solenna, a sweet and spicy, candy-apple Belgian-style beer.

SALVATION
AVERY BREWING COMPANY, BOULDER, COLORADO

A very's Belgian golden ale, Salvation, was introduced in 2002 as part of Avery's Holy Trinity of strong ales that also includes Hog Heaven Barleywine and The Reverend Belgian Style Quadrupel Ale. Salvation is a classic of the style. Sweet highlights of apricot and peach stone-fruit flavors intertwine with contrasting notes of herbs, cinnamon, and white pepper. The mouth-filling, cotton-candy character from the Belgian yeast strain gives a backdrop to both. It's a strong beer, but true to the Belgian way it remains light and drinkable.

INGREDIENTS

10 ounces (280 g) Dingemans Cara-8 malt

10 ounces (280 g) Dingemans Cara-20 malt

6 pounds (2.7 kg) Pilsner liquid malt extract

2.5 pounds (1.1 kg) light dry malt extract

14.5 ounces (411 g) light Belgian candy sugar

1.4 ounces (39.7 g) Sterling hop pellets (5.5% AA) *(60 minutes)*

0.6 ounces (17 g) Sterling hop pellets (5.5% AA) *(30 minutes)*

0.8 ounces (23 g) Sterling hop pellets (5.5% AA) *(post boil, off the heat)*

2 ounces (55 g) Fuggles hop pellets (4.8% AA) *(post boil, off the heat)*

Wyeast 3787 Trappist High Gravity or WLP530 Abbey Ale

6 ounces (170 g) corn sugar

1 Crush the Dingemans malts and steep in 1 gallon (3.8 L) of water at 160°F (71°C) for 30 minutes.

2 Strain the grain into your brewpot and sparge with 0.5 gallon (1.9 L) of water at 160°F (71°C). Add water as needed to bring the total volume to 1.5 gallons (5.7 L). Bring the water to a boil, remove from the heat, and add the liquid and dry malt extracts and the Belgian candy sugar.

3 Stir well until the extract is completely dissolved. Add water to bring the total volume to 3 gallons (11.4 L). Bring the wort to a rolling boil. Boil for 60 minutes. Add the hops according to the times indicated in the ingredients list.

4 Chill the wort as quickly as possible to below 80°F (27°C) using an ice bath or wort chiller. Transfer the wort to the fermentor and add cold water to bring the total volume to 5 gallons (19 L). Aerate the wort. Add the yeast.

Starting gravity:	Final gravity:	Final target alcohol by volume (ABV):	IBU:	SRM:
1.080	1.013	8.9%	33	6.4

5 Ferment at 68°F (20°C) for the first half of fermentation and then let the temperature rise as high as possible until final gravity is achieved. Siphon to a secondary fermentor.

6 Allow the beer to condition for 7 days. When fermentation is complete, bottle with the corn sugar.

ALL-GRAIN INSTRUCTIONS

Replace the malt extract with 14.5 pounds (6.6 kg) pale two-row malt. Crush the grains and mash at 149°F (65°C) for 60 minutes. Sparge with 170°F (77°C) until you reach a total volume of 6 gallons (22.7 L) in the brewpot. Reduce the 60-minute Sterling hop addition to 1.2 ounces (34 g). Reduce the 30-minute Sterling hop addition to 0.4 ounces (11 g).

HELLION

TRVE BREWING, DENVER, COLORADO

Founded in 2011, TRVE (think of those legends chiseled over the entrances to ancient Greek buildings; in other words, think *true*) prides itself on disavowing set or expected guidelines when it comes to ingredients and styles. Witness Hellion, a unique American session ale loaded down with oats—more than three-quarters of a pound (340 g) in the case of TRVE's 5-gallon (19 L) batch. As TRVE bluntly proclaims in describing this summer lawnmower beer, it's a brew "you can drink the shit out of without worrying about your ability to remember which way's up. Notes of strawberry, blueberry, and a subtle lingering bitterness." Before you dive in, take note that this recipe must be made as either partial mash or all grain.

INGREDIENTS

1 pound (455 g) American two-row malt

1.5 pounds (680 g) Munich II malt

13 ounces (370 g) Simpsons Golden Naked Oats

6 ounces (170 g) Crystal 60L malt

3.15 pounds (1.4 kg) pale liquid malt extract

0.75 pounds (340 g) light dry malt extract

45 ounces (12.8 kg) Columbus pellet hops (15% AA) *(60 minutes)*

3 ounces (85 g) Centennial pellet hops (10.5% AA) *(end of boil, off heat)*

White Labs WLP001 California Ale

5 ounces (140 g) corn sugar

1 Heat 2 gallons (7.6 L) of water to 152°F (67°C). Crush and place the grains in a nylon-mesh bag. The temperature should be within a degree or two of 149°F (65°C). Maintain that temperature and steep for 60 minutes.

2 While the mash rests, heat 1 gallon (3.8 L) of water to 168°F (76°C) in a separate pot. When the mash is finished, return the pot to the heat and slowly raise the temperature to 168°F (76°C).

3 Strain the grain into your brewpot and sparge with the water from the second pot. Bring the wort to a boil, remove from the heat, and add the liquid and dry malt extracts. Stir well until the extract is completely dissolved. Add water as needed to bring the total volume to 3 gallons (11.4 L). Bring the wort to a rolling boil. Boil for 60 minutes. Add the hops according to the times indicated in the ingredients list.

Starting gravity:	Final gravity:	Final target alcohol by volume (ABV):	IBU:	SRM:
1.041	1.010	4%	30	11

4 Chill the wort as quickly as possible to 66°F (19°C) using an ice bath or wort chiller. Transfer the wort to the fermentor and add cold water to bring the total volume to 5 gallons (19 L). Aerate the wort. Add the yeast.

5 Ferment at 66°F (19°C) until final gravity is achieved. Allow the beer to condition for 1 week. When fermentation is complete, bottle with the corn sugar.

ALL-GRAIN INSTRUCTIONS

Replace the malt extract with 6 pounds (2.7 kg) American two-row malt for a total of 7 pounds (3.2 kg). Crush the grains and mash at 149°F (65°C) for 60 minutes. Sparge with 168°F (76°C) water to reach a total volume of 6 gallons (22.7 L) in the brewpot. Reduce the 60-minute Columbus hop addition to 0.4 ounces (11.34 g).

TRVE BREWING, DENVER, COLORADO

TRVE (pronounced "true") Brewing was founded during the summer solstice of 2011. A raging, roaring peal of thunder ripped across the Colorado sky as the silhouette of a pale horseman could be seen through the rain, wind, and moonlight. He raised a bony hand, summoning the most fervent beer drinkers and homebrewers in all the mountainous land, chanting long-forgotten, infernal brewing incantations to the dark lord of barley and hops. OK, it may not have happened *quite* like that, but TRVE Brewing was indeed founded on that warm summer night, inspired by and brewed for lovers of black metal and good, good beer. The mission, according to the company website, "has always been to create beers that are beyond the pale . . . channeling Loki and embracing chaos." Self-described "style blasphemers and category agnostics," TRVE Brewing has something for every saint and sinner.

Founder and homebrewer Nick Nunns is proud that the beers and people behind TRVE Brewing represent "being a part of a counter culture without immersing yourself to the point of taking it too seriously." From behind one of the longest single tables in Colorado—a 30-foot (9 m) oaken beauty on the main floor of his taproom—he pours beer produced in a 250-square-foot (23 m²) brewhouse behind the bar, where his three-barrel system is housed. With a smaller system, Nunns believes he can exercise greater flexibility among the flavors and styles of his beers and eschew traditional guidelines if they brew up something worth saving.

All of TRVE Brewing's beers are named after famous black metal songs or albums. From the 4 percent summer seasonal Prehistoric Dog wheat all the way up the ABV scale to the 10 percent Nazareth double IPA, the beers are intended to challenge and invigorate the senses, defying what typical beer drinkers may think of as a standard IPA, saison, or stout. Hellion, an American table beer, is a local favorite; at 4.4 percent ABV, it's a beer "you can drink the shit out of," according to the website. But don't stop there. With a constantly changing lineup of six to eight beers on tap and more available in special-edition or limited batches, there's always something new to try at TRVE Brewing's busy Baker neighborhood locale in Fort Collins.

LEVITATION
STONE BREWING COMPANY, ESCONDIDO, CALIFORNIA

T here are few names bigger in craft beer than Stone Brewing, a brewery known for bold, assertive beers that pull no punches. Levitation proves that Stone Brewing can make a session beer with as much flavor and style as its bigger brethren. Coming in at just 4.5 percent ABV, Levitation is a beer that packs a lot of flavor and depth into a "small" package.

INGREDIENTS

11.2 ounces (318 g) Crystal 75L malt

6.4 ounces (181 g) Crystal 150L malt

1 ounce (28 g) Black Patent malt

6.5 pounds (2.9 kg) pale liquid malt extract

5 ounces (140 g) Columbus hop pellets (15% AA) *(90 minutes)*

1.2 ounces (34 g) Amarillo hop pellets (9.5% AA) *(10 minutes)*

9 ounces (255 g) Crystal hop pellets (4.5% AA) *(end of boil)*

9 ounces (255 g) Simcoe hop pellets (13% AA) *(end of boil)*

0.77 ounces (22 g) Amarillo hop pellets (9.5% AA) *(dry hops)*

White Labs WLP007 Dry English Ale or WLP002 English Ale

5 ounces (140 g) corn sugar

1 Crush the grains and steep in 1 gallon (3.8 L) of water at 160°F (71°C) for 30 minutes.

2 Strain the grain into your brewpot and sparge with 0.5 gallon (1.9 L) of water at 160°F (71°C). Bring the water to a boil, remove from the heat, and add the liquid malt extract. Stir well until the extract is completely dissolved. Add water to bring the total volume to 3 gallons (11.4 L). Bring the wort to a rolling boil. Boil for 90 minutes. Add the hops at the times indicated in the ingredients list.

3 Chill the wort as quickly as possible to below 80°F (27°C) using an ice bath or wort chiller. Transfer the wort to the fermentor and add cold water to bring the total volume to 5 gallons (19 L). Aerate the wort. Add the yeast.

Starting gravity:	Final gravity:	Final target alcohol by volume (ABV):	IBU:	SRM:
1.048	1.013	4.5%	45	18

STONE'S HOP-FORWARD BEERS...

4 Ferment at 72°F (22°C) until final gravity is achieved. Siphon to a secondary fermentor and add the dry hops.

5 Allow the beer to condition for 7 days. When fermentation is complete, bottle with the corn sugar.

ALL-GRAIN INSTRUCTIONS

Replace the malt extract with 9.25 pounds (4.2 kg) of two-row pale ale malt. Crush the grains and mash at 157°F (69°C) for 60 minutes. Sparge with 170°F (77°C) water to reach a total volume of 6.5 gallons (24.6 L) in the brewpot for a 90-minute boil. Reduce the 90-minute Columbus hop addition to 0.43 ounces (12 g) and the 10-minute Amarillo addition to 1.1 ounces (31 g).

STONE BREWING COMPANY, ESCONDIDO, CALIFORNIA

The Escondido headquarters of Stone Brewing Company is also home to a 300-plus capacity restaurant and beer garden, and in the spring of 2013, Stone opened another brewing facility in the Point Loma neighborhood of San Diego. At over 20,000 square feet (1858 m²), this facility can host over 700 sud-soaked patrons at a time.

By several measures, Stone Brewing is one of the foremost leaders of craft beer you can find. But it wasn't always so—founders Steve Wagner and Greg Koch built upon their burgeoning friendship as scholars of lager at a weekend "Sensory Evaluation of Beer" conference at UC Davis in the early 1990s. They kept in touch and decided to open a brewery a few short years later using Koch's business acumen coupled with Wagner's brewing know-how. Their first full year of brewing was 1996, and Stone's yield was about 440 barrels. In 2017, they output 388,000 barrels, a 9.3 increase over the year before. Such is the power of good beer and good friends.

Like many West Coast breweries, many of Stone's beers have a strong emphasis on hops and flavor. Several of the Stone Brewing Company's beers rate well above average in ABV, with 4 percent ABV constituting the low end of the spectrum—many beers are over 8 and even 10 percent. Stone serves several beers on tap year round, including Stone Pale Ale (the flagship beer); Arrogant Bastard Ale, a brash American-style lager ("Hated by many. Loved by few. You're not worthy."); Stone IPA; Ruination IPA 2.0 (a double IPA); and many more. Many special- and limited-edition styles and reserves are brewed and available at select times throughout the year.

NUGGET NECTAR

TRÖEGS BREWING COMPANY, HERSHEY, PENNSYLVANIA

B rothers Chris and John Trogner opened Tröegs Brewing Company in 1997. Although living nearly 2,000 miles (3,219 km) apart—one in Boulder, Colorado, and the other in Philadelphia—the two hit on a love of craft beer simultaneously. That love eventually turned into a business plan. After several years of cleaning tanks, managing restaurants, and taking classes, the plan turned into a business. The seasonal Nugget Nectar is an amped-up version of the brewery's popular HopBack Amber. It delivers a bracing pine and citrus hop wallop, tempered by an ample dose of toasty and caramel malt.

INGREDIENTS

1.75 pounds (794 g) Pilsner malt

8 ounces (225 g) Dark Munich 20L malt

8 ounces (225 g) Vienna malt

8 ounces (225 g) Crystal 60L malt

6 pounds (2.7 kg) light liquid malt extract

26 ounces (737 g) light dry malt extract

1.5 ounces (43 g) Nugget hop pellets (13% AA) *(90 minutes)*

0.5 teaspoon Irish moss *(30 minutes)*

0.5 ounce (15 g) Columbus hop pellets (15% AA) *(20 minutes)*

0.5 teaspoon yeast nutrient *(15 minutes)*

0.75 ounce (21 g) Palisade hop pellets (8.25% AA) *(10 minutes)*

1 ounce (28 g) Nugget hop pellets (13% AA) *(1 minute)*

1.5 ounces (43 g) Simcoe hop pellets (13% AA) *(1 minute)*

0.5 ounce (15 g) Columbus hop pellets (15% AA) *(1 minute)*

Wyeast 1056 American Ale, WLP 001 California Ale, or Safale US-05

0.25 ounce (7 g) Columbus hop pellets (15% AA) *(dry hop)*

1 ounce (28 g) Nugget hop pellets (13% AA) *(dry hop)*

1 ounce (28 g) Simcoe hop pellets (13% AA) *(dry hop)*

6 ounces (170 g) corn sugar

1 Crush the grains and steep in 2 gallons (7.6 L) of water at 152°F (67°C) for 30 minutes.

2 Strain the grain into your brewpot and sparge with 0.5 gallon (1.9 L) of water at 160°F (71°C). Bring the water to a boil, remove from the heat, and add the liquid and dry malt extracts. Stir well until the extract is completely dissolved. Add water to bring the total volume to 3 gallons (11.4 L). Bring the wort to a rolling boil. Boil for 90 minutes. Add the hops, Irish moss, and yeast nutrient at the times indicated in the ingredients list.

3 Chill the wort as quickly as possible to below 80°F (27°C) using an ice bath or wort chiller. Transfer the wort to the fermentor and add cold water to bring the total volume to 5 gallons (19 L). Aerate the wort. Add the yeast.

Starting gravity:	Final gravity:	Final target alcohol by volume (ABV):	IBU:	SRM:
1.072	1.014	7.5%	91	12

4 Ferment at 68°F (20°C) until final gravity is achieved. Siphon to a secondary fermentor and add the dry hops.

5 Allow the beer to condition for 7 to 10 days. When fermentation is complete, bottle with the corn sugar.

ALL-GRAIN INSTRUCTIONS

Replace the malt extract with 9.5 pounds (4.3 kg) Pilsner malt, 2.5 pounds (1.1 kg) dark Munich malt, and 2.5 pounds (1.1 kg) Vienna malt. Crush the grains and mash at 152°F (67°C) for 60 minutes. Sparge with 175°F (79°C) water until you reach a total volume 6.5 gallons (24.6 L) in the brewpot. Reduce the 90-minute nugget hop addition to 1.25 ounces (35 g).

TRÖEGS BREWING COMPANY, HERSHEY, PENNSYLVANIA

Tröegs Brewing Company is the brainchild of brothers Chris and John Trogner. The name *Tröegs* comes from an old family nickname, from a portmanteau of the founders' surname—*Trogner*—and the Flemish word for *pub*, which is "Kroeg." Put together, Tröegs is what you get.

And *together* is a great way to describe the founders. Just eighteen months apart, Chris and John were more than 100 times that number apart in miles during the late 1990s, when Chris moved to Boulder, Colorado, for school and skiing, and John worked in real estate in Philadelphia. As the microbrewing scene exploded in both states, the brothers Trogner nursed the small dream of one day opening a business together. John moved to Boulder to learn the beer business, taking classes at UC Davis and Chicago's Siebel Institute of Technology. Chris kept his focus on marketing and business and hopped the pond to England to take some of the best beer classes in the world at the University of Sunderland, just south of Edinburgh on the eastern coast of the United Kingdom.

In 1997, Chris and John decided to return to their native state of Pennsylvania to establish their business, and Tröegs Brewing Company has been producing beer ever since. Tröegs produces "handcrafted world-class beers that combine traditional English brewing techniques" with good, old-fashioned American ingenuity.

One of the most popular beers Tröegs produces is a seasonal named Nugget Nectar, an orange, hopped-up "nirvana of hops," intensifying the same malt and hop flavors that make the flagship HopBack Amber Ale so popular. At 7.5 percent ABV and rated at 93 IBUs, Nugget Nectar's seasonal availability from about February to April make it a hot commodity. A wide variety of Tröegs' other offerings have been perpetual Great American Beer Award winners since 2007.

CHAPTER 3

EXTREME BREWING RECIPES

IMPERIAL PALE ALE

The pale ale style originated in the United Kingdom and the fruity, estery profile of these beers was gained, in part, by the mineral-rich water found in the regions where it was brewed. American craft brewing traditions have often revolved around taking storied continental styles and amplifying the flavors and alcohol components to make for bigger, more robust beers. The following recipe celebrates this new-world tradition.

INGREDIENTS

1 pound (455 g) 60 Lovibond Crystal malt

8 pounds (3.6 kg) pale liquid malt extract or 6.5 pounds (2.9 kg) dry light malt extract *(65 minutes)*

4.5 gallons (17 L) water

2 teaspoons (28 g) gypsum

1.5 ounces (43 g) Centennial hops (bittering) *(60 minutes)*

1 teaspoon (5 g) Irish Moss *(20 minutes)*

1 ounce (28 g) Cascade hops (flavoring) *(10 minutes)*

0.5 ounce (15 g) Cascade hops (aroma) *(end of boil)*

1 ounce (28 g) Cascade hops *(dry hop, 5 to 7 days)*

Wyeast 1056 or 1272; or White Labs WLP001 or WLP051; Safale US-05

0.5 pound (225 g) light brown sugar *(day 2 in primary)*

5 ounces (140 g) priming sugar

1 Place the crushed crystal malt in a grain bag. Tie off the top and place the bag in the brewpot filled with 4.5 gallons (17 L) of cool water. Add the gypsum. Heat the pot and stir the water and grain bag every 5 minutes.

2 Just as the water reaches 170°F (77°C), pull the grain bag out of the water using a large stirring spoon. Hold the bag above the brewpot for a minute allowing most of the liquid to drain into the pot. Do not squeeze the grain bag.

3 As the water begins to boil, remove the pot from the heat. Add the pale malt extract. Stir to prevent clumping and scorching on the bottom of the pot. Return the pot to the heat.

4 Allow the wort to come up to a boil. After preboiling for 5 minutes, add the Centennial bittering hops and stir. Start timing the 1-hour boil at the point that you make this hop addition.

Starting gravity:	Final gravity:	Final target alcohol by volume (ABV):
1.069	1.014	8.5%

5 At 20 minutes from the end of the boil, add the Irish moss and stir for 1 minute.

6 At 10 minutes before the end of the boil, add the Cascade flavoring hops and stir for 1 minute.

7 At the 60-minute mark (end of boil), add the Cascade aroma hops, stir for 1 minute, and turn off heat source. Stir the wort clockwise for 2 minutes as you build up a whirlpool effect. Stop stirring and allow the wort to sit for 10 minutes.

8 Chill the wort in a cold water bath to a temperature of 70°F to 75°F (21°C to 24°C).

9 Transfer the wort into fermentor; aerate for 1 minute.

10 Top up the wort to the 5-gallon (19 L) level with cold water.

11 Pitch the yeast into the carboy and aerate for another minute.

12 After fermentation takes off (1 or 2 days), add the light brown sugar to the fermentor by dissolving it in 2 cups (480 ml) of boiling water.

13 Once fermentation is over (no more bubbling in the air lock), add the Cascade hops for dry hopping.

14 In about 10 days, your beer should be ready to package.

15 Before bottling, clean and sanitize bottles and caps and create a priming solution of 1 cup (240 ml) boiling water and priming sugar. Siphon the beer into a sterilized bottling bucket, add the water-diluted priming solution, and gently stir. Bottle and cap the beer.

16 Allow the beer to bottle condition for about 2 weeks, and it should then be ready to drink.

DARK STAR LICORICE STOUT

A stout is a very dark ale that has a more assertive roasty malt character than a porter. The dark grains used in brewing this beer tend to give it a relatively bitter taste profile. Licorice root contains a natural acid called glycyrrhizin, which is quite sweet, even in small doses. This will act as a pleasant counterbalance to the bitterness of the dark barley.

INGREDIENTS

9 ounces (255 g) crushed black patent malt

6 ounces (170 g) crushed roasted barley malt

9.9 pounds (4.5 kg) dark liquid malt extract or 8 pounds (3.6 kg) of dark dry malt extract *(65 minutes)*

1 pound (455 g) light dry malt extract *(65 minutes)*

4.5 gallons (17 L) water

2 teaspoons (10 g) gypsum

3 ounces (85 g) Fuggles hop pellets (bittering) *(60 minutes)*

1 ounce (28 g) licorice root shredded into small pieces *(20 minutes)*

1 teaspoon (5 g) Irish moss *(20 minutes)*

0.5 ounce (15 g) Willamette hop pellets *(10 minutes)*

0.5 ounce (15 g) Fuggles hop pellets (aroma) *(end of boil)*

White Labs WLP004/1084 Irish Ale Yeast, WLP001/1056 American Ale Yeast, or Safale US-05

5 ounces (140 g) priming sugar

Starting gravity:	Final gravity:	Final target alcohol by volume (ABV):
1.084	1.020	8%

1 Fill a grain bag with the crushed black patent malt and the crushed roasted barley. Tie off the top and place the bag in your brewpot filled with 4.5 gallons (17 L) of cool water. Heat the pot and stir the water and grain bag every 5 minutes.

2 Just as the water reaches 170°F (77°C), pull out the grain bag using a large stirring spoon. Hold the bag above the brewpot for a minute, allowing most of liquid to drain into the pot. Do not squeeze the grain bag.

3 As the water begins to boil, remove the pot from the heat. Add all the malt extract. Stir well to prevent clumping and scorching on the bottom of the pot. Return the pot to heat.

4 Allow the wort to come up to a boil. After preboiling for 5 minutes, add the Fuggles bittering hop pellets and stir. Start timing the 1-hour boil at the point that you make this hop addition.

5 At 20 minutes before the end of the boil, add the chunks of licorice root and Irish moss. Stir for 1 minute.

6 At 10 minutes before the end of the boil, add the Willamette hop pellets and stir for 1 minute.

7 At the 60-minute mark, add the Fuggles aroma hop pellets, stir for 1 minute, and turn off heat source. Stir wort clockwise for 2 minutes as you build up a whirlpool effect. Stop stirring and allow wort to sit for 10 minutes.

8 Chill the wort in a cold water bath to a temperature of 70°F to 75°F (21°C to 24°C).

9 Transfer the wort into carboy. Aerate for 1 minute.

10 Pitch the yeast into the fermentor and aerate for another minute. Top up the carboy to the 5-gallon (19 L) mark with cool water.

11 In about 10 days, your beer should be ready to package.

12 Before bottling, clean and sanitize bottles and caps and create a priming solution of 1 cup (240 ml) boiling water and priming sugar. Siphon the beer into a sterilized bottling bucket, add the water-diluted priming solution, and gently stir. Bottle and cap the beer.

13 Allow the beer to bottle condition for another 10 days, and it should then be ready to drink.

BLOOD ORANGE HEFEWEIZEN

Hefeweizen is a centuries-old German style wheat beer. Because it is light, refreshing, and thirst quenching, it is traditionally drunk in the summer months, although it is a year-round staple of many commercial and homebrewers. The grain bill (the list of grain ingredients) for hefeweizens usually calls for half barley and half wheat. Hefeweizen beers are typically lightly hopped to allow the wheat and yeast characters to shine through. It's important to use a traditional German weissbier yeast and to ferment at slightly warmer temperatures if possible. Both the yeast strain and the warmer fermentation temperature will contribute the estery, fruity character so typical of hefeweizens. This recipe will magnify the traditional fruit profile of this style with the addition of blood orange meat and peels. The pectin in the fruit will make this beer a bit more cloudy, which is fine since the style is characteristically cloudy due to the wheat.

INGREDIENTS

6.6 pounds (3 kg) light liquid wheat extract (55% wheat malt and 45% barley malt) *(65 minutes)*

4 gallons (15.1 L) water

0.5 ounce (15 g) Hallertau hop pellets *(60 minutes)*

0.5 ounce (15 g) Saaz hop pellets *(20 minutes)*

4 average-sized blood oranges *(20 minutes in another pot)*

0.5 ounce (15 g) Hallertau hop pellets *(10 minutes)*

Wyeast 3068 or 3638; or White Labs WLP300, WLP320 or WLP380 or Fermenting Safebrew W306 or T58

5 ounces (140 g) priming sugar

1 Heat 4 gallons (15.1 L) of water in the brewpot. As the water begins to boil, remove it from heat. Add the light wheat malt extract. Stir to prevent clumping and scorching on the bottom of the pot. Return the pot to heat.

2 Allow the wort to come up to a boil. After preboiling for 5 minutes, add the first Hallertau hop pellets and stir. Start timing the 1-hour boil at the point that you make this hop addition.

3 At 20 minutes before the end of the boil, add the Saaz hop pellets.

4 Peel the blood oranges and separate sections of fruit. Discard half of the peels. Use a grater on the remainder of peel and cut the fruit sections into small pieces. When grating, you only want the orange part of the rind. The white will add extreme bitterness. The fruit pieces should be small enough to allow easy entry into the carboy in a later step. An alternative is to use a plastic fermentation

Starting gravity:	Final gravity:	Final target alcohol by volume (ABV):
1.050	1.12	4.8%

bucket that would allow easier addition of the fruit. When using a plastic fermentor with a large lid, the size of the fruit is not a concern. The fruit may be placed in a straining bag for easy removal after fermentation. Heat fruit and peels in 0.5 gallon (1.9 L) of water to 160°F (71°C) and then turn off heat. Let it steep as it cools.

5 At 10 minutes before the end of the boil, add the second Hallertau hop pellets and stir for 1 minute.

6 At the 60-minute mark, turn off the heat source. Stir the wort clockwise for 2 minutes as you build up a whirlpool effect. Stop stirring and allow the wort to sit for 10 minutes.

7 Chill the wort in a cold water bath to a temperature of 70°F to 75°F (21°C to 24°C).

8 Transfer the wort into a carboy or a plastic fermentor. Pour blood orange peels and fruit into the wort.

9 Aerate for 1 minute.

10 Pitch the yeast into the carboy and aerate for another minute. Top up the carboy to a 5-gallon (19 L) mark with cool water.

11 In about 10 days, your beer should be ready to package.

12 Before bottling, clean and sanitize bottles and caps and create a priming solution of 1 cup (240 ml) boiling water and priming sugar. Siphon the beer into a sterilized bottling bucket, add the water-diluted priming solution, and gently stir. Bottle and cap the beer.

13 Allow the beer to bottle condition for another 10 days, and it should then be ready to drink.

GINGER SAISON

Saisons are traditional Belgian farmhouse-style ales that are relatively light in body and color. They are usually dry and spicy from fermenting with Belgian ale yeast and contain a healthy dose of hops. They also tend to be a bit stronger in alcohol than the average beer. This version will get some additional fermentable sugars from the use of light Belgian candi (beet) sugar and the spiciness will be enhanced with a bit of crystallized ginger root.

INGREDIENTS

4.5 gallons water (17 L)

1 pound (455 g) crushed Cara-Munich barley

2 teaspoons (10 g) gypsum

6.6 pounds (3 kg) light liquid malt extract *(65 minutes)*

1 pound (455 g) light dry malt extract *(65 minutes)* (or 6 pounds [2.7 kg] light dry malt extract)

1.5 ounces (43 g) Hallertau hop pellets (bittering) *(60 minutes)*

1 pound (455 g) light Belgian candi sugar *(15 minutes)*

0.5 ounce (15 g) Hallertau hop pellets (flavor) *(10 minutes)*

1 teaspoon (5 g) Irish moss *(10 minutes)*

0.5 ounce (15 g) Styrian Golding hop pellets (aroma) *(5 minutes)*

4 ounces (115 g) crystallized ginger cut into pea size pieces *(end of boil)*

Wyeast 3724 Saison, 3725 Biere de Garde, 3726 Farm House Ale; or White Labs WLP565 Saison

5 ounces (140 g) priming sugar

1 Fill a grain bag with the crushed Cara-Munich barley. Tie off the top and place the bag in the brewpot filled with 4.5 gallons (17 L) gallons of cool water. Add the gypsum to the water. Heat the pot and stir the water and grain bag every 5 minutes.

2 As the water begins to reach 170°F (77°C), pull out the grain bag using a large stirring spoon. Hold the bag above the brewpot for a minute, allowing most of the liquid to drain into the pot. Do not squeeze the grain bag.

3 As the water begins to boil, remove the pot from the heat. Add all the malt extract (liquid and/or dry). Stir to prevent clumping and scorching on the bottom of the pot. Return the pot to heat.

4 Allow the wort to come up to a boil. After preboiling for 5 minutes, add the bittering Hallertau hop pellets and stir. Start timing the 1-hour boil at the point that you make this hop addition.

Starting gravity:	Final gravity:	Final target alcohol by volume (ABV):
1.072	1.015	7%

5 At 15 minutes before the end of the boil, add the Belgian candi sugar. Stir until all of the candi sugar is dissolved into the wort.

6 At 10 minutes before the end of the boil, add the flavoring Hallertau hop pellets and the Irish moss and stir for 1 minute.

7 At 5 minutes before the end of the boil, add the aroma Styrian Golding hop pellets and stir for 1 minute.

8 At the 60-minute mark, add the crystallized ginger, stir for 1 minute, and turn off heat source. Stir wort clockwise for 2 minutes as you build up a whirlpool effect. Stop stirring and allow the wort to sit for 10 minutes.

9 Chill the wort in a cold water bath to a temperature of 70°F to 75°F (21°C to 24°C).

10 Transfer the wort into the fermentor and aerate for 1 minute.

11 Pitch the yeast into the carboy and aerate for another minute. Top up the carboy to the 5-gallon (19 L) mark with cool water. Ferment at 68°F to 80°F (20°C to 27°C). The higher temperature will accentuate the characteristics of these Belgium yeasts.

12 In about 10 days, your beer should be ready to package.

13 Before bottling, clean and sanitize bottles and caps and create a priming solution of 1 cup (240 ml) boiling water and priming sugar. Siphon the beer into a sterilized bottling bucket, add the water-diluted priming solution, and gently stir. Bottle and cap the beer.

14 Allow the beer to bottle condition for another 10 days, and it should then be ready to drink.

TRIPEL 'ROUND THE WORLD'

Tripel Round the World can best be described as a traditional strong, pale, Belgian-style ale on an exotic road trip. In most instances, the malt sugars in Belgian tripel ales are augmented with white, brown, or candi sugar. For this version, you will venture to the Far East (or at least an Asian grocery store . . . or Amazon) for Chinese rock sugar. Usually used to braise meats, this sugar is a mixture of refined sugar, brown sugar, and honey that has a subtle pleasant spiciness. For a finishing touch, add a bit of dried chamomile to give a fruity finish that will complement the estery profile of the Belgian yeast. A vigorous yeast strain will be needed to ferment this strong brew.

INGREDIENTS

4.5 gallons (17 L) cool water

1 pound (455 g) crushed Cara-pils barley

2 teaspoons (10 g) gypsum

9.9 pounds (4.5 kg) light liquid malt extract plus 1 pound (455 g) light dry malt extract or 8 pounds (3.6 kg) light dry malt extract *(65 minutes)*

1 ounce (28 g) Saaz hop pellets (bittering) *(60 minutes)*

1 pound (455 g) Chinese rock sugar *(30 minutes)*

1 teaspoon (5 g) Irish moss *(20 minutes)*

1 ounce (28 g) East Kent Golding hop pellets (flavor) *(20 minutes)*

0.5 ounce (15 g) Saaz hop pellets (aroma) *(10 minutes)*

1 pound (455 g) Chinese rock sugar *(5 minutes)*

1.5 ounces (43 g) dried chamomile *(end of boil)*

Wyeast 1762 Belgian Abbey Yeast or 3787 Trappist High Gravity; or White Labs WLP530 or WLP575

1 pound (455 g) light brown sugar *(day 2 in primary)*

5 ounces (140 g) priming sugar

1 Fill a grain bag with the crushed Cara-pils malt. Tie off the top and place the bag in the brewpot filled with 4.5 gallons (17 L) of cool water. Add the gypsum. Heat the pot and stir the water and grain bag every 5 minutes.

2 When the water reaches 170°F (77°C), pull out the grain bag using a large stirring spoon. Hold the bag above the brewpot for a minute, allowing most of the liquid to drain into the pot. Do not squeeze the grain bag.

3 As the water begins to boil, remove the pot from the heat. Add all the malt extract. Stir to prevent clumping and scorching on the bottom of the pot. Return the brewpot to the heat.

4 Allow the wort to come to a boil. After preboiling for 5 minutes, add the Saaz hop pellets for bittering and stir. Start timing the 1-hour boil at the point that you make this hop addition.

Starting gravity:	Final gravity:	Final target alcohol by volume (ABV):
1.090	1.018	9%

5 At 30 minutes before the end of the boil, add 1 pound (455 g) of the Chinese rock sugar and stir for a minute.

6 At 20 minutes before the end of the boil, add the East Kent Golding hop pellets and the Irish moss and stir for 1 minute.

7 At 10 minutes before the end of the boil, add the aroma Saaz hop pellets and stir for 1 minute.

8 At 5 minutes before the end of the boil, add the last pound (455 g) of Chinese rock sugar and stir for 1 minute.

9 At the 60-minute mark, add the dried chamomile. Stir for 1 minute and turn off the heat source. Stir the wort clockwise for 2 minutes as you build up a whirlpool effect. Stop stirring and allow the wort to sit for 10 minutes.

10 Chill the wort in a cold-water bath to a temperature of 70°F to 75°F (21°C to 24°C).

11 Transfer the wort with the chamomile into the carboy. Aerate for 1 minute.

12 Top up the carboy with cool water to the 5-gallon (19 L) mark and aerate for another minute.

13 Pitch the yeast into the carboy.

14 After fermentation takes off (1 or 2 days), bring 2 cups (480 ml) of water to a boil and add the brown sugar. When dissolved, add this to the fermenting beer in the carboy.

15 In about 10 days, your beer should be ready to package.

16 Before bottling, clean and sanitize bottles and caps and create a priming solution of 1 cup (240 ml) boiling water and priming sugar. Siphon the beer into a sterilized bottling bucket, add the water-diluted priming solution, and gently stir. Bottle and cap the beer.

17 Allow the beer to bottle condition for another 2 weeks, and it should then be ready to drink.

KIWIT

Wit, or white, beers are traditional Belgian beers made with wheat and a variety of spices. They are relatively light in body and alcohol and are very refreshing. The style dates back to before hops were domestically grown and brewers were forced to spice or bitter their beer with whatever ingredients were handy. Modern wit beers are usually spiced with Curaçao orange peel and crushed coriander. Since Kiwi is such a refreshing tropical fruit, it works well with a wit style beer; in this recipe, the coriander will remain but Kiwi will replace the orange peel. Make sure the fresh kiwis you find for this beer are nice and firm and not mushy and browning. Soak them in hot water for a few minutes and it should be easier to peel the skin off of them.

INGREDIENTS

0.5 pound (225 g) Torrified wheat grain

0.5 pound (225 g) six-row pale malt

6.6 pounds (3 kg) wheat-barley liquid malt extract *(65 minutes)* (or 5 pounds [2.3 kg] dry wheat malt extract)

4.5 gallons (17 L) cool water

2 teaspoons (10 g) gypsum

1 ounce (28 g) Tettnanger hop pellets *(60 minutes)*

0.5 ounce (15 g) Willamette hop pellets *(10 minutes)*

0.5 ounce (15 g) crushed coriander *(10 minutes)*

1 teaspoon (5 g) Irish moss *(10 minutes)*

4 pounds (1.8 kg) fresh kiwi fruit peeled and cubed (0.5 inch [1.3 cm] cubes) *(end of boil)*

White Labs WLP400 Belgian Wit Ale or WLP410 Belgian Wit II; or Wyeast 3944 Belgian Wit or 3463 Forbidden Fruit or Safale S-33

5 ounces (140 g) priming sugar

1 Mix the grains together before filling a grain bag with the crushed six-row pale malt and the crushed Torrified wheat. Torrified grains are heated to explode the cell walls and make the grain pop, similar to puffed rice or wheat. It makes the interior of the grain more usable for the brewing process. Tie off the top and place the bag in the brewpot filled with 4.5 gallons (17 L) of cool water. Add the gypsum to the water. Heat the pot and stir the water and grain bag every few minutes.

2 When the water reaches 170°F (77°C), pull out the grain bag using a large stirring spoon. Hold the bag above the brewpot for a minute, allowing most of the liquid to drain into the pot. Do not squeeze the grain bag.

3 As the water begins to boil, remove the pot from the heat. Add the wheat-barley malt extract. Stir to prevent clumping and scorching on the bottom of the pot. Return the pot to the heat.

Starting gravity:	Final gravity:	Final target alcohol by volume (ABV):
1.052	1.014	5%

4 Allow the wort to come up to a boil. After preboiling for 5 minutes, add the Tettnanger bittering hop pellets and stir. Start timing the 1-hour boil at the point that you make this hop addition.

5 At 10 minutes before the end of the boil, add the Willamette hop pellets, coriander, and Irish moss and stir for 1 minute.

6 At the 60-minute mark in the boil, add the cubed kiwi fruit, and shut off the heat source. Stir the wort clockwise for 2 minutes as you build up a whirlpool effect. Stop stirring and allow the wort to sit for 20 minutes.

7 Chill the wort in a cold water bath to a temperature of 70°F to 75°F (21°C to 24°C). Transfer the wort and fruit into the carboy and aerate for 1 minute.

8 Pitch the yeast into the carboy or bucket and aerate for another minute. Top up the fermentor with cool water to the 5-gallon (19 L) mark.

9 Primary fermentation will take a little longer than usual (this beer should be done fermenting in 15 to 20 days). When the kiwis rise to the top of the carboy and are almost white in color, this will signify that they have been successfully stripped of their flavors and sugars.

10 Before bottling, clean and sanitize bottles and caps and create a priming solution of 1 cup (240 ml) boiling water and priming sugar. Siphon the beer into a sterilized bottling bucket, add the water-diluted priming solution, and gently stir. Bottle and cap the beer.

11 After bottling, allow the beer to bottle condition for another 10 days; it should then be ready to drink.

LAGERS

When it comes to brewing lagers, there has been significantly less experimentation in the commercial and homebrewing worlds than there has been with ales. Part of the reason for this is that it's more difficult to achieve ideal fermenting temperatures with lagers than it is with ales. The history of lager brewing plays a role in this reality as well. The German Purity Act mandates that beer can be made with *only* yeast, hops, barley, wheat, and water. This militant position has affected the lager culture in a way that stifled creative brewing with nontraditional ingredients. As homebrewers and commercial brewers outside of Germany are not obligated to obey the Purity Act, experimentation with lager brewing is on the rise. Lagers are as easy and as much fun to brew as ales. However, as lagers ferment from the bottom up at cooler temperatures, you'll need a bit more patience and access to a cooler area in order to ferment them.

The extreme lager recipes in this chapter acknowledge the genesis of the styles, but incorporate extreme ingredients and techniques.

LAGER TEMPERATURES

Ale yeasts ferment from the top down in ideal temperatures of around 70°F (21°C), and lager yeasts ferment from the bottom up in ideal temperatures of around 50°F (10°C). Because commercial breweries use brewing tanks that have cooling coils or jackets to regulate temperature, there is less challenge with maintaining proper lager temperatures. Your homebrewing carboy does not have a temperature-control system. For this reason, many homebrewers tend to brew lagers in the cooler months when cellar or garage temperatures are between 40°F and 50°F (4°C and 10°C). The easiest way to ferment lagers at the proper temperature, without having to wait around for Mother Nature, is

to convert an old refrigerator into a fermenting place. This will take some space and money but is quite effective. Look in the classified ads for a cheap but functioning used refrigerator. Once you have a suitable unit, remove the top shelves. This will create space to store your carboy comfortably and safely in the bottom of the refrigerator. Plug in the refrigerator, set the thermostat for 48°F (9°C), and wait a few hours to see if the temperature in the refrigerator will stabilize there. Most refrigerators will not control the temperature above 40°F (4°C). If this is the case with your refrigerator, an external temperature controller will be required. These are available from most homebrew stores.

REFRIGERATOR CONVERSION,
DOUG GRIFFITH, XTREMEBREWING.COM

I have found that a consistent fermentation temperature of about 68°F (20°C) makes ales taste better. I prefer the lower end of the recommended fermenting temperatures, as I've found that those temperatures work well with most ale yeasts for beers of normal gravity. To me, it is one of the main variables in brewing that most helps consistency. A few years ago, I was only making ales and in order to maintain a consistently cool temperature during the warmer months, I acquired an old refrigerator. I thought that I would be able to plug it in, adjust the thermostat for a temperature about 68°F (20°C), and be ready to ferment. Well, it wasn't quite that easy. I found that the thermostats in most refrigerators are not designed to be set for anything above 40°F (4°C); they're designed to keep food cold, not cool. After moving the heavy unit, I was determined to make it work. I discovered that an external temperature controller, available at most homebrew stores, would do exactly what I needed. The temperature controller is a device that sits or hangs on the outside of the refrigerator. The refrigerator power cord usually plugs into the backside of the temperature controller power cord. The controller has an attached temperature sensor tube that's about 3 feet (90 cm) long and gets placed inside the refrigerator. Most of the sensor tubing is about 0.125 inches (3 mm) in diameter and easily runs under the door seal to the interior of the refrigerator. Some controllers have sensors designed to be inserted into your brew in the fermentor for optimal accuracy.

Two types of controllers are available: digital display and dial. Both are sufficiently accurate. The digital display units usually have some additional features (direct-read temperature on the display and adjustable high and low temperature differential), but either will work well. When using a dial type, a thermometer inside the refrigerator helps to confirm the correct temperature setting. I set the temperature to the desired setting and put my wort inside to ferment. Now that I had a space where I could control my temperature between about 34°F (1°C) (the coldest the refrigerator fermentation space will get) and 80°F (27°C) (the warmest the temperature controller will control), I have been doing two or three lagers a year. I still like the shorter turnaround time of the ales, but many of my friends enjoy the crisp, clean taste of a lager occasionally. I make my lagers during the winter using the refrigerator and temperature controller and, at the same time, I can ferment my ales in a cool area in my house. When it starts getting warm, I usually go back to using the refrigerator for my ales. Originally, I thought that I would be able to use my newly acquired refrigerator for storing and dispensing my finished brews because I now put most of my beers in corny kegs to force-carbonate and dispense. But I found that it was difficult to juggle between finished product and fermenting. I now have a second refrigerator for dispensing, but that is another story. I am extremely pleased with my fermenting refrigerator setup, the consistency it provides, and the fact that I can now do lagers.

IMPERIAL PILSNER

A good Pilsner is quite pale in color, with a pronounced malt character. Its hop profile, however, is further forward than the malt in both taste and aroma. This recipe will be a true all-barley version of the style. In order to bring this rendition into the realm of the extreme, significantly more barley and hops than the average Pilsner calls for will be used. Since lager beers require more aging time than ales, you will need to transfer this beer to the sterilized bottling bucket, clean and sanitize the carboy, and then transfer it back into the carboy on more hops for aging. By adding the hops after fermentation is complete, the beer will maintain more of the wonderful hop aromas that would have dissipated with the CO_2 gas had the hops been added during the height of primary fermentation. You may even want to goose this Pilsner with more hop complexity by preparing the bottle-conditioning priming sugar as a hop tea.

INGREDIENTS

0.5 pound (225 g) Cara-pils crushed malt

8 pounds (3.6 kg) Pilsner or light liquid malt extract (65 minutes)

3 pounds (1.4 kg) extra light dry malt extract (65 minutes) (or 9.5 pounds [4.3 kg] Pilsner extra light dry malt extract)

4 gallons (15.1 L) cool water

2 teaspoons (10 g) gypsum

1 ounce (28 g) Saaz hop pellets (bittering) (60 minutes)

0.5 ounce (15 g) Saaz hop pellets (flavor) (20 minutes)

0.5 ounce (15 g) Saaz hop pellet (aroma) (10 minutes)

1 teaspoon (5 g) Irish moss (10 minutes)

0.5 ounce (15 g) Saaz hop pellets (aroma) (end of boil)

1 ounce (28 g) whole-leaf Hallertau hops (dry hop, 2 to 3 weeks)

1 ounce (28 g) whole-leaf Hallertau hops (final hop tea, at bottling)

Wyeast 2035 American Lager or 2124 Bohemian Lager; White Labs WLP840 or WLP830 or Saflager S-23 or S-34/70

5 ounces (140 g) priming sugar

1 Fill a grain bag with the crushed Cara-pils malt. Tie off the top and place the bag in the brewpot filled with 4 gallons (15.1 L) of cool water. Add the gypsum. Heat the pot and stir the water and grain bag every 5 minutes.

2 As the water reaches 170°F (77°C), pull out the grain bag using a large stirring spoon. Hold the bag above the brewpot for a minute, allowing most of the liquid to drain into the pot. Do not squeeze the grain bag.

3 As the water begins to boil, remove the pot from the heat. Add the lager malt extract syrup and dry malt extract. Stir to prevent clumping and scorching on the bottom of the pot. Return the pot to the heat.

4 Allow the wort to come up to a boil. After preboiling for 5 minutes, add the bittering Saaz hop pellets and stir. Start timing the 1-hour boil at the point that you make this hop addition.

Starting gravity:	Final gravity:	Final target alcohol by volume (ABV):
1.089	1.016	9%

5 At 20 minutes before the end of the boil, add the flavoring Saaz hop pellets.

6 At 10 minutes before the end of the 1-hour boil, put in the third Saaz hop pellets addition and the Irish moss and stir for 1 minute.

7 At the 60-minute mark of the boil, add the last of the Saaz hops and remove the pot from the heat source. Stir the wort clockwise for 2 minutes as you build up a whirlpool effect. Stop stirring and allow the wort to sit for 10 minutes.

8 Chill the wort in a cold water bath to just below 55°F (13°C). Use some ice in the water bath to help cool the wort to the lager fermentation temperature.

9 Transfer the wort into the carboy. Aerate for 1 minute.

10 Pitch the yeast into the carboy and aerate for another minute. Top up with water to 5 gallons (19 L).

11 Store the carboy in a cool place (at or under 50°F [10°C]) for the duration of fermentation.

12 After primary fermentation is complete (about 2 to 3 weeks), transfer the wort into a sanitized bottling bucket and then sanitize your now-empty carboy. A hydrometer gravity of around 1.015 will indicate that primary fermentation is complete. Place 1 ounce (28 g) of whole-leaf Hallertau hops in a grain bag and make sure it's well sealed. Push the grain bag through the neck of the empty carboy before transferring your beer back into it. If possible, reduce the temperature to around 40°F (4°C) for the extended lagering (storage).

13 In about 2 or 3 weeks, your beer should be ready to package.

On bottling day, boil 6 ounces (170 ml) of water and add the sugar and the final Hallertau hops. Let it steep for a good 20 minutes before straining it through a cheesecloth-lined colander (to catch the hop leafs and solids) on its way into your bottling bucket.

14 Before bottling, clean and sanitize bottles and caps and create a priming solution of 1 cup (240 ml) boiling water and priming sugar. Siphon the beer into a sterilized bottling bucket, add the water-diluted priming solution, and gently stir.

15 Allow the beer to bottle condition for about 2 weeks, and it should then be ready to drink.

PEPPERCORN RYE-BOCK

The bock beer style has been made in northern Germany and Austria for centuries. The Dutch version of a bock beer is usually a bit darker in color than those from other countries, and there is evidence that the Dutch used rye in making some versions of their bock beers. Bock beers tend to lean more on the barley than the hops for their signature character. The rye that will be used in this recipe will give the beer a nice, spicy, woody edge to cut the sweetness of the barley. Black and green peppercorns will be added to further accentuate the spicy notes in this beer.

INGREDIENTS

1 pound (455 g) flaked rye

0.5 pound (225 g) crushed Munich malt

6.6 pounds (3 kg) Pilsner or light liquid malt extract (*65 minutes*)

1 pound (455 g) light dry malt extract (*65 minutes*) (or 6 pounds [2.7 kg] extra light dry malt extract)

4.5 gallons (17 L) cool water

1 ounce (28 g) cluster hop pellets (*60 minutes*)

1 ounce (28 g) Hallertau hop pellets (*10 minutes*)

1 teaspoon (5 g) Irish moss (*10 minutes*)

1 teaspoon (2 g) milled black peppercorns (*end of boil*)

1 teaspoon (2 g) milled green peppercorns (*end of boil*)

Wyeast 2308 Munich or 2206 Bavarian Lager; or White Labs WLP838 Southern German Lager yeast

Saflager S-23 or S-34/70

5 ounces (140 g) priming sugar

1 Fill a grain bag with the flaked rye and Munich malt. Tie off the top and place the bag in your brewpot filled with 4.5 (17 L) gallons of cool water. Heat the pot, and stir the water and grain bag every 5 minutes.

2 As the water reaches 170°F (77°C), pull out the grain bag using a large stirring spoon. Hold the bag above the brewpot for a minute, allowing most of the liquid to drain into the pot. Do not squeeze the grain bag.

3 As the water begins to boil, remove the pot from the heat. Add all the malt extract. Stir to prevent clumping and scorching on the bottom of the pot. Return the pot to the heat.

4 Allow the wort to come up to a boil. After preboiling for 5 minutes, add the cluster hop pellets and stir. Start timing the 1-hour boil at the point that you make this hop addition.

Starting gravity:	Final gravity:	Final target alcohol by volume (ABV):
1.063	1.014	5.5%

5 At 10 minutes before the end of the 1-hour boil, add the Hallertau hop pellets and the Irish moss and stir for 1 minute.

6 At the 60-minute mark, add the black and green peppercorns and turn off the heat source. Stir the wort clockwise for 2 minutes as you build up a whirlpool effect. Stop stirring and allow the wort to sit for 10 minutes.

7 Chill the wort in a cold water bath to a temperature of under 55°F (13°C).

8 Transfer the wort into the carboy and aerate for 1 minute.

9 Pitch the yeast into the carboy and aerate for another minute. Top up with water to 5 gallons (19 L).

10 Store in a cool place (at or under 50°F [10°C]) for the duration of fermentation.

11 After primary fermentation is complete (about 2 to 3 weeks), transfer the wort into a sanitized bottling bucket and then sanitize your now-empty carboy. Variation: Place 1 ounce (28 g) whole-leaf Hallertau hops in a grain bag and make sure it is well sealed. Push the grain bag through the neck of the sanitized carboy.

12 In about 2 more weeks, your beer should be ready to package.

13 Before bottling, clean and sanitize bottles and caps and create a priming solution of 1 cup (240 ml) boiling water and priming sugar. Siphon the beer into a sterilized bottling bucket, add the priming sugar solution, and gently stir. Fill bottles 1 to 1.5 inches (2.5 to 3.8 cm) from the top and cap.

14 Allow the beer to bottle condition for another 2 weeks, and it should then be ready to drink.

VARIATION FOR PRIMING SUGAR:

On bottling day, boil 12 ounces (340 ml) water and 5 ounces (140 g) priming sugar. Let the temperature of the priming sugar solution drop to about 160°F (71°C) and then place 1 ounce (28 g) Hallertau leaf hops in a hop bag and put in the pot and cover. Let it steep for 20 minutes before removing the bagged hops. Add to bottling bucket and stir gently.

MOLASSES MARZEN

Marzen beers are German in heritage, have a relatively sweet malt character, and tend to have a reddish hue. Traditionally, Marzen beers were brewed in the spring to lager through the warm summer months. This method was the result of brewing these beers in the days before modern refrigeration. After fermentation, the beers were transferred into barrels and rolled deep into caves and cellars where they were packed with ice to age over the summer. The extended lagering time gives Marzen their smooth but crisp malt character. This Marzen will be a bit stronger than the standard 5 to 6 percent ABV continental version. To bump up the ABV to 8.5 percent, this recipe will use molasses. Brewing with molasses is a tradition that is actually more prevalent in Britain than in Germany, but allowing the worlds to collide can be a fun way to make an ordinary beer a bit more extreme. Be sure to use high-grade, light molasses, which is about 90 percent fermentable. In addition to sugars, molasses contains aromatics that will contribute to the flavor and complexity of this beer.

INGREDIENTS

1 pound (455 g) 60 Lovibond Crystal malt

6.6 pounds (3 kg) Pilsner or light liquid malt extract (*65 minutes*)

2 pounds (900 g) light brown sugar (*65 minutes*)

4.5 gallons (17 L) cool water

2 teaspoons (10 g) gypsum

1.5 ounces (43 g) Chinook hop pellets (*60 minutes*)

1 teaspoon (5 g) Irish moss (*20 minutes*)

1 pound (455 g) light molasses (*20 minutes*)

1 ounce (28 g) Saaz hop pellets (*10 minutes*)

1 teaspoon (5 g) Irish moss (*10 minutes*)

Wyeast 2042 Danish Lager yeast or White Labs WLP830; or Saflager S-23

8 ounces (225 g) molasses for priming

1 Fill a grain bag with the crushed 60 Lovibond crystal malt. Tie off the top and place the bag in your brewpot filled with 4.5 gallons (17 L) of cool water. Heat the pot and stir the water and grain bag every 5 minutes.

2 As the water reaches 170°F (77°C), pull out the grain bag using a large stirring spoon. Hold the bag above the brewpot for a minute, allowing the last of liquids to drain into the pot. Do not squeeze the grain bag.

3 As the water begins to boil, remove the pot from the heat. Add the light liquid malt extract and brown sugar. Stir to prevent clumping and scorching on the bottom of the pot. Return the pot to the heat.

4 Allow the wort to come up to a boil. After preboiling for 5 minutes, add the Chinook hop pellets and stir. Start timing the 1-hour boil at the point that you make this hop addition.

Starting gravity:	Final gravity:	Final target alcohol by volume (ABV):
1.080	1.016	8%

5 At 20 minutes before the end of your boil, add the light molasses; stir to prevent clumping.

6 At 10 minutes before the end of your 1-hour boil, add the Saaz hop pellets and the Irish moss and stir for 1 minute.

7 At the 60-minute mark, turn off your heat source. Stir the wort clockwise for 2 minutes as you build up a whirlpool effect. Stop stirring and allow the wort to sit for 10 minutes.

8 Chill the wort in a cold water bath to just below 55°F (13°C).

9 Transfer the wort into the carboy and aerate for 1 minute.

10 Pitch the yeast into the carboy and aerate for another minute. Top up with water to 5 gallons (19 L).

11 Store in a cool place (at or under 50°F [10°C]) for the duration of fermentation. In about 4 weeks, your beer should be ready to package.

12 On bottling day, boil 6 ounces (170 ml) of water and 1 cup (240 ml) of light molasses. Stir until the molasses is completely mixed into the solution. Pour it into bottling bucket and transferring the beer into it. Stir to mix well. The beer is now ready to bottle.

13 Allow the beer to bottle condition for another 2 weeks, and it should then be ready to drink.

PUNKIN' PORTER

Porters have been brewed in Britain and Ireland for centuries. The style is similar to a stout in color but is usually a bit lighter in alcohol content and body. Porters are also usually a bit sweeter and less roasty than a stout. This porter also has a bit more alcohol (why not?) than the garden-variety porter and will be made with both pumpkin meat and pumpkin pie spices. As with any homebrew recipe, it's always better to use natural, raw ingredients than artificial flavors. Obviously, this is a great beer to share with family and friends during the holiday season.

INGREDIENTS

Extra equipment: potato masher, food processor or blender, and a large cheesecloth-lined colander or strainer

1 to 2 gallons (3.8 to 7.6 L) water to cover pumpkin

2 pounds (900 g) fresh pumpkin, peeled and cut into 1-inch (2.5 cm) cubes

0.5 gallon (1.9 L) water

1 pound (455 g) crushed black patent malt

1.5 pounds (680 g) crushed pale six-row malt

3.3 pounds (1.5 kg) light liquid malt extract (65 minutes)

3 pounds (1.4 kg) amber dry malt extract (65 minutes)

1 pound (455 g) dark dry malt extract (65 minutes)

4.5 gallons (17 L) water

2 teaspoons (10 g) gypsum

1 ounce (28 g) Hallertau hop pellets (bittering) (60 minutes)

2 teaspoons (10 g) Irish moss (20 minutes)

1 ounce (28 g) Cascade hop pellets (20 minutes)

0.5 ounce (15 g) Hallertau hop pellets (10 minutes)

1 teaspoon (5 g) allspice (5 minutes)

1 teaspoon (5 g) cinnamon (5 minutes)

1 teaspoon (5 g) nutmeg (5 minutes)

White Labs WLP001 or Wyeast 1056 American Ale Yeast or Safale US-05

5 ounces (140 g) priming sugar

1 Wash the pumpkin and cut it in half. Remove the seeds and stringy innards. Peel the outer skin and cut it into roughly 1-inch (2.5 cm) cubes. Place the cubes in the brewpot, cover them with water—1 to 2 gallons (3.8 to 7.6 L)—and bring the pot to a low boil for 20 minutes. Mash or run the pumpkin meat through a food processor or blender. Do not discard the boiled water. Return the pumpkin to the brewpot. **Note:** A 30-ounce (850 g) can of plain pumpkin and 0.5 gallon (1.9 L) of water can be substituted if a pumpkin is not available or not in season.

2 Add 0.5 gallon (1.9 L) of cool water, the crushed black patent malt, and the crushed six-row malt to the brewpot mixture. The six-row malt has enzymes that are not in the crystal malts and will help convert most of the starches in the pumpkin into sugars. Heat the water to 155°F (68°C) and hold at that temperature for about 45 minutes. This process is called mashing, and on a large scale, it's how all the barley sugars are extracted from the grains for brewing beers at our brewery. Stir occasionally.

Starting gravity:	Final gravity:	Final target alcohol by volume (ABV):
1.078	1.014	8%

After the 45-minute mash, pour the grain, pumpkin, and water mixture through the cheesecloth-lined colander or strainer into another pot or temporarily into your fermentor. Sometimes a strainer works well and other times the pumpkin tends to clog the strainer. You are trying to remove as much of the grain as possible. Return everything that went through the strainer to the brewpot. Top up the brewpot with more water to about 4.5 (17 L) gallons. Return the pot to the heat.

3 As the water begins to boil, remove the pot from the heat. Add the malt extracts (liquid and dry). Stir to prevent clumping and scorching on the bottom of the pot. Return the pot to the heat.

4 Allow the wort to come up to a boil. After preboiling for 5 minutes, add the Hallertau hop pellets and stir. Start timing the 1-hour boil at the point that you make this hop addition.

5 At 20 minutes before the end of the boil, add the Cascade hops and the Irish moss, and stir for 1 minute.

6 At 10 minutes before the end of the boil, add the last of Hallertau aroma hop pellets and stir for 1 minute. At 5 minutes before the end of your boil, add the spices (allspice, cinnamon, and nutmeg) and stir for 1 minute.

7 At the 60-minute mark of the boil, turn off the heat source. Stir the wort clockwise for 2 minutes as you build up a whirlpool effect. Stop stirring and allow the wort to sit for 10 minutes.

8 Chill the wort in a cold water bath to a temperature of 70°F to 75°F (21°C to 24°C).

9 Transfer the wort into the carboy. Aerate for 1 minute.

10 Pitch the yeast into the carboy and aerate for another minute. Top up with water to the 5-gallon (19 L) mark.

11 After primary fermentation is complete (about 7 days), transfer the beer into a sanitized bottling bucket and then sanitize your now-empty carboy before transferring the beer back into it. This will remove much of the sediment from the pumpkin.

12 In about 2 weeks, your beer should be ready to package.

13 Before bottling, clean and sanitize bottles and caps and create a priming solution of 1 cup (240 ml) boiling water and priming sugar. Siphon beer into a sterilized bottling bucket, add the water-diluted priming solution, and gently stir. Bottle and cap the beer.

14 Allow the beer to bottle condition for another 10 days, and it should then be ready to drink.

SOUR CHERRY ALE

Belgian cherry beers are called Kriek, and they are usually brewed with wild yeast and specific bacteria strains. Later recipes in this chapter will incorporate this lambic fermentation process, but this is a more straightforward fruit beer. Because this beer is fermented with the cherry meat and pits in the fermentor, there will be some beer loss as the fruit solids absorb some of the beer. The pits will add a subtle woody character to the beer. It would be nice to have two carboys for this beer, but it is not necessary if you use your bottling bucket to transfer the beer out of the carboy (so it can be cleaned) between primary fermentation and conditioning. With its subtle red hue and excellent pairing with dark chocolate, this is a great beer for romantic occasions.

INGREDIENTS

8 ounces (225 g) crushed wheat malt

8 ounces (225 g) crushed Munich malt

6.6 pounds (3 kg) light malt extract *(65 minutes)*

4.5 gallons (17 L) cool water

2 teaspoons (10 g) gypsum

1 ounce (28 g) Northern Brewer hop pellets *(60 minutes)*

0.5 ounce (15 g) Fuggles hop pellets *(20 minutes)*

0.5 ounce (15 g) Tettnanger hop pellets *(10 minutes)*

1 teaspoon (5 g) Irish moss *(10 minutes)*

10 pounds (4.5 kg) crushed sour red cherries, 7 pounds (3.2 kg) of cherries if using frozen, or 2 pounds (900 g) dried cherries *(end of boil)*

4 teaspoons (20 g) pectic enzyme *(end of boil)*

Wyeast 1968 ESB or 1388 Belgian Strong Ale; or White Labs WLP002 English ale/ESB or Safale S-04

5 ounces (140 g) priming sugar

1 Fill a grain bag with the crushed grains (Munich and wheat). Tie off the top and place the bag in the brewpot filled with 4.5 (17 L) gallons of cool water. Add the gypsum to the water. Heat the pot and stir the water and grain bag every 5 minutes.

2 As the water reaches 170°F (77°C), pull out the specialty grain bag using a large stirring spoon. Hold the bag above the brewpot for a minute, allowing most of the liquid to drain into the pot. Do not squeeze the grain bag.

3 As the water begins to boil, remove the pot from the heat. Add the light malt extract syrup. Stir to prevent clumping and scorching on the bottom of the pot. Return the pot to the heat.

4 Allow the wort to come up to a boil. After preboiling for 5 minutes, add the Northern Brewer hop pellets and stir. Start timing the 1-hour boil at the point that you make this hop addition.

Starting gravity:	Final gravity:	Final target alcohol by volume (ABV):
1.066	1.016	6.5%

5 Add the Fuggles hops 20 minutes before the end of your boil and stir for 1 minute.

6 Add the Tettnanger hop pellets and the Irish moss 10 minutes before the end of the boil and stir for 1 minute.

7 At the 60-minute mark of the boil, turn off the heat source. Let the beer come down below 170°F (77°C). Placing the brewpot in the water bath will speed up the cooling time. Add your cherries of choice. You don't want to add the fruit to boiling beer, as the high temperature will set the natural fruit pectin, which may adversely affect the taste and clarity of your beer. Stir the wort clockwise for 2 minutes as you build up a whirlpool effect. Stop stirring and allow the wort to sit for 10 minutes.

8 Chill the wort in a cold water bath until it is below 75°F (24°C).

9 For the primary fermentation, a plastic bucket fermentor would be easier to use for this brew, as it will be difficult to get the cherries in and out of the glass carboy. To aerate, pour the wort back and forth between the plastic fermentor and your sanitized bottling bucket 4 or 5 times. Add the pectic enzyme.

10 Pitch the yeast into the fermentor and aerate for another minute. Top up to the 5-gallon (19 L) mark.

11 After primary fermentation is over (your airlock has stopped bubbling), if using the plastic fermentor, transfer your beer into the sanitized carboy, leaving behind all of the fruit, pits, and yeast solids that have settled to the bottom; if using a carboy, transfer your beer to the sanitized bottling bucket, clean the carboy, and move the beer back to the carboy.

12 In about 2 weeks, your beer should be ready to package. Rack your beer to another container to leave all sediment behind. Boil priming sugar in 1 cup (240 ml) of water. Add to racked beer. Stir to disperse sugar. Sanitize bottles and caps. Fill bottles 1 to 1.5 inches (2.5 to 3.8 cm) from top and cap.

13 Allow the beer to bottle-condition for another 2 weeks, and it should be fully carbonated.

BIG MAMA'S BARLEY WINE

B arley wines get their name because they have alcohol levels more closely associated with wine than traditional beer. They tend to follow a simple grain recipe and gain their complexity through the heightened alcohol levels, esters of the yeast, and profound hop presence in both the nose and the mouth. To bump up the alcohol in this recipe, a good amount of brown sugar and some raisins will be added. To bump up the hop profile, you will do some wort hopping (adding hops before the beer starts boiling) in addition to dry hopping the beer in the carboy during primary fermentation. Regular ale yeast might have a tough time fermenting this beer all the way down. At 11 percent alcohol by volume, this beer will not ferment completely with the ale yeast. For this reason, a Champagne yeast will be added late in fermentation (along with a bit more brown sugar to get the yeast working more quickly) and yeast nutrient (available from homebrew supply stores) to ensure complete fermentation.

INGREDIENTS

Extra equipment: food processor, a second small cooking pot, and a second stirring spoon

2 pounds (900 g) crushed 20 Lovibond Crystal malt

9.9 pounds (4.5 kg) light malt extract (*65 minutes*)

2 pounds (900 g) light brown sugar (*65 minutes*)

4 gallons (15.1 L) cool water

2 ounces (55 g) Warrior hop pellets (*60 minutes*)

0.5 ounce (15 g) whole-leaf Cascade hops (*60 minutes in a separate pot*)

1 pound (455 g) golden raisins (*60 minutes in a separate pot*)

2 ounces (55 g) Centennial hop pellets (*20 minutes*)

1 teaspoon (5 g) Irish moss (*20 minutes*)

Hop bags (*10 minutes*)

0.5 ounce (15 g) Cascade leaf hops (*10 minutes*)

Wyeast 1056 or White Labs WLP001 American Ale

Wyeast 4021 Safale US-05 or Red Star Champagne or Lalvin EC-1118 (*for secondary fermentation, 4 or 5 days after start of fermentation*)

5 teaspoons (25 g) yeast nutrient (*4 or 5 days after start of fermentation*)

0.5 pound (225 g) light brown sugar (*4 or 5 days after start of fermentation*)

1 ounce (28 g) Centennial hop pellets (*4 or 5 days after start of fermentation*)

5 ounces (140 g) priming sugar

1 Fill a grain bag with the crushed 20 Lovibond Crystal malt. Fill a second bag with 1 ounce (28 g) of whole-leaf Cascade hops. Tie off the tops and place the bags in your brewpot filled with 4 gallons (15.1 L) of cool water. Add 2 teaspoons gypsum to the water. Heat the pot and stir the water and grain bag every 5 minutes.

2 Just as the water reaches 170°F (77°C), pull out the specialty grain bag using a large stirring spoon. Hold the bag above the brewpot for a minute, allowing most of the liquid to drain into the pot. Do not squeeze the grain bag. Leave the bag with hops in the brewpot.

3 As the water begins to boil, remove the pot from the heat. Add the malt extracts (liquid and dry) and the light brown sugar. Stir to prevent clumping and scorching on the bottom of the pot. Return the pot to the heat.

Starting gravity:	Final gravity:	Final target alcohol by volume (ABV):
1.105	1.020	11%

4 Allow the wort to come up to a boil. After preboiling for 5 minutes, add the Warrior hop pellets and stir. Start timing the 1-hour boil at the point that you make this hop addition.

5 Heat 12 ounces (340 ml) of water in a second pot to a boil and shut off heat source. Add 0.5 pound (225 g) of golden raisins and the whole-leaf Cascade (loose, not in a bag) to this water to hydrate. Stir occasionally as it cools.

6 At 20 minutes before the end of your boil, add 2 ounces (55 g) of Centennial hop pellets and Irish moss and stir for 1 minute.

7 At 10 minutes before the end of the boil, add the Cascade leaf hops in a hop bag. Stir for 1 minute.

8 At 5 minutes before the end of your boil, purée the mixture of raisins, hops, and water that was in your second cooking pot. Once this mixture is a thin paste in consistency, add it to your brewpot. Stir for 1 minute.

9 At the 60-minute mark, turn off the heat source. Stir the wort clockwise for 2 minutes as you build up a whirlpool effect. Stop stirring and allow the wort to sit for 10 minutes.

10 Chill the wort in a cold water bath to a temperature of 70°F to 75°F (21°C to 24°C).

11 Transfer the wort into a carboy. Aerate for 1 minute.

12 Pitch the ale yeast into the carboy and aerate for another minute. Top up to the 5-gallon (19 L) mark with cool water.

13 After the vigorous primary fermentation slows down (around 4 or 5 days), hydrate your packet of Champagne yeast in 1 cup (240 ml) of warm water (less than 95°F [35°C]) and stir well with a sanitized spoon. Put the brown sugar in 2 cups (480 ml) 170°F (77°C) of water to dissolve. Add the hot sugar water to the carboy. Aerate. Dump the Champagne yeast mixture into the carboy along with the final ounce (28 g) of Centennial hop pellets, and replace the airlock. Aerate. Secondary fermentation should last another 2 to 3 weeks. In another 2 weeks or so, your beer should be clear and ready to package.

14 Before bottling, clean and sanitize bottles and caps and create a priming solution of 1 cup (240 ml) boiling water and priming sugar. Siphon the beer into a sterilized bottling bucket, add the water-diluted priming solution, and gently stir. Bottle and cap the beer.

15 In another 3 to 4 weeks, your beer should be ready to drink. Due to its higher alcohol content, this beer is slow to carbonate. This is a long keeper and because of the high alcohol content will age well.

CRANDADDY BRAGGOT

A braggot is a mixed-alcohol beverage of beer and mead. Traditional meads consist of nothing but fermented honey and water. Meads fermented with fruits or spices are called melomels. This braggot will be subtly spicy and have a pleasant fruitiness in both aroma and taste. To achieve this profile, orange blossom honey will be used for the desired citrus note. Additional fruit flavors will also be gained by adding rehydrated dried cranberries at the end of the boil. The honey won't be boiled as long as the barley extract syrup, as the boiling action drives off so many of the volatiles that give good meads their nice perfumey nose. But the honey does need to be heated for a while to gain sterility and drop out proteins that would contribute to a haze in the final braggot. Honey beers sometimes need a little prodding to complete a healthy fermentation because fewer of the yeast nutrients in barley are naturally present. For that reason, you will be adding some yeast nutrients (available from any good homebrew supply store) at the time that you pitch the yeast in the carboy. While the braggot will ferment at ale temperatures, the duration of the fermentation will probably be a bit longer than that of traditional beers. Allow a month or so before bottling.

INGREDIENTS

Extra equipment: second pot and a food processor or blender

6.6 pounds (3 kg) light malt extract syrup (*65 minutes*)

3 gallons (11.4 L) water

1 ounce (28 g) Hallertau hop pellets (*60 minutes*)

2 pounds (900 g) dried cranberries (*60 minutes in a separate pot*)

32 ounces (946 ml) water (*60 minutes in a separate pot*)

1 teaspoon (5 g) Irish moss (*10 minutes*)

6 pounds (2.7 kg) unfiltered orange blossom honey (*end of boil*)

1 teaspoon (5 g) pectic enzyme

5 teaspoons (25 g) yeast nutrient

Wyeast 4021; Red Star or Lalvin EC-1118; White Labs WLP715

5 ounces (140 g) priming sugar

1 Add 3 gallons (11.4 L) of water to your brewpot.

2 As the water begins to boil, remove the pot from the heat. Add the light malt extract syrup. Stir to prevent clumping and scorching on the bottom of the pot. Return the pot to the heat.

3 Allow the wort to come up to a boil. After preboiling for 5 minutes, add the Hallertau hop pellets and stir. Start timing your 1-hour boil at the point that you make this hop addition.

4 Heat 32 ounces (946 ml) of water in a second pot to a boil and shut off heat source. Add the dried cranberries to this water to rehydrate. Stir the mixture occasionally as it cools.

5 At 10 minutes before the end of the boil, add the Irish moss and stir for 1 minute. At 7.5 minutes before the end of the boil, purée the mixture of dried cranberries in a grain bag and water. Once this mixture is a thin paste in consistency, add it to the brewpot.

Starting gravity:	Final gravity:	Final target alcohol by volume (ABV):
1.082	1.010	8.5%

6 At the 60-minute mark, turn off heat source, and add the unfiltered orange blossom honey. Stir until all the honey is dissolved. Stir the wort clockwise for 2 minutes as you build up a whirlpool effect. Stop stirring and allow the wort to sit for 10 minutes.

7 Chill the wort in a cold water bath until it is just below 75°F (24°C).

8 Transfer the wort into a fermentor and aerate for 1 minute. Top up to the 5-gallon (19 L) mark with water. A bucket fermentor allows easy transfer of cranberries.

9 Pitch the Pasteur Champagne yeast, pectic enzyme, and yeast nutrient into the carboy. Aerate for another minute. In about 4 weeks, your beer should be ready to package.

10 Before bottling, clean and sanitize bottles and caps and create a priming solution of 1 cup (240 ml) boiling water and priming sugar. Siphon the beer into a sterilized bottling bucket, add the water-diluted priming solution, and gently stir. Bottle and cap the braggot. Store in a warm place.

11 In another 2 weeks, your beer should be ready to drink.

HONEYMOONS?

Mead is a honey-based, fermented drink that has been enjoyed since the dark ages. In eighteenth-century England, mead was the drink of choice at weddings as it was believed to have great fertility properties. The term "honeymoon" was born from this tradition.

PORT BARREL-AGED BELGIAN BROWN ALE

Produced for centuries in southwestern Belgium, this style of beer offers great complexity derived from wood aging, exotic fermentation, and subtle notes of fruit. An acidic mixed-yeast culture gives this beer its signature tart flavor. A healthy bit of bacteria will be incorporated into the sugar-eating process for this beer. There will be a primary fermentation on Belgian ale yeast and a secondary fermentation on a prepackaged *lactobacillus* strain. This secondary fermentation will last for about 1 month. During secondary fermentation, you will also add American oak chips that have been soaked in port (for both sterilizing and flavoring reasons). This process will add the final touches of complexity to this very unique and memorable beer.

INGREDIENTS

Extra equipment: quart jar (946 ml) to hold oak chips

4.5 gallons (17 L) cool water

1.5 pounds (680 g) Cara-pils crushed barley malt

2 teaspoons (10 g) gypsum

6.6 pounds (3 kg) light malt extract syrup *(65 minutes* (or 5 pounds [2.3 kg] dry malt extract)

1 pound (455 g) dark Belgian candy sugar *(65 minutes)*

1.5 ounces (43 g) Kent Goldings hop pellets *(60 minutes)*

0.5 ounce (15 g) Saaz hop pellets *(20 minutes)*

1 teaspoon (5 g) Irish moss *(20 minutes)*

8 ounces (225 g) molasses *(10 minutes)*

Wyeast 1388 or White Labs WLP570 Belgian Strong/ Golden Ale Primary

0.25 pounds (115 g) American oak chips, medium roast

6 ounces (170 ml) quality red port wine

Wyeast 5335 *Lactobacillus delbruecki* or White Labs WLP655 Sour (secondary fermentation)

5 ounces (140 g) priming sugar

1 Fill a grain bag with the crushed Cara-pils barley. Tie off the top and place the bag in your brewpot filled with 4.5 gallons (17 L) of cool water. Add the gypsum to the water. Heat the pot and stir the water and grain bag every 5 minutes.

2 As the water reaches 170°F (77°C), pull out the specialty grain bag using a large stirring spoon. Hold the bag above the brewpot for a minute, allowing most of the liquid to drain into the pot. Do not squeeze the grain bag.

3 As the water begins to boil, remove the pot from the heat. Add the light malt extract and the dark Belgian candy sugar. Stir to prevent clumping and scorching on the bottom of the pot. Return the pot to the heat.

4 Allow the wort to come up to a boil. After preboiling for 5 minutes, add the Kent Goldings hop pellets and stir. Start timing your 1-hour boil at the point that you make this hop addition.

Starting gravity:	Final gravity:	Final target alcohol by volume (ABV):
1.068	1.014	6.8%

5 At 20 minutes before the end of your boil, add the Saaz hop pellets and the Irish moss and stir for 1 minute.

6 At 10 minutes before the end of the boil, add the molasses and stir for 1 minute.

7 At the 60-minute mark, turn off heat source. Stir the wort clockwise for 2 minutes to build up a whirlpool effect. Stop stirring and allow the wort to sit for 10 minutes.

8 Chill the wort in a cold water bath to a temperature of 70°F to 75°F (21°C to 24°C).

9 Transfer the wort into a carboy. Aerate for 1 minute.

10 Pitch the strong ale yeast into the carboy and aerate for another minute. Top up to the 5-gallon (19 L) mark with water.

11 Place the American oak chips in a 1-quart (946 ml) jar and pour the port over the chips. Close the jar tightly and allow it to sit at room temperature for 3 weeks or as long as the beer goes through fermentation.

12 After the vigorous primary fermentation slows down (around 5 or 6 days), pitch the secondary yeast into the fermenting beer. Allow the beer to continue fermenting in a warm place (75°F [24°C]) for 2 or 3 weeks. Transfer your beer into the sterilized bottling bucket and clean and sanitize the carboy. Transfer the beer back into the carboy for the extended aging and acidification needed for this style of beer and add the port-soaked oak chips. In about 3 or 4 months, your beer should be ready to package.

13 Before bottling, clean and sanitize the bottles and caps and create a priming solution of 1 cup (240 ml) boiling water and priming sugar. Siphon the beer into a sterilized bottling bucket, add the water-diluted priming solution, and gently stir. Bottle and cap the beer.

14 In another 2 weeks, it should be ready to drink.

DEMA-GODDESS ALE

T o make this particular recipe, you will be conducting high-gravity brewing. White or light beet sugars are more highly fermentable than barley sugars, so mix in small amounts of sugar during fermentation. However, using too much of these sugars will make a beer overly dry, cidery, and hot (boozy with no body). To reduce this effect, high-quality Demerara sugar will be added during the initial boil, as well as intermittently during fermentation, to keep the body of the beer up and the dryness down. With big beers, high volumes of hops need to be added just to counterbalance the sweetness that will inevitably be left via the unfermented sugars. To fully ferment this beer, two different yeast strains and a special aerating method will be used. The boiling process drives nearly all of the oxygen out of the beer as it's being made, but yeast works best in an oxygen-rich environment. Aerating your beer is therefore recommended at the start of fermentation. However, with strong beers, sometimes that isn't enough.

For this beer, and all beers with a target alcohol by volume of over 12 percent, it's recommended to use an aquarium air pump, hose, and aerating stone to add high levels of oxygen just before pitching the primary yeast and just before adding the secondary yeast. This extreme aeration method can give your beer undesired, oxygenated, or cardboard flavors if done too late in the fermentation process. But stronger beers require extended periods of time to properly ferment. For primary and secondary fermentation periods lasting 6 to 8 weeks for the combined processes, it is not recommended to use this method of aeration beyond the third week of total fermentation. Since you will be adding sugar repeatedly during fermentation, it will be difficult to gauge the initial and final specific gravity. However, it will be important to take hydrometer readings to measure this parameter, as you add sugars during fermentation to make sure that the yeast is still performing optimally in the alcohol-rich environment.

Starting gravity:	Final gravity:	Final target alcohol by volume (ABV):
1.100 - - - - - - - - - - - - - - - - - (at the start of primary fermentation)	With this many small sugar additions and this big a beer, final gravity is anybody's guess! - - - - - - - - - - - - - - - - -	14 to 16% - - - - - - - - - - - - - - - - -

INGREDIENTS

Extra equipment: aquarium pump/hose/aerating stone setup

0.5 pound (225 g) crushed Cara-Munich barley

0.5 pound (225 g) crushed Special B barley

13.2 pounds (6 kg) light liquid malt extract or 11 pounds (5 kg) dry light malt extract *(65 minutes)*

4 gallons (15.1 L) cool water

2 teaspoons (10 g) gypsum

2 ounces (55 g) Warrior hop pellets *(60 minutes)*

2 ounces (55 g) Chinook hop pellets *(20 minutes)*

0.5 pound (225 g) cane sugar *(20 minutes)*

2 teaspoon (10 g) Irish moss *(20 minutes)*

0.5 pound (225 g) Demerara sugar *(10 minutes)*

5 teaspoons (25 g) yeast nutrient *(after cooling)*

Wyeast 1214 Abbey Ale or White Labs WLP570 Belgian Strong/Golden Ale or Safbrew T-58

1 ounce (28 g) pure cane sugar *(primary day 8)*

1 ounce (28 g) Demerara sugar *(primary day 9)*

1 ounce (28 g) pure cane sugar *(primary day 10)*

1 ounce (28 g) Demerara sugar *(primary day 11)*

1 ounce (28 g) pure cane sugar *(primary day 12)*

1 ounce (28 g) Cascade hop pellets *(primary day 13)*

Distillers yeast (secondary) *(primary day 13)*

1 ounce (28 g) pure cane sugar *(primary day 13)*

1 ounce (28 g) Demerara sugar *(primary day 14)*

1 ounce (28 g) pure cane sugar *(primary day 15)*

1 ounce (28 g) Demerara sugar *(primary day 16)*

1 ounce (28 g) pure cane sugar *(primary day 17)*

Champagne Yeast; Wyeast 4021; White Label WLP 715; Red Star Champagne or Lalvin EC-1118

5 ounces (140 g) priming sugar

Note: Day references in the recipe above are approximations. The day that you actually begin your postprimary fermentation sugar additions may vary depending upon fermentation temperatures.

1 Fill a grain bag with the crushed Cara-Munich malt and the crushed Special B malt. Tie off the top and place the bag in your brewpot filled with 4 gallons (15.1 L) of cool water. Add the gypsum to the water. Heat the pot and stir the water and grain bag every 5 minutes.

2 As the water reaches 170°F (77°C), pull out the specialty grain bag using a large stirring spoon. Hold the bag above the brewpot for a minute, allowing most of the liquid to drain into the pot. Do not squeeze the grain bag.

3 As the water begins to boil, remove the pot from the heat. Add the light malt extract. Stir to prevent clumping and scorching on the bottom of the pot. Return to heat.

4 Allow the wort to come up to a boil. After preboiling for 5 minutes, add the Tomahawk hop pellets and stir. Start timing the 1-hour boil at the point that you make this hop addition.

5 At 20 minutes before the end of the boil, add the Chinook hop pellets, 0.5 pound (225 g) of cane sugar, and the Irish moss. Stir for 1 minute.

6 At 10 minutes before the end of the boil, add 0.5 pound (225 g) of Demerara sugar and stir for 1 minute.

7 At the 60-minute mark of the boil, turn off the heat source. Stir the wort clockwise for 2 minutes as you build up a whirlpool effect. Stop stirring and allow the wort to sit for 10 minutes.

8 Chill the wort in a cold water bath to a temperature of 70°F to 75°F (21°C to 24°C).

9 Transfer the wort into a carboy. Add the yeast nutrient.

10 Pitch the primary strong ale yeast into carboy. Top up the wort to the 5-gallon (19 L) mark with water. Set up the aquarium pump, hose, and aeration stone, and oxygenate beer for 1 hour.

11 After the vigorous primary fermentation slows down (around 8 to 10 days), you will hear the airlock bubbling less frequently. Once this slowdown occurs, alternate between 1 ounce (28 g) of pure cane sugar and 1 ounce (28 g) of Demerara sugar additions to the carboy every day for 5 days straight.

12 A few days after the primary fermentation slows down, transfer your beer into the sterilized bottling bucket while you clean out the carboy. Many yeast cells have grown in this sugar-rich environment, and you want to leave the layer of dead/dormant yeast cells that have dropped to the bottom of the carboy behind as you transfer to the bottling bucket.

13 Add the Cascade hop pellets to the empty, sterilized carboy. Transfer the beer back into your sterilized carboy and pitch your secondary super high-gravity yeast. A yeast starter is a good idea. Set up your aquarium pump/hose/aerating stone unit once again and aerate the beer for 1 full hour. Again, you will be adding 1 ounce (28 g) of pure cane sugar followed by 1 ounce (28 g) of Demerara sugar the next day for 5 straight days. The difference here is that you begin the sugar additions the day that you transfer and aerate the beer for secondary fermentation. Secondary fermentation should last 1 to 3 weeks. Two weeks after all fermentation activity subsides, your beer should be ready to package.

14 For this high-gravity beer, you will be adding additional yeast at bottling to make sure that the beer has fresh yeast for the bottle conditioning. While transferring the beer to the bottling bucket, use a cup of the beer to dissolve the Champagne yeast. Add the Champagne yeast mixture to the bottling bucket and stir well. Now add the priming sugar dissolved in 1 cup (240 ml) boiling water to the bottling bucket, and stir well before bottling.

15 In another 4 to 6 weeks, your beer should be ready to drink. Due to its higher alcohol content, this beer is slow to carbonate. This is another long keeper, and it will mature well with age. It will be better after a year of aging, if you can wait that long.

WILDFLOWER WHEAT

MIKE GERHART, FORMERLY OF DOGFISH HEAD CRAFT BREWERY

The addition of chamomile flowers and honey lends this American style wheat beer a soothing character that complements warm weather and relaxation. This brew was originally made in the summer of 2005 at Dogfish Head Brewery & Eats in Rehoboth Beach, Delaware.

INGREDIENTS

6.6 pounds (3 kg) wheat/barley liquid malt extract *(75 minutes)* (or 5 pounds [2.3 kg] wheat/barley dry malt extract)

6 gallons (22.7 L) water

1 pound (455 g) honey *(75 minutes)*

1 ounce (28 g) Vanguard hops *(60 minutes)*

2 ounces (55 g) whole chamomile flowers *(60 minutes)*

White Lab WLP320 or Wyeast 1010 or Safebrew WB-06

5 ounces (140 g) priming sugar

1 In a brew kettle, heat 6 gallons (22.7 L) of water to a boil. Remove from heat and add malt extract and honey. Return to a boil.

2 Place the chamomile flowers into a mesh sack and seal. After 15 minutes, add Vanguard hops and chamomile to the kettle. Boil for 60 minutes.

3 Remove from heat and swirl the contents of the kettle to create a whirlpool.

4 Cool the wort and rack to a fermentor, leaving as much of the solids behind in the kettle as possible. (It's okay to get some of the sediment into the fermentor as it is beneficial to yeast health.)

Final gravity:	Final target alcohol by volume (ABV):	IBUs:
1.008	5.5%	15

5 Pitch the cooled wort with American wheat yeast and ferment at around 68°F to 71°F (20°C to 22°C). Allow to sit for 24 hours after fermentation is complete.

6 Cool and rack to secondary fermentor and allow 5 more days of conditioning.

7 Before bottling, clean and sanitize bottles and caps and create a priming solution of 1 cup (240 ml) boiling water and priming sugar. Siphon beer into a sterilized bottling bucket, add the water-diluted priming solution, and gently stir. Bottle and cap beer. Beer will be ready to drink in about 2 weeks.

IMPERIAL STOUT

ADAM AVERY, AVERY BREWING COMPANY

This is a souped-up interpretation on a traditional beer that has been brewed in Europe for centuries. An early example in the American craft brewing renaissance was brewed by Grant's Brewery in Washington State.

INGREDIENTS

6 ounces (170 g) Dingemans Cara 8 (caramel-pils) malt, crushed

5 ounces (140 g) Dingemans Debittered Black malt, crushed

5 ounces (140 g) Dingemans Chocolate malt, crushed

5 ounces (140 g) Weyerman Dehusked Carafa III malt, crushed

12 ounces (340 g) Gambrinus honey malt, crushed

12 ounces (340 g) Dingemans Cara 45 malt, crushed

4.5 gallons (17 L) water

12 pounds (5.4 kg) dry dark malt extract

0.5 pound (225 g) Turbinado or brown sugar (60 minutes)

0.5 ounce (15 g) Magnum hops (60 minutes)

0.5 ounce (15 g) Magnum hops (30 minutes)

1.5 ounces (43 g) Sterling hops (end of boil)

Wyeast 1056 or White Labs WLP001 ale yeast or Safale US-05

5 ounces (140 g) priming sugar

1 Steep the crushed Dingemans Cara 8, Dingemans Debittered Black, Dingemans Chocolate, Weyermans Dehusked Carafa III, Gambrinus honey malt, and Dingemans Cara 45 malt at 155°F (68°C) in 4.5 gallons (17 L) of water for 30 minutes in 2 grain bags.

2 Remove the crushed grains and add the dark malt extract and the Turbinado. Stir well. Bring to a boil.

3 Add 0.5 ounce (15 g) of the Magnum hops and boil for 30 minutes.

4 Add the remaining 10.5 ounce (15 g) of Magnum hops and boil for 30 more minutes.

5 Remove from heat and add 1.5 ounces (43 g) of Sterling hops.

Starting gravity:	Final gravity:	Final target alcohol by volume (ABV):	IBUs:
1.104	1.024	10.7%	46

6 Cool to 70°F (21°C), oxygenate, and rack to fermentor adding the necessary cold water to achieve gravity of 1.104.

7 Pitch yeast ferment at 70°F (21°C).

8 When fermentation is complete, rack to secondary vessel for 4 weeks.

9 Before bottling, clean and sanitize bottles and caps and create a priming solution of 1 cup (240 ml) boiling water and priming sugar. Siphon beer into a sterilized bottling bucket, add the water-diluted priming solution, and gently stir. Bottle and cap beer. Beer will be ready to drink in about 2 weeks.

BELGIAN WIT
ROB TOD, ALLAGASH BREWING COMPANY

This is a traditional Belgian-style wit that can be enjoyed all year. It's very refreshing served ice cold in the summer, and during the cooler seasons, it can be served at cellar temperatures where it will nicely express a subtle spice character. Wits are traditionally spiced; in addition to orange peels, this recipe calls for coriander freshly crushed from whole seeds just before the brew. When making this, try experimenting by adding your own "secret spice." Some suggestions for spices are anise, cinnamon, vanilla, pepper, or ginger. Just use a tiny pinch. Character added by the spice should only be a barely identifiable note in the background.

INGREDIENTS

6 gallons (22.7 L) water

6.6 pounds (3 kg) 40% wheat/60% barley liquid malt extract (or 5 pounds [2.3 kg] wheat/barley dry malt extract) *(75 minutes)*

0.75 ounce (21 g) Tettnanger hops (bittering) *(60 minutes)*

0.75 ounce (21 g) Saaz hops (flavor) *(30 minutes)*

0.25 ounce (7 g) Saaz hops (aroma) *(end of boil)*

0.25 ounce (7 g) freshly crushed coriander *(end of boil)*

0.25 ounce (7 g) bitter orange peel *(end of boil)*

1 pinch "secret spice" *(end of boil)*

White Labs WLP400 Belgian Wit Ale or WLP410 Belgian Wit II; or Wyeast 3944 Belgian Wit beer or 3463 Forbidden Fruit Yeast or Safbrew T-58

5 ounces (140 g) priming sugar

Note: The key to the proper flavor profile (and a nice complement to the spices) is the use of a traditional Belgian wit yeast. Most commercial yeast suppliers have yeast strains specifically designed for Belgian wits. Or, if you're feeling adventurous, you can try culturing some yeast from a bottle. Many commercial producers of these beers don't filter out the yeast, and a healthy yeast culture often rests at the bottom of a fresh bottle.

1 In a brew kettle, heat 6 gallons (22.7 L) of water to a boil. Remove from heat and add the malt extract. Return to a boil.

2 After 15 minutes, add the Tettnanger bittering hops.

3 Boil for 30 minutes.

4 Add first Saaz (flavor) hops and boil for 30 minutes.

Starting gravity:	Final gravity:	Final target alcohol by volume (ABV):	IBUs:
1.048	1.010	4.8%	18

5 At end of boil, add second Saaz aroma hops, coriander, orange peel, and a pinch of a "secret spice."

6 Remove from heat, swirl contents of kettle to create whirlpool, and allow to rest for 15 minutes.

7 Cool the wort and rack to fermentor, leaving as many of the solids behind in the kettle as possible.

8 Pitch cooled wort with Belgian wit yeast and ferment at 70°F (21°C) until fermentation is complete.

9 Before bottling, clean and sanitize bottles and caps and create a priming solution of 1 cup (240 ml) boiling water and priming sugar. Siphon beer into a sterilized bottling bucket, add the water-diluted priming solution, and gently stir. Bottle and cap beer. Beer will be ready to drink in about 2 weeks.

60-MINUTE IPA

BRYAN SELDERS, DOGFISH HEAD CRAFT BREWERY

This is a DIY version of Dogfish Head's best-selling beer. This beer uses a unique method called continual hopping. Traditionally, beers are brewed with two major hop additions: one early in the boil for bitterness and one at the end of the boil for aroma. We asked ourselves: "What would happen if we add a series of minor hop additions that occur evenly throughout the length of the boil?" From this, the idea of continual hopping was born. This recipe calls for adding the small doses of hops by hand, but you may also make your own continual-hopping device.

INGREDIENTS

6 gallons (22.7 L) water

6 ounces (170 g) crushed amber malt

7 pounds (3.2 kg) light dry malt extract *(75 minutes)*

0.5 ounce (15 g) Warrior hops *(add gradually over 60 minutes)*

0.5 ounce (15 g) Simcoe hops *(add gradually over 60 minutes)*

0.5 ounce (15 g) Amarillo hops *(add gradually over 60 minutes)*

1 teaspoon (5 g) Irish moss

0.5 ounce (15 g) Amarillo hops *(end of boil)*

Wyeast 1187 Ringwood Ale or Safale S-04; or White Labs WLP 005

1 ounce (28 g) Amarillo hops *(6 to 7 days)*

0.5 ounce (15 g) Simcoe hops *(6 to 7 days)*

5 ounces (140 g) priming sugar

1 In a brew kettle, heat 6 gallons (22.7 L) of water to 150°F (66°C). In a grain bag, add the crushed British amber malt. Allow to steep for 15 minutes.

2 Remove the grain bag and bring water to a boil. While waiting for a boil, blend together the Warrior hops with 0.5 ounce (15 g) of Simcoe and 0.5 ounce (15 g) of Amarillo hops.

3 Remove from heat and add the light malt extract.

4 Return to a boil.

5 After 15 minutes, begin adding the hop blend a little at a time so it takes 60 minutes to add all of the hops to the kettle.

6 After 60 minutes, remove the kettle from the heat and stir the wort to create a whirlpool while adding another 0.5 ounce (15 g) of Amarillo hops to the liquid. Cover and allow to settle for 20 minutes.

Starting gravity:	Final gravity:	Final target alcohol by volume (ABV):	IBUs:
1.064	1.017	6%	60

7 Cool the wort and rack to a fermentor, leaving as many of the solids behind in the kettle as possible. (It's okay to get some of the sediment into the fermentor as it's beneficial to yeast health.)

8 Pitch the cooled wort with ale yeast and ferment at around 68°F to 71°F (20°C to 22°C). "Rock the baby" to aerate the wort.

9 After 6 to 7 days, rack the beer to the secondary fermentor leaving behind as much yeast and trub as possible and add 1 (28 g) ounce of Amarillo hops and 0.5 ounce (15 g) of Simcoe hops.

10 Allow beer to condition in a secondary fermentor for 12 to 14 days

11 Before bottling, clean and sanitize bottles and caps and create a priming solution of 1 cup (240 ml) boiling water and priming sugar. Siphon beer into a sterilized bottling bucket, add the water-diluted priming solution, and gently stir.

Note: A hop bag or some type of coarse clothing over the end of the racking cane will help prevent it from getting stopped up by the hops from dry hopping. Bottle and cap beer. Beer will be ready to drink in about 2 weeks.

MIDAS TOUCH

BRYAN SELDERS, DOGFISH HEAD CRAFT BREWERY

T he recipe for Midas Touch was discovered in a 2,700-year-old tomb in Turkey, believed to belong to King Midas. In addition to its exotic pedigree, the saffron, honey, white Muscat grapes, and higher-than-average alcohol content are what make this recipe so special.

INGREDIENTS

6 gallons (22.7 L) water

8 pounds (3.6 kg) light liquid malt extract *(75 minutes)* (or 5.5 pounds [2.5 kg] light dry malt extract)

2 pounds (900 g) clover honey *(75 minutes)*

0.25 ounce (7 g) Simcoe hops *(60 minutes)*

10 Saffron threads *(end of boil)*

White Labs WLP001 or Wyeast 1056 ale yeast or Safale US-05

1 quart (946 ml) White Muscat grape juice concentrate *(3 days)*

5 ounces (140 g) priming sugar

1 In a brew kettle, heat 6 gallons (22.7 L) of water to a boil. Remove from heat and add light malt extract and honey. Return to a boil.

2 After 15 minutes, add Simcoe hops. Boil for 60 minutes.

3 Remove from heat and add saffron threads and swirl contents of kettle to create a whirlpool.

4 Cool the wort and rack to a fermentor leaving as much of the solids behind in the kettle as possible. (It's okay to get some of the sediment into the fermentor as it is beneficial to yeast health.)

5 Pitch the cooled wort with a fairly neutral ale yeast and ferment at around 68°F to 71°F (20°C to 22°C). Aerate the wort.

Starting gravity:	Final gravity:	Final target alcohol by volume (ABV):	IBUs:
1.086	1.026	9%	12

6 After the most vigorous fermentation subsides (about 3 days), add the White Muscat grape juice concentrate. Aerate again.

7 Ferment for 5 to 7 more days and then rack to secondary fermentor. Allow beer to condition for 12 to 14 days.

8 Before bottling, clean and sanitize bottles and caps and create a priming solution of 1 cup (240 ml) boiling water and priming sugar. Siphon beer into a sterilized bottling bucket, add the water-diluted priming solution, and gently stir. Bottle and cap beer. Beer will be ready to drink in about 2 weeks.

CHAPTER 4
VINTAGE BREWING RECIPES

ABOUT THE WRITER: RON PATTINSON

This section of the book will look at the origins of some of the most influential beer styles in the world that originated in Europe. The historical background and recipes in this chapter were created by Ron Pattinson, who writes extensively on the history of beer in Britain and in Europe, with particular emphasis on London, Scotland, and Germany. He is the author of several books on beer history and has worked with brewers in the United Kingdom, United States, and Europe to re-create beers from the past. These interests are covered in his expansive blog, *Shut up About Barclay Perkins*. He also maintains a website—www.europeanbeerguide.net—with pub guides to towns across Europe. He writes a regular column for *BeerAdvocate* magazine and has given lectures on subjects as diverse as the history of Lager brewing in the United Kingdom and the beers of Poughkeepsie brewer, Vassar.

Deviations from recipe standardizations (see page 12) are noted in each recipe.

NOTES ON THE RECIPES

THE COOLERS AND REFRIGERATORS AT SALT

THE REFRIGERATORS AT BASS

Before we get to the meat of the recipes that follow, there are a few things to know. Every attempt was made to make them as true as possible to the originals, but there are times when certain details are lacking in the brewing records. This will explain any modifications that were done in those cases and why. A small number of recipes were not taken from brewing records directly. Those are clearly identified as such. All the others are based on my analysis of the original brew-day document.

INGREDIENTS

These present a few challenges, mostly with colored malts. There was a huge variation in the character and color of brown and amber malt. Attempting to exactly match the one in the original recipe is a hopeless task, even if you make the malt yourself. Using what's available is really your only option. Crystal malt offers the same difficulty. In brewing records, it's recorded just as crystal malt, with no indication of its color. The one specified in these recipes is just a guess. Feel free to change it at your discretion.

MASHING

The mashing schemes have all been simplified to a single infusion followed by a sparge. That's not the way most of the beers were originally brewed. Before 1860, most beers from London had multiple mashes, sometimes combined with sparges, but sometimes not.

BOILING

Many of the original brews had much longer boil times than homebrewers usually perform. Two, three, or even four hours were not that uncommon, especially for porter and stout. In general, the boil times have been reduced it to just 90 minutes in these recipes, really just for your convenience.

There are cases where a long boil was an important part of the brewing process. Porter Brewers performed long boils to concentrate a wort to raise its gravity and to darken the wort's color.

The first isn't so relevant if you're homebrewing. You don't need to worry about wringing the last few ounces (grams) of extract out of your grains. The second is more relevant, especially in early nineteenth-century recipes, where a significant amount of color seems to have come from the boil.

HOP ADDITIONS

Almost no brewing records contain details of hop additions. In the rare occasions where they do, it is noted in the text accompanying the recipe. For the vast majority, additions were an educated guess. That guess is based upon descriptions of typical hopping schemes in old technical manuals.

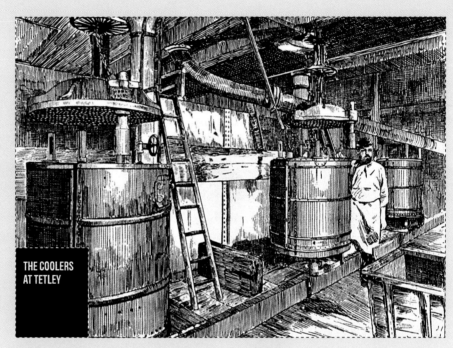

THE COOLERS AT TETLEY

Feel free to play around with the additions as you see fit. There are a couple of points to bear in mind. Very late additions are a modern technique. Where additions have been recorded, the last is no later than 30 minutes.

IBU VALUES

The (International Bitterness Unit) IBU numbers in the recipes are the theoretical values, based on the quantity of hops used. Due to physical limitations, the actual IBU numbers will be lower.

COLOR

Many beers after World War I were color adjusted with caramel at racking time. To match the color as it would have been in the pub, you'll need to do the same.

It's easy to spot recipes where this is true—I've included caramel in the ingredients, but without a quantity. The idea is that if you want to match the color of the original, you simply add enough caramel to hit the SRM number in the recipe. The amount you'll need to add will vary depending on the color of the caramel, which is why I've not filled in a quantity.

PORTER

HISTORY

Porter holds a unique place in brewing history as the world's first beer to be produced on a truly industrial scale and the first to become a global phenomenon. Yet despite its fame, the origins of porter are still clouded in mystery and obscured by myth.

EARLY EIGHTEENTH CENTURY

No source for the first half of the eighteenth century confirms the tale story that porter was an attempt to re-create a mix of three different draft beers called "three threads, and the main piece of evidence used to support the theory was written the best part of a century later.

More reliable sources like Obadiah Poundage's letter (see page 155) and *The London and Country Brewer* tell us what early porter was really like. The innovation was in creating a beer that was aged at the brewery rather than in the pub. Before porter, London brewers had shipped their beer immediately after the end of primary fermentation, leaving any aging to publicans or third parties. It was a 1720s development of the brown beer (see the section on mild beers for an explanation of the difference between beer and ale) that had been popular in London for a century or so.

A LOADED DRAY AT TRUMAN

THE PORTER VAT AT BARCLAY PERKINS

"And where such Malt-liquors are kept in Butts, more time is required to ripen, meliorate and fine them, than those kept in Hogsheads, because the greater quantity must have the longer time; so also a greater quantity will preserve itself better than a lesser one, and on this account the Butt and Hogshead are the two best sized Casks of all others; but all under a Hogshead hold rather too small a quantity to keep their Bodies." — *The London and Country Brewer, 1736*

Early porter was a standard-strength (about 1070°) beer brewed from 100 percent brown malt that was brewery aged for about 6 months before sale. Like all beers, it was heavily hopped, though the aging would have mellowed its bitterness.

The fact that tuns stood on their ends was also seen as an advantage. As the 1700s progressed, porter brewers built larger and larger barrels to mature their beer in, but always in the form of a tun.

LATE EIGHTEENTH CENTURY

Some of the most important technological developments in brewing came in the second half of the eighteenth century. Thermometers, hydrometers, steam engines, and attemperators transformed the way beer was brewed and made brewing more scientific. These developments had an impact not just on the quality of porter but also on the ingredients used to brew it.

Once the hydrometer had revealed how much greater the yield of pale malt was than brown malt, porter grists quickly began to change. The transformation was given an extra boost by the long conflict with France in the 1790s. To pay for the war with France, the tax on malt was drastically increased. Brewers eagerly accepted any way of reducing their malt usage. They began to replace some of the brown malt with pale malt.

The pressure of taxation also forced porter's gravity down to around 1050° by 1800.

EARLY NINETEENTH CENTURY

The process of increasing the pale malt content at the expense of brown malt continued, as did the war with France. The changes in grist left porter brewers with a growing concern about the color of their beer.

For a while, substances other than malt were allowed to color porter, but these were banned again in 1816. The next year, the solution was found with the development of patent or black malt. Being highly roasted, only a small quantity of it was needed to turn porter pitch black. As it was a form of malt, it was perfectly legal. It was immediately adopted, and the brown malt content could be reduced even further.

In much of Britain, brewers moved to a simpler porter grist, consisting of just pale and black malt, or sometimes pale, black, and amber malt. In London, they remained faithful to brown malt, and it was a major element in the flavor of their porters. The difference between London and Irish porter in the nineteenth century was defined by the lack of brown malt in the latter.

EAST INDIA PORTER

It's ironic that, despite the romance of its story, IPA wasn't the most popular type of beer in India. More porter was shipped to India than pale ale. If you think about it, the reason is obvious. It all has to do with class. IPA was the drink of wealthier classes, officers, and East India Company officials. Porter was drunk by the ordinary British soldiers, who numbered far more. IPA was an expensive product, beyond the means of ordinary soldiers, most of whom, in any case, were accustomed to drinking porter.

The East India Company invited tenders to supply it with both pale ale and porter. The porter was supplied by London brewers, most notably Barclay Perkins and Whitbread. East India porter, much like IPA, was tweaked to survive the journey. It was the same strength as the domestic version but more heavily hopped. The trade continued for the whole of the nineteenth century and even a little beyond. Barclay Perkins was still brewing theirs in 1910.

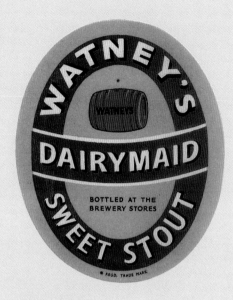

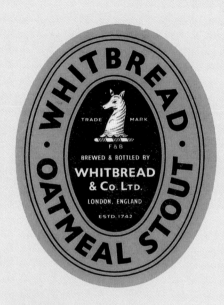

WORLD WAR I

The Great War was a disaster for British brewing in general, but for porter in particular. In 1917 and 1918, London brewers drastically cut back on their range of beers, and many dropped porter and retained stout. When they resumed brewing porter after the end of hostilities, it was at a gravity far lower than before the war. Looking at the sales figures of Whitbread, it seems that many drinkers switched from porter to stout. Not all that surprising, as the stout of the 1920s was much like prewar porter.

Porter limped along between the wars as a cheap, low-gravity beer drunk by old men in the public bar. Sales fell every year, and by the eve of World War II, only tiny quantities were being brewed. Poor sales didn't help its quality. Whitbread's Gravity Book (where they record analyses of their competitors' beers) has comments on the condition of the beer they sampled in the 1920s. Almost every sample of porter was poor.

THE END

It was another war that finally killed off porter, at least in London. Shortages of materials forced brewers to rationalize their product ranges, and a cheap, low-volume beer like porter was an obvious one to drop. Whitbread and Barclay Perkins, breweries that had made their name and their fortune brewing the style, produced their last porter in 1940.

Guinness porter managed to hang on until the 1970s, ending its days as a low-gravity beer brewed exclusively for the Northern Ireland market.

WHITBREAD PORTER GRAVITY		
YEAR	**GRAVITY**	**ABV**
1805	1051.2	–
1809	1049.3	4.58
1815	1055.7	4.98
1821	1057.6	5.35
1825	1059	5.68
1830	1059.8	5.39
1835	1061.2	5.64
1840	1062.9	5.83
1845	1063.2	5.35
1850	1065.9	5.97
1855	1059.8	5.50
1860	1055.4	5.35
1865	1057.1	5.09
1870	1058.4	5.64
1875	1055.4	4.98
1880	1056.5	5.90
1885	1056	5.72
1890	1056.5	6.02
1895	1057.6	5.51
1900	1056	5.55
1905	1055.1	5.44
1910	1053.5	5.22
1914	1053	4.89
1915	1052.4	5.47
1916	1050.4	5.21
1917	1049	4.90
1918	1036.1	3.58
1919	1042.9	4.09
1919	1044.8	4.21
1920	1041	4.10
1921	1029.4	2.96
1925	1028	2.52
1930	1028.2	2.67
1936	1029.9	2.63
1940	1028.8	2.82

1804 BARCLAY PERKINS

This is a transitional recipe, between the 100 percent brown malt eighteenth-century grists and the overwhelmingly pale malt ones of the nineteenth century. War with France had forced down porter gravities, and the brown malt content here is below 50 percent for the first time. Barclay Perkins, the second-largest brewery in the world, produced 130,000 barrels annually.

INGREDIENTS

4 pounds 3.7 ounces (1.9 kg) pale malt

4 pounds 12.9 ounces (2.18 kg) Brown malt

1 pound 5.5 ounces (0.6 kg) amber malt

1.96 ounces (59 g) Goldings pellet hops *(90 minutes)*

1.96 ounces (59 g) Goldings pellet hops *(60 minutes)*

Wyeast 1099 Whitbread Ale or Wyeast 1098 British Ale yeast

5 ounces (140 g) corn sugar

1 Mash the grains at 150°F (66°C) for 60 minutes.

2 Sparge with 179°F (82°C) water and collect 6.5 gallons (24.6 L) of wort.

3 Boil the wort for 90 minutes, adding the hops at the times indicated in the ingredients list.

4 Chill the wort as quickly as possible to 64°F (18°C) using an ice bath or wort chiller. Aerate the wort. Add the yeast.

5 Ferment at 64°F (18°C) until final gravity is achieved. Allow the beer to condition for 1 week. Bottle with corn sugar.

Starting gravity:	Final gravity:	Final target alcohol by volume (ABV):	IBUs:	SRM:
1.055	1.015	5.29%	67	27

EXTRACT INSTRUCTIONS

1 Replace the pale malt with 7 pounds 3.3 ounces (3.3 kg) pale liquid malt extract. Replace the brown and amber malts with 4 pound 2.1 ounces (1.9 kg) Crystal 60L malt and 2 pounds 7.5 ounces (1.1 kg) Crystal 20L malt. Increase both of the hop additions to 2.25 ounces (64 g).

2 Crush the crystal and black malts and steep them in a grain bag in 2.5 gallons (9.5 L) of water at 160°F (71°C) for 30 minutes. Strain the grain into your brewpot and sparge with 0.5 gallon (1.9 L) of water at 160°F (71°C). Bring the wort to a boil, remove from the heat, and add the liquid malt extract. Stir well until the extract is completely dissolved. Add water to bring the total volume to 3 gallons (11.4 L). Bring the wort to a rolling boil. Boil for 90 minutes. Add the hops at the times indicated in the ingredients list.

3 Chill the wort to 64°F (18°C). Transfer the wort to the fermentor and add cold water to bring the total volume to 5 gallons (19 L). Follow the fermentation and packaging instructions from the all-grain recipe.

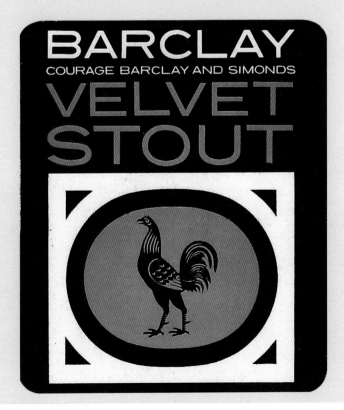

1831 TRUMAN KEEPING

There were two types of porter: keeping and running (or runner). Keeping was aged before sale; running is sold young. The two kinds of porters were the same, except keeping was much more heavily hopped. Hops were used to help preserve the beer between 6 months and 1 year aging. Brewers blended one-third keeping to two-thirds running before sale.

INGREDIENTS

7 pounds 14.2 ounces (3.6 kg) pale malt

2 pounds 14.2 ounces (1.3 kg) brown malt

3.1 ounces (88 g) black malt

3 ounces (85 g) Golding pellet hops (90 minutes)

3 ounces (85 g) Golding pellet hops (60 minutes)

Wyeast 1098 British Ale or Wyeast 1099 Whitbread Ale yeast

5 ounces (140 g) corn sugar

1 Mash the grains at 158°F (70°C) for 60 minutes.

2 Sparge with 176°F (80°C) water and collect 6.5 gallons (24.6 L) of wort.

3 Boil the wort for 90 minutes, adding the hops at the times indicated in the ingredients list.

4 Chill the wort as quickly as possible to 64°F (18°C) using an ice bath or wort chiller. Aerate the wort. Add the yeast.

5 Ferment at 64°F (18°C) until final gravity is achieved. Allow the beer to condition for 1 week. When fermentation is complete, bottle with the corn sugar.

Starting gravity:	Final gravity:	Final target alcohol by volume (ABV):	IBUs:	SRM:
1.059	1.015	5.82%	116	24

EXTRACT INSTRUCTIONS

1 Replace the pale malt with 7 pounds 3.9 ounces (3.3 kg) pale liquid malt extract. Replace the brown malt with 2 pounds 9.9 ounces (1.2 kg) Crystal 60L malt and scale the black malt to 3 ounces (85 g). Increase both of the hop additions to 3 ounces (85 g).

2 Crush the crystal and black malts and steep them in a grain bag in 2.5 gallons (9.5 L) of water at 160°F (71°C) for 30 minutes. Strain the grain into your brewpot and sparge with 0.5 gallon (1.9 L) of water at 160°F (71°C). Bring the wort to a boil, remove from the heat, and add the liquid malt extract. Stir well until the extract is completely dissolved. Add water to bring the total volume to 3 gallons (11.4 L). Bring the wort to a rolling boil. Boil for 90 minutes. Add the hops at the times indicated in the ingredients list.

3 Chill the wort to 64°F (18°C). Transfer the wort to the fermentor and add cold water to bring the total volume to 5 gallons (19 L). Follow the fermentation and packaging instructions from the all-grain recipe.

1910 FULLER'S PORTER

F uller's used flaked corn and brewing sugars enthusiastically. This recipe simplifies the several types of sugar and caramel originally used to just No. 3. This is the first time a porter gravity fell below 1050°.

INGREDIENTS

2 pounds 8 ounces (1.1 kg) pale malt two-row

1 pound 5.5 ounces (0.6 g) pale malt six-row

12.3 ounces (349 g) brown malt

12.3 ounces (349 g) black malt

3.1 ounces (88 g) flaked corn

2 pounds 1.8 ounces (1 kg) invert sugar (No. 3)

1.15 ounces (33 g) Fuggles pellet hops (*90 minutes*)

1.15 ounces (33 g) Goldings pellet hops (*60 minutes*)

Wyeast 1098 British Ale yeast

5 ounces (140 g) corn sugar

1 Mash the grains at 151°F (66°C) for 60 minutes.

2 Sparge with 170°F (77°C) water and collect 6.5 gallons (24.6 L) of wort. Add the invert sugar.

3 Boil the wort for 90 minutes, adding the hops at the times indicated in the ingredients list.

4 Chill the wort as quickly as possible to 59°F (15°C) using an ice bath or wort chiller. Aerate the wort. Add the yeast.

5 Ferment at 59°F (15°C) until final gravity is achieved. Allow the beer to condition for 1 week. When fermentation is complete, bottle with the corn sugar.

Starting gravity:	Final gravity:	Final target alcohol by volume (ABV):	IBUs:	SRM:
1.049	1.011	5.03%	44	28

EXTRACT INSTRUCTIONS

1 Replace the pale malts with 3 pounds 12.8 ounces (1.7 kg) pale liquid malt extract. Replace the brown malt with 11.3 ounces (320 g) Crystal 60L malt and scale the black malt to 11.9 ounces (337 g). Scale the invert sugar to 1 pound 12.8 ounces (0.8 kg) and add 2.4 ounces (68 g) of sucrose (table sugar). Increase both of the hop additions to 1.15 ounces (33 g).

2 Crush the crystal and black malts and steep them in a grain bag in 2.5 gallons (9.5 L) of water at 160°F (71°C) for 30 minutes. Strain the grain into your brewpot and sparge with 0.5 gallon (1.9 L) of water at 160°F (71°C). Bring the wort to a boil, remove from the heat, and add the liquid malt extract, invert sugar, and table sugar. Stir well until the extract is completely dissolved. Add water to bring the total volume to 3 gallons (11.4 L). Bring the wort to a rolling boil. Boil for 90 minutes. Add the hops at the times indicated in the ingredients list.

3 Chill the wort to 59°F (15°C). Transfer the wort to the fermentor and add cold water to bring the total volume to 5 gallons (19 L). Follow the fermentation and packaging instructions from the all-grain recipe.

STOUT

HISTORY

Much of what the preceding section says about porter applies equally to stout. Don't worry about what modern style guidelines might tell you about the differences between the two. Historically, the difference was very simple: Stout was the name given to all porter stronger than standard strength. In all respects other than strength, porter and stout were identical.

EIGHTEENTH CENTURY

The use of the word *stout* to describe strong beer preceded the development of porter, and even after its arrival wasn't used exclusively for dark beers. Brown stout (or brown stout porter) was the first name of what we now consider stout. But there was also pale stout, a beer of similar strength brewed from pale rather than brown malt. Pale stout just about lasted until the nineteenth century, dying out between 1800 and 1810.

Like porter, the original brown stouts were brewed from 100 percent brown malt. Just as with porter, the grist gradually changed to a base of pale malt with a combination of brown, black, and amber malt for color and flavor.

NINETEENTH CENTURY

While London brewers brewed only one strength of porter, stouts were produced in a range of gravities, starting at single stout and moving up through double stout and triple stout to imperial stout. Add to these keeping (beers aged before sale), running (beers sold young), and export versions and a brewer might have as many as ten different stouts in their portfolio.

WORLD WAR I

Stout wasn't spared the chaos World War I wrought on British brewing. Rationalization of their product range left many brewers with just one stout, replacing a porter and several stouts. Drinkers complained that the same beer was sold as both porter and stout:

"Porter, apparently, is no longer sold as such, but very often there is no difference between the draught stout sold and the porter excepting the price." — *Weekly Dispatch, September 9, 1917*

SWEET STOUT

Long before the use of lactose in brewing, Scottish brewers had developed a substyle of stout that was characterized by a very low degree of attenuation and minimal hopping. Often, no fresh hops were used at all, just ones that had already been boiled once in another brew. Porter and stout had never been as popular in Scotland as they had been in England, and after 1860, Scottish stouts began to diverge from those brewed south of the border.

An example is Younger's S2 from the 1880s, which had an OG of 1064 but an FG of 1030, meaning it was only 4.5 percent ABV. With its high terminal gravity and less than a quarter of the hops of a beer of the same gravity brewed in London, it must have tasted very sweet.

OATMEAL STOUT

In the 1890s, Maclay of Alloa, Scotland, developed a new type of stout that included oats in the grist. Called Oat Malt Stout, about 30 percent of the grist consisted of malted oats. They were so proud of their new invention that they placed advertisements in newspapers throughout Britain. To protect it, they also patented it.

That patent probably explains why brewers that tried to copy their success used the term oatmeal stout and used flaked rather than malted oats. It was all the rage between 1900 and 1940 with many brewers producing versions. Many were little more than a sham. London brewers Barclay Perkins and Whitbread both marketed oatmeal stouts that were in fact identical to their standard stouts. A tiny amount of flaked oats was included in the grist, and some was packaged up as oatmeal stout, the rest as just stout.

MILK STOUT

Just before World War I, Mackeson came up with a startling innovation. By adding lactose they were able to produce a reliably sweet stout without having to worry about fermentation progressing too far and drying it out. The technique was widely copied by other brewers, and the type became known as milk stout.

Early milk stouts could be surprisingly strong with gravities over 1060°. It was only after World War II that the strength dropped to around 3 percent ABV or even less.

But it would be a mistake to think that milk stout and sweet stout completely drove out the older, drier type. Many breweries continued to produce several different bottled stouts. Drier versions were 70 to 75 percent attenuated, much the same as the Guinness of the period.

LONDON STOUT

Porter may have gone into terminal decline after World War I, but stout remained popular, especially in London. Brewers there continued to make several different stouts. The majority of these were not sweet or milk stouts, but the direct descendants of nineteenth-century stouts. The gravity might have dropped, but the character remained generally the same. Stout remained popular in London right up until World War II and beyond. While draft stout had disappeared from many parts of England by the 1930s, it continued to be one of the staples of London pubs.

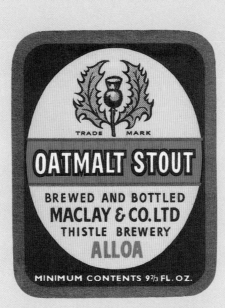

"During the last few years Younger, Charrington, Watney and other brewers have produced sweet stouts, for which there is strong demand. Some are new brews, some are a new name and label to replace the pre-1939 milk stout, now illegal unless the brew actually contains milk."
— *The Book of Beer* by Andrew Campbell, 1956

1805 BARCLAY PERKINS BST

Brown stout, the original eighteenth-century name for stout, continued to be used in London in the nineteenth century. This recipe uses a typical grist of the period with over 40 percent brown malt.

INGREDIENTS

7 pounds 11.1 ounces (3.5 kg) pale malt two-row

5 pounds 6.2 ounces (2.4 kg) brown malt

3 ounces (85 g) Goldings pellet hops *(90 minutes)*

3 ounces (85 g) Goldings pellet hops *(60 minutes)*

Wyeast 1098 British Ale or Wyeast 1099 Whitbread Ale yeast

5 ounces (140 g) corn sugar

1 Mash the grains at 150°F (66°C) for 60 minutes.

2 Sparge with 179°F (82°C) water and collect 6.5 gallons (24.6 L) of wort.

3 Boil the wort for 90 minutes, adding the hops at the times indicated in the ingredients list.

4 Chill the wort as quickly as possible to 67°F (19°C) using an ice bath or wort chiller. Aerate the wort. Add the yeast.

5 Ferment at 67°F (19°C) until final gravity is achieved. Allow the beer to condition for 1 week. When fermentation is complete, bottle with the corn sugar.

Starting gravity:	Final gravity:	Final target alcohol by volume (ABV):	IBUs:	SRM:
1.070	1.026	5.82%	92	28

EXTRACT INSTRUCTIONS

1 Replace the pale malt with 8 pounds 6 ounces (3.8 kg) pale liquid malt extract. Replace the brown malt with 4 pounds 8.2 ounes (1.3 kg) Crystal 60L malt. Increase both of the hop additions to 3 ounces (85 g).

2 Crush the crystal malt and steep in a grain bag in 2.5 gallons (9.5 L) of water at 160°F (71°F) for 30 minutes. Strain the grain into your brewpot and sparge with 0.5 gallon (1.9 L) of water at 160°F (71°C). Bring the wort to a boil, remove from the heat, and add the liquid malt extract. Stir well until the extract is completely dissolved. Add water to bring the total volume to 3 gallons (11.4 L). Bring the wort to a rolling boil. Boil for 90 minutes. Add the hops at the times indicated in the ingredients list.

3 Chill the wort to 67°F (19°C). Transfer the wort to the fermentor and add cold water to bring the total volume to 5 gallons (19 L). Follow the fermentation and packaging instructions from the all-grain recipe.

1840 TRUMAN RUNNING STOUT

This version of stout was meant to be sold unaged. It was hopped very heavily. It uses a typical London nineteenth-century stout grist.

INGREDIENTS

12 pounds 1.8 ounces (5.5 kg) pale malt two-row

1 pound 11.7 ounces (0.8 kg) brown malt

6.2 ounces (176 g) black malt

4.62 ounces (130 g) Goldings pellet hops *(90 minutes)*

4.62 ounces (130 g) Goldings pellet hops *(30 minutes)*

Wyeast 1098 British Ale or Wyeast 1099 Whitbread Ale yeast

5 ounces (140 g) corn sugar

1 Mash the grains at 160°F (71°C) for 60 minutes.

2 Sparge with 170°F (77°C) water and collect 6.5 gallons (24.6 L) of wort.

3 Boil the wort for 90 minutes, adding the hops at the times indicated in the ingredients list.

4 Chill the wort as quickly as possible to 64°F (18°C) using an ice bath or wort chiller. Aerate the wort. Add the yeast.

5 Ferment at 64°F (18°C) until final gravity is achieved. Allow the beer to condition for 1 week. When fermentation is complete, bottle with the corn sugar.

Starting gravity:	Final gravity:	Final target alcohol by volume (ABV):	IBUs:	SRM:
1.078	1.026	6.88%	92	26

EXTRACT INSTRUCTIONS

1 Replace the pale malt with 9 pounds 12.6 ounces (4.4 kg) pale liquid malt extract, replace the brown malt with 1 pound 7.7 ounces (0.7 kg) Crystal 60L malt, and scale the black malt to 5.6 ounces (159 g). Increase the 90-minute hop addition to 4.62 ounces (130 g) and the 60-minute hop addition to 4.62 ounces (130 g).

2 Crush the crystal and black malts and steep them in a grain bag in 2.5 gallons (9.5 L) of water at 160°F (71°C) for 30 minutes. Strain the grain into your brewpot and sparge with 0.5 gallon (1.9 L) of water at 160°F (71°C). Bring the wort to a boil, remove from the heat, and add the liquid malt extract. Stir well until the extract is completely dissolved. Add water to bring the total volume to 3 gallons (11.4 L). Bring the wort to a rolling boil. Boil for 90 minutes. Add the hops at the times indicated in the ingredients list.

3 Chill the wort to 64°F (18°C). Transfer the wort to the fermentor and add cold water to bring the total volume to 5 gallons (19 L). Follow the fermentation and packaging instructions from the all-grain recipe.

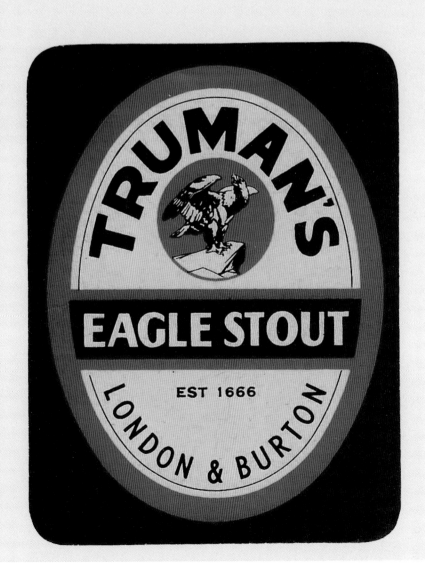

1850 TRUMAN IMPERIAL

 his recipe has a lunatic level of hopping. All the hops in the original recipe were from the 1850 crop.

INGREDIENTS

14 pounds 9.8 ounces (6.6 kg) pale malt two-row

3 pounds 4.3 ounces (1.5 kg) brown malt

6.2 ounces (170 g) black malt

4.81 ounces (136 g) Goldings pellet hops *(90 minutes)*

4.62 ounces (130 g) Goldings pellet hops *(60 minutes)*

4.62 ounces (130 g) Goldings pellet hops *(30 minutes)*

Wyeast 1098 British Ale or Wyeast 1099 Whitbread Ale yeast

5 ounces (140 g) corn sugar

1 Mash the grains at 164°F (73°C) for 60 minutes.

2 Sparge with 175°F (79°C) water and collect 6.5 gallons (24.6 L) of wort.

3 Boil the wort for 90 minutes, adding the hops at the times indicated in the ingredients list.

4 Chill the wort as quickly as possible to 62°F (17°C) using an ice bath or wort chiller. Aerate the wort. Add the yeast.

5 Ferment at 62°F (17°C) until final gravity is achieved. Allow the beer to condition for 1 week. When fermentation is complete, bottle with the corn sugar.

Starting gravity:	Final gravity:	Final target alcohol by volume (ABV):	IBUs:	SRM:
1.099	1.028	9.39%	174	31

EXTRACT INSTRUCTIONS

1 Replace the pale malt with 12 pounds 6.2 ounces (5.6 kg) pale liquid malt extract. Replace the brown malt with 2 pounds 13.8 ounces (1.3 kg) Crystal 60L malt. Scale the black malt to 5 ounces (162 g). Increase both the 90-minute hop addition to 4.81 ounces (136 g) and the 60- and 30-minute additions to 4.62 ounces (130 g).

2 Crush the crystal and black malts and steep in a grain bag in 2.5 gallons (9.5 L) of water at 160°F (71°F) for 30 minutes. Strain the grain into your brewpot and sparge with 0.5 gallon (1.9 L) of water at 160°F (71°C). Bring the wort to a boil, remove from the heat, and add the liquid malt extract. Stir well until the extract is completely dissolved. Add water to bring the total volume to 3 gallons (11.4 L). Bring the wort to a rolling boil. Boil for 90 minutes. Add the hops at the times indicated in the ingredients list.

3 Chill the wort to 62°F (17°C). Transfer the wort to the fermentor and add cold water to bring the total volume to 5 gallons (19 L). Follow the fermentation and packaging instructions from the all-grain recipe.

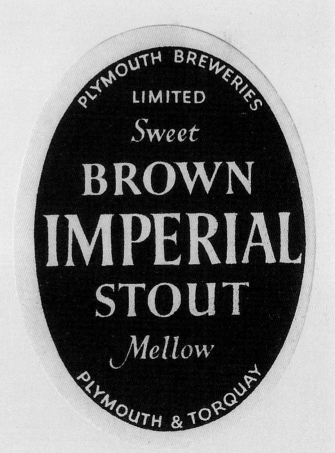

PLYMOUTH BREWERIES
LIMITED
Sweet
BROWN
IMPERIAL
STOUT
Mellow
PLYMOUTH & TORQUAY

1883 GUINNESS EXTRA STOUT

This recipe is one of the few in this collection that is not based on a brewing record. The grist, hopping rate, and the OG are from *A Bottle of Guinness, Please* by David Hughes. The FG is from a nineteenth-century analysis. Unlike London stouts, this has no brown malt. Fresh beer, aged beer, and high-gravity unfermented wort are blended together.

INGREDIENTS

12.69 pounds (5.8 kg) pale malt two-row

1.46 pounds (662 g) amber malt

0.86 pound (390 g) black malt

2.53 ounces (72 g) Fuggle pellet hops *(90 minutes)*

2.53 ounces (72 g) Fuggle pellet hops *(60 minutes)*

2.11 ounces (60 g) Goldings pellet hops *(30 minutes)*

Wyeast 1098 British Ale or Wyeast 1099 Whitbread Ale yeast

5 ounces (140 g) corn sugar

1 Mash the grains at 156°F (69°C) for 60 minutes.

2 Sparge with 165°F (74°C) water and collect 6.5 gallons (24.6 L) of wort.

3 Boil the wort for 90 minutes, adding the hops at the times indicated in the ingredients list.

4 Chill the wort as quickly as possible to 60°F (16°C) using an ice bath or wort chiller. Aerate the wort. Add the yeast.

5 Ferment at 60°F (16°C) until final gravity is achieved. Allow the beer to condition for 1 week. When fermentation is complete, bottle with the corn sugar.

Starting gravity:	Final gravity:	Final target alcohol by volume (ABV):	IBUs:	SRM:
1.076	1.018	7.67%	94	31

EXTRACT INSTRUCTIONS

1 Replace the pale malt with 11.85 pounds (5.4 kg) pale liquid malt extract. Replace the amber malt with 1.65 pounds (748 g) Crystal 20L malt. Scale the black malt to 11.8 ounces (335 g). Increase both the 90-minute and 60-minute Fuggle hop additions to 2.76 ounces (78 g) and the final 30-minute Goldings addition to 2.3 ounces (65 g).

2 Crush the crystal and black malts and steep in a grain bag in 2.5 gallons (9.5 L) of water at 160°F (71°C) for 30 minutes. Strain the grain into your brewpot and sparge with 0.5 gallon (1.9 L) of water at 160°F (71°C). Bring the wort to a boil, remove from the heat, and add the liquid malt extract. Stir well until the extract is completely dissolved. Add water to bring the total volume to 3 gallons (11.4 L). Bring the wort to a rolling boil. Boil for 90 minutes. Add the hops at the times indicated in the ingredients list.

3 Chill the wort to 60°F (16°C). Transfer the wort to the fermentor and add cold water to bring the total volume to 5 gallons (19 L). Follow the fermentation and packaging instructions from the all-grain recipe.

1910 FULLER'S BROWN STOUT

The original recipe included a tiny quantity of oats. The last iteration before World War I drastically reduced its strength. Sugars have been simplified from the original recipe.

INGREDIENTS

4 pounds 6.8 ounces (2 kg) pale malt two-row

1 pound 8.6 ounces (0.7 kg) pale malt two-row

1 pound (0.45 kg) brown malt

6.2 ounces (176 g) black malt

4.1 ounces (116 g) flaked corn

12.3 ounces (349 g) invert sugar (No. 3)

1 pound 8.6 ounces (0.7 kg) invert sugar (No. 4)

1.35 ounces (38 g) Goldings pellet hops *(90 minutes)*

0.96 ounces (27 g) Goldings pellet hops *(60 minutes)*

0.96 ounces (27 g) Goldings pellet hops *(30 minutes)*

Wyeast 1098 British Ale or Wyeast 1099 Whitbread Ale yeast

5 ounces (140 g) corn sugar

1 Mash the grains at 146°F (63°C) for 60 minutes.

2 Sparge with 180°F (82°C) water and collect 6.5 gallons (24.6 L) of wort.

3 Boil the wort for 90 minutes, adding the hops at the times indicated in the ingredients list.

4 Chill the wort as quickly as possible to 60°F (16°C) using an ice bath or wort chiller. Aerate the wort. Add the yeast.

5 Ferment at 60°F (16°C) until final gravity is achieved. Allow the beer to condition for 1 week. When fermentation is complete, bottle with the corn sugar.

Starting gravity:	Final gravity:	Final target alcohol by volume (ABV):	IBUs:	SRM:
1.070	1.022	6.35%	51	39

EXTRACT INSTRUCTIONS

1 Replace the pale malts with 5 pounds 1.2 ounces (2.3 kg) pale liquid malt extract. Replace the brown malt with 13.6 ounces (386 g) Crystal 60L malt. Scale the black malt to 5.8 ounces (164 g). Scale the No. 3 invert sugar to 1.63 pounds (739 g), the No. 4 invert sugar to 13 ounces (370 g) and add 2.9 ounces (82 g) of sucrose (table sugar). Increase the 90-minute hop addition to 1.35 ounces (38 g) and both the 60-minute and 30-minute hop additions to 0.96 ounces (27 g).

2 Crush the crystal and black malts and steep in a grain bag in 2.5 gallons (9.5 L) of water at 160°F (71°F) for 30 minutes. Strain the grain into your brewpot and sparge with 0.5 gallon (1.9 L) of water at 160°F (71°C). Bring the wort to a boil, remove from the heat, and add the liquid malt extract and sugars. Stir well until the extract is completely dissolved. Add water to bring the total volume to 3 gallons (11.4 L). Bring the wort to a rolling boil. Boil for 90 minutes. Add the hops at the times indicated in the ingredients list.

3 Chill the wort to 60°F (16°C). Transfer the wort to the fermentor and add cold water to bring the total volume to 5 gallons (19 L). Follow the fermentation and packaging instructions from the all-grain recipe.

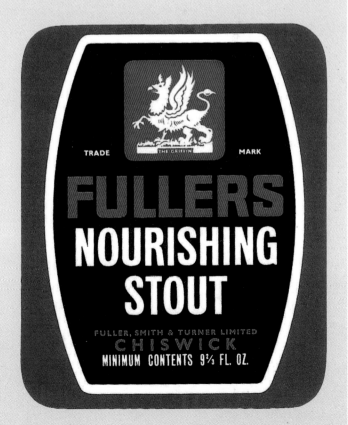

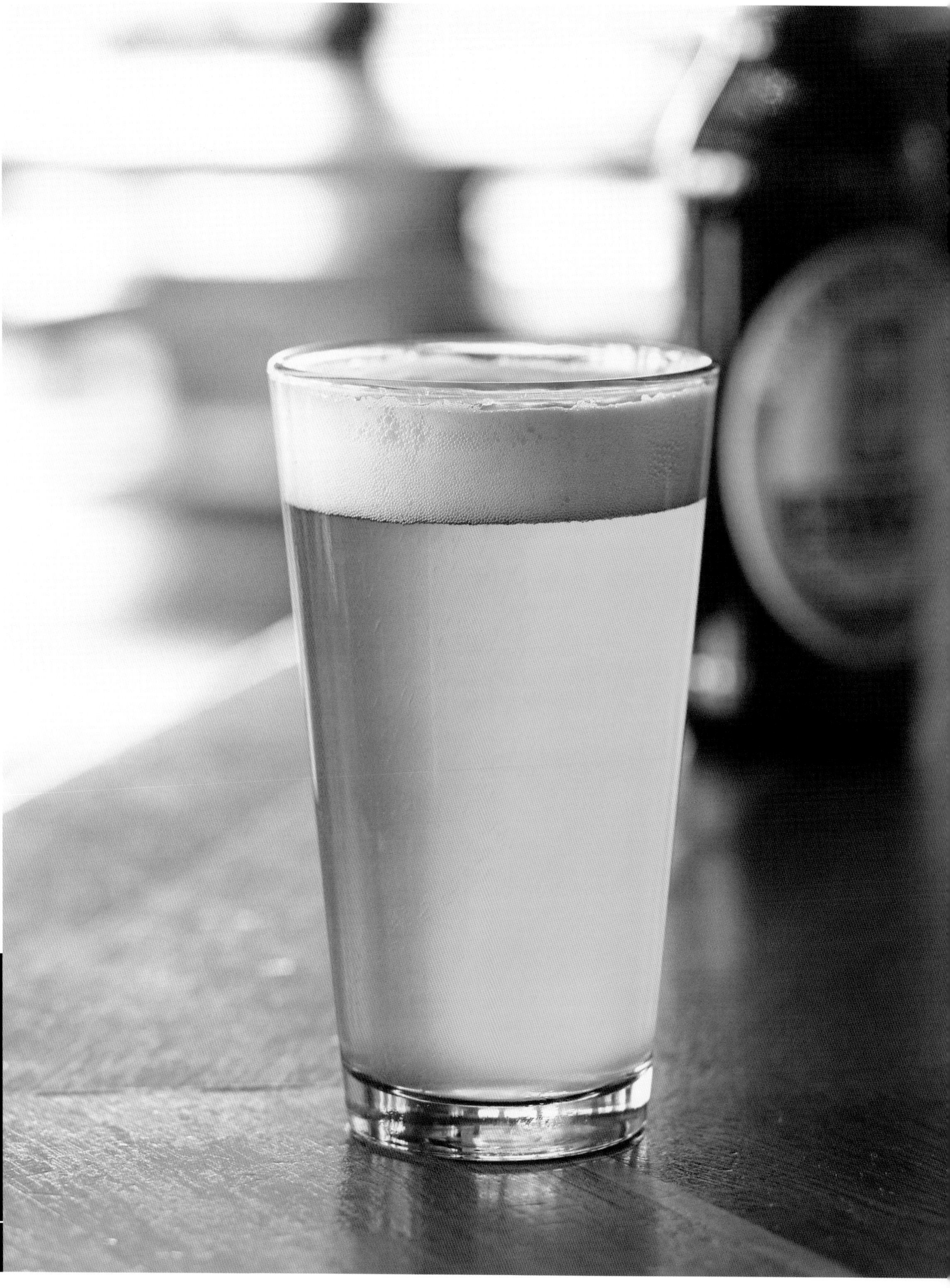

IPA

HISTORY

The story of IPA is one of the most romantic in brewing history. But much of what you think you know about IPA isn't true. Myths have grown up through the years that shroud the real history of the style.

The first pale ales were exported to India in the second half of the eighteenth century. The term IPA wasn't coined immediately, with clumsy designations like "pale ale prepared for India" being used initially. The first recorded use of India pale ale is in a newspaper article of 1829. After that date, the term soon passed into common usage. No one really knows what these early pale ales for India were like, as no brewing records still exist. There has been much speculation that they evolved from pale October beer. This was a type of strong stock ale, brewed from 100 percent pale malt and aggressively hopped. But it is only speculation, as the exact details have been lost to time.

NINETEENTH CENTURY

A brewery called Hodgson was able to establish a near monopoly in the trade of pale ale to India in the early years of the nineteenth century. The brewery was handily situated close to the docks where the East India Company's ships loaded up. The captains and crew of the East India Company's ships were allowed to trade on their own behalf. Hodgson was canny enough to let them have beer on extended credit, not requiring payment until they returned.

When Hodgson began to demand cash up front for their beer in 1821, the East India Company looked for other sources of pale ale. In 1822, Campbell Marjoribanks, an official of the company, suggested to brewer Samuel Allsopp that India might be a suitable replacement export market for the Russian one that he had just lost through increases in tariffs.

Back in Burton, Allsopp got his head brewer to make some very pale malt and brew up a trial batch of this newfangled beer. The experiment was a great success, and the first shipment to India was dispatched in 1823. The British expats loved it, preferring it over Hodgson's beer. The rise of Burton had begun.

"The cause of all the commotion in the brewing trade was East India pale ale, and many strange tales have been told of its origin, all of which refer to a consignment of beer sent out in a cloudy condition, which, after travelling round the world, came back to the country of its birth, in a condition so excellent, bright and sparkling, that it was said to be superior to a glass of Madeira or sparkling champagne."
— *Noted Breweries of Great Britain and Ireland*, Vol. 2, Alfred Barnard, 1889, pages 421–422

The same year, two other Burton brewers, Bass and Salt, also began brewing IPA and shipping it to India. Very quickly, Bass, Allsopp, and Salt dominated the trade in pale ale to India, though it should be pointed out that the total amount of IPA sold in India was modest. In the 1840s, Bass and Allsopp sent only around 20,000 barrels a year between them.

To put that into perspective, in 1843, Barclay Perkins brewed 389,835 barrels and Truman 344,342—around 1,000 barrels a day. The combined annual sales of Bass and Allsopp in India were less than a week's production of the five largest London porter breweries.

The beer they exported had several defining characteristics. It was very pale, brewed from only the highest-quality and palest malt. It was heavily hopped, both in the kettle and in the form of dry hops. Around 6 pounds (2.7 kg) of hops per UK barrel were used. That's the equivalent of 1 pound (455 g) per 6 U.S. gallons (22.7 L). They were the best quality hops available: Goldings or Farnhams.

THE UNION ROOM AT BASS

One of the most important characteristics is often overlooked: an extremely high degree of attenuation. This was vital to stop the beer from bursting its casks or becoming infected. With almost all the sugars fermented out, there was nothing for any bacteria to eat. At a time when the apparent attenuation of mild ales was 65 percent, IPA's was 85 percent.

The one thing IPA wasn't was strong, at least not by the standards of the day. The weakest mild ales brewed in London had a gravity of over 1070° in the 1830s and 1840s. Even porter, the staple of the poor, was around 1062°.

An important aspect of the journey to India was the maturation that took place on the way. The high temperatures in the hold and the rocking motion of the ship made IPA mature at an accelerated rate. The 3 or 4 months at sea were the equivalent of 2 years aging on land. When it arrived in India, if all had gone well, IPA was in wonderful condition.

IPA IN THE UNITED KINGDOM

How did IPA come to be sold back home in Britain? The tale usually told is another romantic one, of a ship bound for India with a load of IPA that was wrecked in the Irish Channel. Its cargo was salvaged and sold in Liverpool, where it was a sensation. There's just one problem. No record exists of such a shipwreck.

The reality is doubtless much more prosaic. Demand was created by officers and officials returning from India. They'd got a taste for IPA and wanted to continue drinking it when they got home. Not as good a story as a shipwreck, but more probable.

The IPAs sold at home were a little weaker than those sent to India, with gravities of 1055° to 1060°. Like the export version, they were extremely heavily hopped and highly attenuated. They were also stock beers, that is, beers that were aged before sale.

Bass aged their beer in a totally crazy way. After filling, barrels were stacked in enormous piles in the brewery yard, completely exposed to the elements, and left for up to twelve months. Beer that had endured a year in the open would not be likely to spoil due to temperature variations once bottled.

LOW-GRAVITY IPA

The relationship between pale ale and IPA was an odd one in Victorian Britain. Breweries that started with an IPA and later introduced a weaker version often chose to dub the newcomer pale ale. But in other areas, for example London, where bitter beers were introduced later, the first was generally called pale ale and its weaker sibling called IPA.

IPA EXPORTED TO INDIA

YEAR	OG	FG	ABV	APPARENT ATTENUATION
1844	1067.6	1007.8	7.6	88.54%
1844	1066.3	1008.0	7.4	87.93%
1844	1062.0	1010.0	6.6	83.86%
1844	1053.8	1006.5	6.0	87.91%
1844	1053.8	1005.0	6.2	90.71%
1844	1054.2	1013.0	5.2	76.00%
1844	1065.6	1012.0	6.8	81.69%
1844	1067.1	1007.3	7.6	89.20%
1844	1070.1	1010.3	7.6	85.38%
1845	1068.5	1010.5	7.4	84.68%
Average	1062.9	1009.0	6.8	85.59%

IPA SOLD IN BRITAIN

YEAR	OG	FG	ABV	APPARENT ATTENUATION
1844	1059.3	1012.0	6.0	79.75%
1844	1044.7	1005.0	5.0	88.81%
1844	1049.9	1004.3	5.8	91.49%
1844	1047.2	1006.0	5.2	87.28%
1845	1053.8	1006.5	6.0	87.91%
1845	1054.8	1006.0	6.2	89.06%
1845	1058.6	1005.0	6.8	91.46%
1845	1060.1	1005.0	7.0	91.68%
1845	1058.8	1005.3	6.8	91.07%
1846	1055.3	1006.5	6.2	88.25%
Average	1054.2	1006.2	6.1	88.68%

THE COPPER STAGE AT BASS

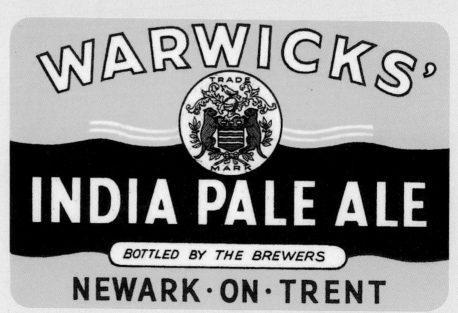

Before World War I, such IPAs had gravities between 1045° and 1050° and a very generous hopping rate of 2 to 2.4 pounds (900 g to 1.1 kg) per barrel. Like higher-gravity IPAs, the grist was simple, mostly just pale malt and invert sugar. Unlike the stronger versions, these running beers were sold young.

TWENTIETH CENTURY

Stock beers had been losing popularity in the final decades of the eighteenth century as drinkers shifted their allegiance to lighter running bitters. The trend accelerated the downward pressure on beer gravity caused by World War I. By the 1920s, just about the only stock IPAs left were those brewed in Burton, such as Bass Red Triangle and Worthington White Shield. Elsewhere, IPA came to signify a low-gravity, hoppy beer, often sold only in bottled form.

Burton IPAs were less affected than other beers, in terms of gravity, by World War I. Prewar they had been 1060° to 1065°, postwar a very respectable 1055° to 1060°. The gravity drop was greater amongst the lighter type of IPA, from 1050° to 1036°, which meant the gap in strength with Burton IPAs grew. They were starting to look like a totally different type of beer.

WORLD WAR II AND BEYOND

The impact on brewing was much the same during World War II as during World War I: ingredient shortages and gravity cuts. Crystal malt began to be used in the weak style of IPA, for example, at Whitbread during the late 1930s. As the war progressed, the percentage of crystal malt increased, presumably to offset reductions in gravity, though some brewers, like Barclay Perkins, continued to use no crystal malt in any of their pale ales. Between 1939 and 1945, the gravity of Whitbread's IPA fell from 1037° to 1032°. At Barclay Perkins, whose IPA had been stronger, the fall was greater: 1044° to 1031°. Postwar, this style of IPA remained in the low 1030°s.

Once again, Burton IPA fared much better than other beers, presumably because of the premium price it commanded. The gravity of Bass's bottled IPA, Red Triangle (or Blue Triangle when filtered and artificially carbonated), dropped only a couple of gravity points, to 1055°. After the end of hostilities, it climbed back to its prewar gravity, or even a little higher, 1058° to 1060°.

1839 REID IPA

Reid brewed several pale ales in the 1830s, then went back to brewing just porter. This is a typical early nineteenth-century recipe—just pale malt and lots of Goldings. All of the hops would have been fresh. The original recipe called for two sparges, which was unusual in London at this time.

INGREDIENTS

11.4 pounds (5.2 kg) pale malt two-row

4.23 ounces (120 g) Goldings pellet hops *(75 minutes)*

4.23 ounces (120 g) Goldings pellet hops *(60 minutes)*

4.23 ounces (120 g) Goldings pellet hops *(30 minutes)*

Wyeast 1098 British Ale or Wyeast 1099 Whitbread Ale yeast

5 ounces (140 g) corn sugar

1 Mash the grains at 152°F (67°C) for 60 minutes.

2 Sparge with 180°F (82°C) water and collect 6.5 gallons (24.6 L) of wort.

3 Boil the wort for 75 minutes, adding the hops at the times indicated in the ingredients list.

4 Chill the wort as quickly as possible to 57°F (14°C) using an ice bath or wort chiller. Aerate the wort. Add the yeast.

5 Ferment at 57°F (14°C) until final gravity is achieved. Allow the beer to condition for 1 week. When fermentation is complete, bottle with the corn sugar.

Starting gravity:	Final gravity:	Final target alcohol by volume (ABV):	IBUs:	SRM:
1.058	1.020	5.03%	196	5

EXTRACT INSTRUCTIONS

1 Replace the pale malts with 6.75 pounds (3 kg) pale liquid malt extract. Increase both the 90-minute and 60-minute hop additions to 1.14 ounces (32 g) and the 30-minute hop addition to 1.59 ounces (45 g).

2 Heat 3 gallons (11.4 L) of water and add the liquid malt extract. Stir well until the extract is completely dissolved. Bring the wort to a boil, remove from the heat, and add the liquid malt extract and sugars. Bring the wort to a rolling boil. Boil for 75 minutes. Add the hops at the times indicated in the ingredients list.

3 Chill the wort to 57°F (14°C). Transfer the wort to the fermentor and add cold water to bring the total volume to 5 gallons (19 L). Follow the fermentation and packaging instructions from the all-grain recipe.

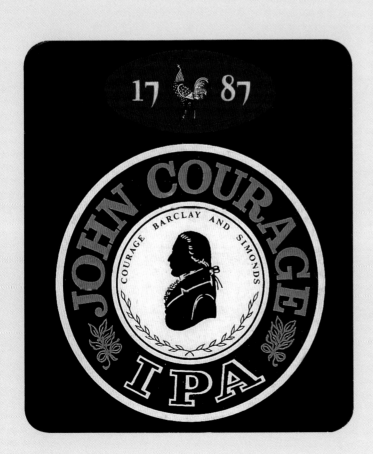

1868 TETLEY EIPA

 etley's brewery in Leeds closed only in 2011. In the 1800s, they were one of the biggest breweries in Yorkshire. This is a typically simple recipe, with just two ingredients.

INGREDIENTS

12.08 pounds (5.5 kg) pale malt two-row

8.45 ounces (240 g) Goldings pellet hops *(90 minutes)*

Wyeast 1469 West Yorkshire Ale yeast

5 ounces (140 g) corn sugar

1 Mash the grains at 153°F (67°C) for 60 minutes.

2 Sparge with 165°F (74°C) water and collect 6.5 gallons (24.6 L) of wort.

3 Boil the wort for 90 minutes, adding the hops at the times indicated in the ingredients list.

4 Chill the wort as quickly as possible to 58°F (14°C) using an ice bath or wort chiller. Aerate the wort. Add the yeast.

5 Ferment at 58°F (14°C) until final gravity is achieved. Allow the beer to condition for 1 week. When fermentation is complete, bottle with the corn sugar.

Starting gravity:	Final gravity:	Final target alcohol by volume (ABV):	IBUs:	SRM:
1.062	1.012	6.61%	146	6

EXTRACT INSTRUCTIONS

1 Replace the pale malt with 10.01 pounds (4.5 kg) pale liquid malt extract. Increase the hop addition to 9.07 ounces (257 g).

2 Heat 3 gallons (11.4 L) of water and add the liquid malt extract. Stir well until the extract is completely dissolved. Bring the wort to a boil, remove from the heat, and add the liquid malt extract. Bring the wort to a rolling boil. Boil for 90 minutes. Add the hops at the times indicated in the ingredients list.

3 Chill the wort to 58°F (14°C). Transfer the wort to the fermentor and add cold water to bring the total volume to 5 gallons (19 L). Follow the fermentation and packaging instructions from the all-grain recipe.

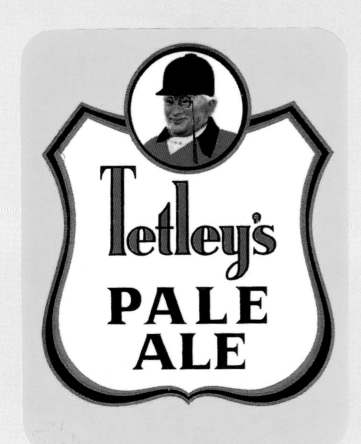

1885 YOUNGER XP

William Younger used lots of continental hops: Spalt, Saaz, and Bohemian and mixed them with Kent hops. Kent hops were brought back by ships that had taken their beer to London. The hopping rate was much lower than in 1853.

INGREDIENTS

10.42 pounds (4.7 kg) pale malt two-row

1.69 ounces (48 g) Cluster hop pellets *(90 minutes)*

1.69 ounces (48 g) Spalt hop pellets *(60 minutes)*

1.69 ounces (48 g) Goldings hop pellets *(30 minutes)*

White Labs WLP028 Edinburgh Ale yeast

1 Mash the grains at 152°F (67°C) for 60 minutes.

2 Sparge with 163°F (73°C) water and collect 6.5 gallons (24.6 L) of wort.

3 Boil the wort for 90 minutes, adding the hops at the times indicated in the ingredients list.

4 Chill the wort as quickly as possible to 59°F (15°C) using an ice bath or wort chiller. Aerate the wort. Add the yeast.

5 Ferment at 59°F (15°C) until final gravity is achieved. Allow the beer to condition for 1 week. When fermentation is complete, bottle with the corn sugar.

Starting gravity:	Final gravity:	Final target alcohol by volume (ABV):	IBUs:	SRM:
1.054	1.013	5.42%	92	5

EXTRACT INSTRUCTIONS

1 Replace the pale malts with 8.63 pounds (3.9 kg) pale liquid malt extract. Increase all three hop additions to 1.8 ounces (51 g).

2 Heat 3 gallons (11.4 L) of water and add the liquid malt extract and invert sugar. Stir well until the extract is completely dissolved. Bring the wort to a rolling boil. Boil for 90 minutes. Add the hops at the times indicated in the ingredients list.

3 Chill the wort to 59°F (15°C). Transfer the wort to the fermentor and add cold water to bring the total volume to 5 gallons (19 L). Follow the fermentation and packaging instructions from the all-grain recipe.

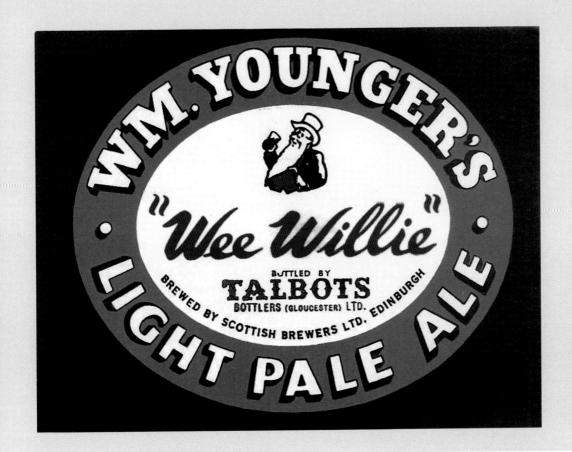

1902 WHITBREAD IPA

This recipe used a more modern grist with a mixture of English two-row and American six-row pale malts. No. 1 invert sugar is used to lighten body and color. Crystal malt was only used after World War I to darken pale ales.

INGREDIENTS

6.88 pounds (3.1 kg) pale malt two-row

1.46 pounds (662 g) pale malt six-row

13.3 ounces (377 kg) invert sugar (No. 1)

1.69 ounces (48 g) Goldings pellet hops *(90 minutes)*

1.27 ounces (36 g) Goldings pellet hops *(60 minutes)*

1.27 ounces (36 g) Goldings pellet hops *(30 minutes)*

Wyeast 1098 British Ale or Wyeast 1099 Whitbread Ale yeast

5 ounces (140 g) corn sugar

1 Mash the grains at 152°F (67°C) for 60 minutes.

2 Sparge with 165°F (74°C) water and collect 6.5 gallons (24.6 L) of wort.

3 Boil the wort for 90 minutes, adding the hops at the times indicated in the ingredients list.

4 Chill the wort as quickly as possible to 58°F (14°C) using an ice bath or wort chiller. Aerate the wort. Add the yeast.

5 Ferment at 58°F (14°C) until final gravity is achieved. Allow the beer to condition for 1 week. When fermentation is complete, bottle with the corn sugar.

Starting gravity:	Final gravity:	Final target alcohol by volume (ABV):	IBUs:	SRM:
1.050	1.013	4.89%	71	5

EXTRACT INSTRUCTIONS

1 Replace the pale malts with 4.51 pounds (2 kg) pale liquid malt extract. Scale up the invert sugar to 2.8 pounds (1.27 kg). Increase both the 90-minute hop addition to 1.79 ounces (51 g) and the 60-minute and 30-minute hop additions to 1.34 ounces (38 g).

2 Heat 3 gallons (11.4 L) of water and add the liquid malt extract and invert sugar. Stir well until the extract is completely dissolved. Bring the wort to a rolling boil. Boil for 90 minutes. Add the hops at the times indicated in the ingredients list.

3 Chill the wort to 58°F (14°C). Transfer the wort to the fermentor and add cold water to bring the total volume to 5 gallons (19 L). Follow the fermentation and packaging instructions from the all-grain recipe.

PALE ALE/ BITTER

The history of pale ale is an odd one. Long a second fiddle to mild ale, pale ale, in its commonest form of draft bitter, eventually fought its way to the peak of popularity in the 1960s, only to be swiftly eclipsed by the unstoppable rise of lager.

A word of warning before we begin: The distinction between IPA and pale ale is historically a very blurred one. Brewers used both terms fairly interchangeably. A beer that one day was called IPA could magically be redubbed a pale ale the next, without any change in recipe. There is no reliable way to differentiate between the two, save for what the brewer decided to call them.

EIGHTEENTH CENTURY

From around 1600, the use of coke as a fuel for malt kilns allowed maltsters to produce much more consistently pale malt. It was initially too expensive to use in any but the most expensive beers, but by the eighteenth century had become one of the three main types of malt.

Pale ales were first brewed in the countryside but spread to London in the early eighteenth century.

It was used to brew two families of malt liquors: pale ale and pale beer. But don't imagine that this pale ale was anything like the ones of today. As an ale, it was lightly hopped, unlike pale beer, which was extremely heavily hopped. Neither has any direct connection with modern pale ales. That connection appears when beers called pale ales began to be exported to India toward the end of the century. These heavily hopped, dry, very pale beers were the inspiration for a whole new family of beers.

NINETEENTH CENTURY

At first, this new breed of pale ale was brewed only for export, the market for which it had been created. By the 1830s, there was also a demand for pale ales similar in character to those shipped to India. As their popularity grew, many brewers began to produce more than one. If you already have a beer called IPA, what do you call the new one? Pale ale was the obvious choice.

Not all brewers immediately dived into the pale ale pool. In the 1840s and 1850s, the trade was dominated in England by the big Burton brewers—Bass, Allsopp, and Salt. In Scotland, it was a slightly different tale, with brewers in Edinburgh and Alloa quick to spot the potential of this new type of beer. Not only did they soon take control of the pale ale trade in Scotland, they also made inroads into northern England and foreign markets.

"About this time [Queen Anne's reign, 1702–1714] the Gentry residing in London more than they had in former times, for them was introduced the pale ales and pale small beers they were habituated to in the country and many of the Brewers took to making drinks of this sort."
—Obadiah Poundage's letter to the *London Chronicle* on November 4, 1760

LEES BREWERY

TWENTIETH CENTURY

In the 1920s, various strengths of pale ale ousted most other styles in Scotland. Mild became very rare, and only small quantities were brewed of strong Scotch ales and stouts. In England, bitter had become the staple of the saloon bar, where the better class of customer drank, but mild continued to dominate overall.

As with all styles, World War I had a big impact. The fall in strength compressed the gravity range of a brewer's pale ales, and most discontinued one or more. This helped blur the distinction between pale ale and light bitter. In London, the most expensive pale ales fared reasonably well in terms of gravity compared to other styles. Typical gravities in the 1920s were between 1048° and 1055°.

Grists remained simple, mostly just pale malt and sugar, though the use of adjuncts such as corn became more common. A few breweries added some crystal malt, but this was by no means the norm. With the fashion changing to darker pale ales, the color was often adjusted with caramel. This is in sharp contrast to the nineteenth century, where the aim was to get such beers as pale as possible.

After 1860, the demand for pale ales was sufficient that most breweries, with the exception of a few large London porter breweries, felt obliged to supply their customers with one. Some brewed them on their existing plant using their normal water supply. Larger brewers sometimes chose either to build a complete new brewery in Burton or to modify their existing brewery.

Nineteenth-century pale ales were very simple beers. Their grists rarely contained more than pale malt and sugar, though after 1880 it might also include an adjunct like flaked corn or flaked rice. The sugar content of pale ales tended to be higher than of other styles. The main concern when brewing pale ale was a color and a body that were both light. Fifteen to twenty percent sugar in the grist helped achieve this.

WORLD WAR II

It was during World War II that pale ale took on its modern form, dropping below 1040°. When the supply situation began to improve after the end of the war, gravities crept up again, though they never reached their prewar levels. Some breweries, keen to profit from the demand (albeit limited) for a stronger bitter, introduced new higher-gravity versions.

Falling gravities are probably the explanation for why crystal malt became common in pale ale grists during the 1940s. Brewers were trying to restore body lost by the weakening of worts. Wartime shortages prompted the government to force the use of unusual ingredients such as malted and flaked oats and even flaked rye. They must have made for some rather unusual bitters.

LEES BREWERY THE GREAT CELLAR AT JOHN SMITH

1858 TETLEY A

Tetley gave this beer the wonderfully vague name of just A. It is a simple combination of pale malt and Kent hops. It was originally fermented in a Yorkshire square.

INGREDIENTS

12.29 pounds (5.6 kg) pale malt two-row

7.6 ounces (215 g) Goldings pellet hops *(60 minutes)*

Wyeast 1469 West Yorkshire Ale yeast

1 Mash the grains at 154°F (68°C) for 60 minutes.

2 Sparge with 175°F (79°C) water and collect 6.5 gallons (24.6 L) of wort.

3 Boil the wort for 90 minutes, adding the hops at the times indicated in the ingredients list.

4 Chill the wort as quickly as possible to 60°F (16°C) using an ice bath or wort chiller. Aerate the wort. Add the yeast.

5 Ferment at 60°F (16°C) until final gravity is achieved. Allow the beer to condition for 1 week. When fermentation is complete, bottle with the corn sugar.

Starting gravity:	Final gravity:	Final target alcohol by volume (ABV):	IBUs:	SRM:
1.063	1.015	6.35%	122	6

EXTRACT INSTRUCTIONS

1 Replace the pale malts with 10.18 pounds (4.6 kg) pale liquid malt extract. Scale the hop addition to 8.17 ounces (232 g).

2 Heat 3 gallons (11.4 L) of water and add the liquid malt extract. Stir well until the extract is completely dissolved. Bring the wort to a rolling boil. Boil for 90 minutes. Add the hops at the times indicated in the ingredients list.

3 Chill the wort to 60°F (16°C). Transfer the wort to the fermentor and add cold water to bring the total volume to 5 gallons (19 L). Follow the fermentation and packaging instructions from the all-grain recipe.

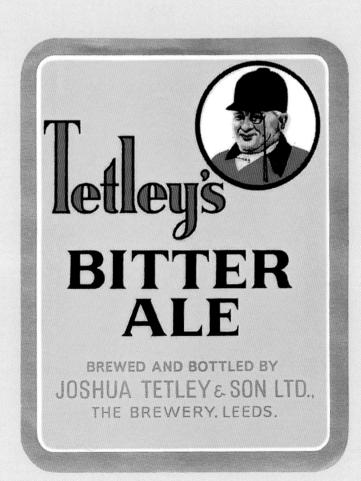

Tetley's
BITTER
ALE

BREWED AND BOTTLED BY
JOSHUA TETLEY & SON LTD.,
THE BREWERY, LEEDS.

1875 WHITBREAD PA

Whitbread first brewed a pale ale in 1865. This was a simple beer of pale malt, sugar, and a huge quantity of hops. All hops were fresh. It was a stock beer so the bitterness would have mellowed before sale.

INGREDIENTS

9 pounds (4 kg) pale malt two-row

1.46 pounds (662 g) invert sugar (No. 1)

3.38 ounces (96 g) cluster pellet hops *(90 minutes)*

5.07 ounces (144 g) Goldings pellet hops *(30 minutes)*

Wyeast 1098 British Ale or Wyeast 1099 Whitbread Ale yeast

5 ounces (140 g) corn sugar

1 Mash the grains at 150°F (66°C) for 60 minutes.

2 Sparge with 170°F (77°C) water and collect 6.5 gallons (24.6 L) of wort.

3 Boil the wort for 90 minutes, adding the hops at the times indicated in the ingredients list.

4 Chill the wort as quickly as possible to 58°F (14°C) using an ice bath or wort chiller. Aerate the wort. Add the yeast.

5 Ferment at 58°F (14°C) until final gravity is achieved. Allow the beer to condition for 1 week. When fermentation is complete, bottle with the corn sugar.

Starting gravity:	Final gravity:	Final target alcohol by volume (ABV):	IBUs:	SRM:
1.060	1.015	5.95%	148	7

EXTRACT INSTRUCTIONS

1 Replace the pale malt with 5.25 pounds (2.4 kg) pale liquid malt extract and increase the invert sugar to 3.37 pounds (1.5 kg). Scale the cluster hop addition to 3.62 ounces (103 g) and the Goldings hop addition to 5.43 ounces (154 g).

2 Heat 3 gallons (11.4 L) of water and add the liquid malt extract and invert sugar. Stir well until the extract is completely dissolved. Bring the wort to a rolling boil. Boil for 90 minutes. Add the hops at the times indicated in the ingredients list.

3 Chill the wort to 58°F (14°C). Transfer the wort to the fermentor and add cold water to bring the total volume to 5 gallons (19 L). Follow the fermentation and packaging instructions from the all-grain recipe.

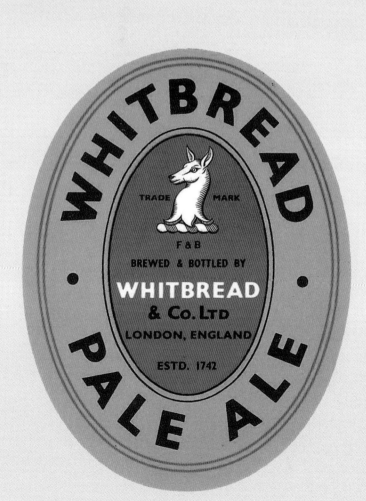

1909 LEES BITTER

 This beer is still brewed in Manchester today. It is the equivalent of an ordinary bitter. A simple recipe of pale malt, sugar, and hops.

INGREDIENTS

7.5 pounds (3.4 kg) pale malt two-row

1.67 pounds (758 g) invert sugar (No. 1)

2.54 ounces (72 g) Fuggles pellet hops *(60 minutes)*

2.54 ounces (72 g) Fuggles pellet hops *(30 minutes)*

Wyeast 1318 London Ale III yeast

5 ounces (140 g) corn sugar

1 Mash the grains at 155°F (68°C) for 60 minutes.

2 Sparge with 168°F (76°C) water and collect 6.5 gallons (24.6 L) of wort.

3 Boil the wort for 90 minutes, adding the hops at the times indicated in the ingredients list.

4 Chill the wort as quickly as possible to 60°F (16°C) using an ice bath or wort chiller. Aerate the wort. Add the yeast.

5 Ferment at 60°F (16°C) until final gravity is achieved. Allow the beer to condition for 1 week. When fermentation is complete, bottle with the corn sugar.

Starting gravity:	Final gravity:	Final target alcohol by volume (ABV):	IBUs:	SRM:
1.054	1.010	5.82%	70	6.3

EXTRACT INSTRUCTIONS

1 Replace the pale malt with 4.64 pounds (2.1 kg) pale liquid malt extract and increase the invert sugar to 3.26 pounds (1.5 kg). Scale both hop additions to 2.7 ounces (77 g).

2 Heat 3 gallons (11.4 L) of water and add the liquid malt extract and invert sugar. Stir well until the extract is completely dissolved. Bring the wort to a rolling boil. Boil for 90 minutes. Add the hops at the times indicated in the ingredients list.

3 Chill the wort to 60°F (16°C). Transfer the wort to the fermentor and add cold water to bring the total volume to 5 gallons (19 L). Follow the fermentation and packaging instructions from the all-grain recipe.

1943 TRUMAN P2

 laked oats were used at insistence of government after a bumper crop in 1942. A gravity of 1042° was quite high for 1943.

INGREDIENTS

7.29 pounds (3.3 kg) pale malt two-row

6.7 ounces (190 g) flaked oats

3.3 ounces (94 g) invert sugar (No. 1)

0.42 ounce (12 g) cluster pellet hops *(60 minutes)*

0.42 ounce (12 g) Northern Brewer pellet hops *(60 minutes)*

0.42 ounce (12 g) Goldings pellet hops *(30 minutes)*

Wyeast 1028 London Ale or White Labs WLP013 London Ale yeast

5 ounces (140 g) corn sugar

1 Mash the grains at 150°F (66°C) for 60 minutes.

2 Sparge with 160°F (71°C) water and collect 6.5 gallons (24.6 L) of wort.

3 Boil the wort for 90 minutes, adding the hops at the times indicated in the ingredients list.

4 Chill the wort as quickly as possible to 60°F (16°C) using an ice bath or wort chiller. Aerate the wort. Add the yeast.

5 Ferment at 60°F (16°C) until final gravity is achieved. Allow the beer to condition for 1 week. When fermentation is complete, bottle with the corn sugar.

Starting gravity:	Final gravity:	Final target alcohol by volume (ABV):	IBUs:	SRM:
1.042	1.008	4.5%	37	4

EXTRACT INSTRUCTIONS

1 Replace the pale malt and flaked oats with 2.43 pounds (1.1 kg) pale liquid malt extract and 4.05 pounds (1.8 kg) Carafoam. Increase the invert sugar to 2.8 pounds (1.3 kg). Scale the first two hop additions to 0.44 ounce (12.5 g); scale the third addition to 0.89 ounce (25 g).

2 Heat 3 gallons (11.4 L) of water and add the liquid malt extract and invert sugar. Stir well until the extract is completely dissolved. Bring the wort to a rolling boil. Boil for 90 minutes. Add the hops at the times indicated in the ingredients list.

3 Chill the wort to 60°F (16°C). Transfer the wort to the fermentor and add cold water to bring the total volume to 5 gallons (19 L). Follow the fermentation and packaging instructions from the all-grain recipe.

EUROPEAN BEERS— BROYHAN & GRATZER

In this section, we'll be taking a look at a few of many top-fermenting styles that existed in Europe before they were swept away by a flood of lager in the late nineteenth century. Once as popular as bitter or mild, few such beers made it past World War I and have slipped almost entirely from memory.

The recipes in this section are slightly different from those for British beers. While in the rest of the book the recipes are based on original brewing records, these are taken from descriptions in technical publications. The details of the ingredients and brewing methods are sometimes rather vague. They shouldn't be considered an exact clone of a specific beer.

1900 GRÄTZER/ GRODZISKIE

GRÄTZER/ GRODZISKIE

Grätzer is a rare survivor of the top-fermenting brewing tradition of Eastern Europe. It managed to hang on not only until the twentieth century but almost into the twenty-first, finally defeated by modern capitalism in 1993. However, it hasn't been forgotten.

Grätzer is an unusual beer in several ways, brewed from 100 percent smoked wheat malt, heavily hopped but light in alcohol, effervescent, and refreshing. A key element in the flavor profile is its own specific type of yeast, which adds another layer of flavor to the finished beer.

HISTORY

Pinning an exact date on Grätzer's origin is a little tricky. They were brewing in Grätz in the Middle Ages, but the town seems to have started to get a good reputation for its beer at the end of the sixteenth century or beginning of the seventeenth century. At this time, both pale and dark beer were brewed, the latter being called *Kuc*, meaning a small horse. Both used 100 percent wheat malt.

In the second half of the nineteenth century, the fame of Grätzer beer began to spread beyond the Posen region through the whole of Germany and even further. In the 1880s, there were five breweries in Grätz, producing between them the very modest quantity of 50,000 barrels (about 80,000 hl) a year. This is when a group of British investors had the unusual idea of forming a limited company to buy all five breweries and corner the market in Grätzer. I'm not sure if it ever went ahead, but there were similar schemes in Prague and Hamburg.

During the Communist period, the remaining brewery in Grodzisk was nationalized, but it continued to brew smoked wheat beer. In addition to the traditional 7.7° Plato version, stronger types were also brewed of 12° and 14° Plato. The brewery was privatized in the 1990s and finally closed in 1993.

Starting gravity:	Final gravity:	Final target alcohol by volume (ABV):	IBUs:	SRM:
1.032	1.007	3.31%	40	3

T he level of hopping in this recipe is greater than in the final days of the style in the 1980s and 1990s. If you want to aim for that version, reduce the IBUs to 20 to 25. You may want to add some rice hulls to the mash to help run off. Since this is a 100% smoked wheat malt recipe, unfortunately, there is not an extract brewing option as there is no commercially available smoked wheat malt extract available at this time.

INGREDIENTS

5.83 pounds (2.6 kg) Smoked wheat malt

0.85 ounce (24 g) Lublin pellet hops *(100 minutes)*

0.85 ounce (24 g) Fuggles pellet hops *(20 minutes)*

White Labs WLP029 Kölsch yeast

5 ounces (140 g) corn sugar

1 Mash the grains at 156°F (69°C) for 60 minutes.

2 Sparge with 165°F (74°C) water and collect 6.5 gallons (24.6 L) of wort.

3 Boil the wort for 120 minutes, adding the hops at the times indicated in the ingredients list.

4 Chill the wort as quickly as possible to 65°F (74°C) using an ice bath or wort chiller. Aerate the wort. Add the yeast.

5 Ferment at 65°F (74°C) until final gravity is achieved. Allow the beer to condition for 1 week. When fermentation is complete, bottle with the corn sugar.

1850 BROYHAN

Broyhan has a rather sad history. It was the most common type of beer in north Germany for 300 years, yet has disappeared virtually without trace. In the preindustrial period, Broyhan was incredibly popular and inspired many similar beers. Berliner Weisse is reckoned by some to be a development of Broyhan.

HISTORY

It was first brewed in Hannover but spread throughout north Germany.

The reality is a little more complicated than that. Broyhan was brewed over a wide area for a long period of time and took many forms. Whatever grains were used, they would be in the form of Luft-Malz, or air-dried malt. Some versions did contain wheat malt or oats, and the exact composition of the grist probably depended on what grains were available. Others contained small amounts of hops and some ground spices such as cloves, cinnamon, and coriander seeds.

As the ancestor of Berliner Weisse, it should come as no surprise that Broyhan was a sour beer, though; as the analyses show, the level of acidity varied. It ranged from the mouth-puckering levels of a lambic to mildly tart. The level of attenuation was quite poor and, combined with a low OG, resulted in a beer of only 2 or 3 percent ABV.

Broyhan is mentioned in technical literature in the early years of the twentieth century and was presumably still being brewed then. It probably finally disappeared around the time of World War I.

"This beer is named after its creator, Cord Broyhahn, who first brewed it in 1526 in the brewhouse of Hans von Sode in Leinstrasse, Hannover. The genuine Broyhahn is very pale, similar in colour to young white wine, has a winey aroma and a pleasant sweetish yet acidic taste. Broyhahn differs from other white beers chiefly in that it is brewed from pure barley malt without the addition of wheat malt or hops."
— *Grundsaetze der Bierbrauerei nach den neuesten technisch-chemischen Entdeckungen* by Christian Heinrich Schmidt, 1853.

Starting gravity:	Final gravity:	Final target alcohol by volume (ABV):	IBUs:	SRM:
1.054	1.023	4.1%	0	3.5

Note that despite containing no hops, the wort was boiled. There were many variations of Broyhan, so feel free to modify this recipe by adding a few hops or spices or use wheat malt and oats in addition to barley malt.

INGREDIENTS

10 pounds (4.5 kg) German Pilsner malt

Wyeast 2565 Kölsch or White Labs WLP029 German Ale/Kölsch yeast

Wyeast 5335 *Lactobacillus Buchneri* or White Labs WLP677 *Lactobacillus Delbrueckii* yeast

5 ounces (140 g) corn sugar

1 Mash the grains at 158°F (70°C) for 60 minutes.

2 Sparge with 170°F (77°C) water and collect 6.5 gallons (24.6 L) of wort.

3 Boil the wort for 60 minutes.

4 Chill the wort as quickly as possible to 64°F (18°C) using an ice bath or wort chiller. Aerate the wort. Add the yeasts.

5 Ferment in the primary at 64°F (18°C) until final gravity is achieved. When fermentation is complete, bottle with the corn sugar.

EXTRACT INSTRUCTIONS

1 Replace the Pilsner malt with 8.6 pounds (3.9 kg) pale liquid malt extract.

2 Heat 3 gallons (11.4 L) of water and add the liquid malt extract. Stir well until the extract is completely dissolved. Bring the wort to a rolling boil. Boil for 60 minutes.

3 Chill the wort to 64°F (18°C). Transfer the wort to the fermentor and add cold water to bring the total volume to 5 gallons (19 L). Follow the fermentation and packaging instructions from the all-grain recipe.

1890 SALVATOR

Styles often begin as a single beer that morphs into a new style. Salvator went one step further, becoming a style and then returning to be the name of one specific beer. Blame Zacherl (the forerunner of Paulaner) and their litigiousness.

HISTORY

Salvator was the original doppelbock, first brewed by Paulist monks in the seventeenth century for their own consumption. During the feast of the Holy Father, they were allowed to sell a special beer to the general population of Munich. This beer came to be known as "Sankt Vaterbier'' (Holy Father beer) after the name of the feast. Eventually, this was corrupted to Salvatorbier or just Salvator.

After Munich's monasteries were secularized in 1799, the brewery was taken over by the Bavarian state and leased to a brewer called Zacherl. He continued to brew Salvator and, seeing its popularity, other brewers in Munich and beyond also started making beers called Salvator.

Like all Munich lagers at the time, Salvator was dark in color. It was also poorly attenuated and not very alcoholic, considering its high OG.

By the 1890s, at least thirty breweries were producing Salvator, a situation that didn't please the Zacherl Brewery. They submitted an application to register Salvator as a trademark and, despite their competitors arguing that it was the name of a type of beer rather than a brand name, it was granted.

Unable to use the name Salvator, breweries came up with a variety of names, all ending in *ator* for their doppelbocks, which is how names like Triumphator and Bajuvator came into existence.

RECIPE

The original would have been brewed using a decoction mash. For any masochists who want to extend their brewing day, this is the type of decoction performed in Munich in the late nineteenth century: For 100 pounds (45.3 kg) of malt, 800 pounds (362.9 kg) of water are used. Half to two-thirds of the water is cold and used to dough in. The rest is brought to a boil in the kettle. After doughing in, the mash is left to rest for 3 or 4 hours. If warm water is used for doughing in, the mash should not be left to rest. When the water has boiled, it is added to the mash. The temperature should rise to 86°F to 99°F (30°C to 37.2°C).

When this temperature has been reached, about a third of the thinner part of the mash is transferred to the kettle and boiled for 30 minutes. (Boiling the first Dickmeisch) The Dickmeisch is returned to the mash tun and mashed for 15 minutes, so that the thinner and thicker parts completely separate. The temperature should now be 113°F to 122°F (145°C to 150°C).

As soon as this is finished, a third of the mash, again the thicker part, is transferred to the kettle and boiled for 30 minutes. (Second Dickmeisch).

The second Dickmeisch is returned to the mash tun and mashed. The temperature should now be 140°F to 145°F (60°C to 62.8°C).

Now, a portion of the thin mash is transferred to the kettle (enough to raise the temperature of the mash to 167°F [75°C] when returned to the mash tun) and boiled for 15 minutes. (Lautermeisch).

The Lautermeisch is returned to the mash tun and there's another round of mashing. The temperature should now be 167°F (75°C). The mash is left to rest for 90 minutes.

Starting gravity:	Final gravity:	Final target alcohol by volume (ABV):	IBUs:	SRM:
1.075	1.034	5.42%	46	22

The original recipe would have been brewed using a decoction mash.

INGREDIENTS

15 pounds (6.8 kg) Munich 20L malt

2.54 ounces (72 g) Hallertauer pellet hops *(45 minutes)*

2.54 ounces (72 g) Hallertauer pellet hops *(45 minutes)*

Wyeast 2308 Munich Lager or White Labs WLP830 German Lager yeast

5 ounces (140 g) corn sugar

1 Mash the grains at 156°F (69°C) for 60 minutes.

2 Sparge with 170°F (77°C) water and collect 6.5 gallons (24.6 L) of wort.

3 Boil the wort for 60 minutes. Add the hops at the times indicated in the ingredients list.

4 Chill the wort as quickly as possible to 50°F (10°C) using an ice bath or wort chiller. Aerate the wort. Add the yeast.

5 Ferment in the primary at 50°F (10°C) until final gravity is achieved. When fermentation is complete, bottle with the corn sugar.

EXTRACT INSTRUCTIONS

1 Replace the Munich malt with 12 pounds (5.4 kg) amber liquid malt extract.

2 Heat 3 gallons (11.4 L) of water and add the liquid malt extract. Stir well until the extract is completely dissolved. Bring the wort to a rolling boil. Boil for 60 minutes. Add the hops at the times indicated in the ingredients list.

3 Chill the wort to 50°F (10°C). Transfer the wort to the fermentor and add cold water to bring the total volume to 5 gallons (19 L). Follow the fermentation and packaging instructions from the all-grain recipe.

1850 KOTBUSSER

KOTBUSSER

Kotbusser is one of the many lost north German top-fermenting styles. It originated in the Silesian town of Cottbus, which is about halfway between Berlin and Dresden, just 10 miles (16 km) from the border with Poland.

HISTORY

Like many north German styles, Kotbusser was a Weissbier, which did not mean "wheat beer" as it does today. Weissbier often did include some wheat, but really indicated that a beer was brewed with air-dried malt.

One characteristic that Kotbusser shared with Broyhan was sourness, which was presumably derived from lactic acid bacteria present in the brewing equipment. And I mean sour. The level of acidity was similar to that in a lambic or Berliner Weisse. Unsurprisingly, given the presence of *lactobacillus* during fermentation, Kotbusser was very lightly hopped. Kotbusser suffered the same fate as most other ancient German top-fermenting styles: slow extinction in the second half of the nineteenth century. The top-fermenting breweries were mostly small, family-run affairs. They were unable to compete with newly founded bottom-fermenting breweries that were run on a much larger scale, usually organized as limited companies on account of the amount of capital involved. The exact date of Kotbusser's disappearance is unclear, but was probably around 1900.

The original mashing method was pretty odd. There was an initial mash with water at 113°F (45°C), followed by a second mash with boiling water. The hop addition was even more bizarre. The hops were boiled separately in a small amount of water for 8 to 10 hours and added to the wort just before it was cooled. Fermentation started in fermenting vessels, but when it had reached its peak, the wort was transferred to barrels with open bungs. When yeast stopped coming out of the bunghole, the cask was bunged and left to condition for another 3 to 4 weeks.

Starting gravity:	Final gravity:	Final target alcohol by volume (ABV):	IBUs:	SRM:
1.057	1.016	5.42%	13	5

B ecause this recipe is already derived from an old, odd mashing method, an extract version of this recipe is not advisable.

INGREDIENTS

6.25 pounds (2.83 kg) German Pilsner malt

3.33 pounds (1.5 kg) pale wheat malt

13.3 ounces (377 g) flaked oats

1.3 ounces (37 g) sucrose (table sugar)

1.4 ounces (40 g) Honey

0.85 ounce (24 g) Spalter pellet hops (90 minutes)

Wyeast 2565 Kölsch or White Labs WLP029 German Ale/Kölsch yeast

Wyeast 5335 *Lactobacillus Buchneri* or White Labs WLP677 *Lactobacillus Delbrueckii* yeast

5 ounces (140 g) corn sugar

1 Mash the grains at 150°F (66°C) for 60 minutes.

2 Sparge with 165°F (74°C) water and collect 6.5 gallons (24.6 L) of wort.

3 Boil the wort for 90 minutes. Add the hops at the time indicated in the ingredients list.

4 Chill the wort as quickly as possible to 64°F (18°C) using an ice bath or wort chiller. Aerate the wort. Add the yeasts.

5 Ferment in the primary at 64°F (18°C) until final gravity is achieved. When fermentation is complete, bottle with the corn sugar.

CHAPTER 5
GARDENING FOR THE HOMEBREWER

HOPS

Hobbyists have one big advantage over corporate breweries: Small batches lend themselves to fresh ingredients and encourage experimentation. After all, the dawn of beer saw brewers using everything from nettles to wormwood. Many of the plants used to make beer can be easily grown in a home garden. Perennial hops, for instance, are incorrigible extroverts. Their botanical name, *Humulus lupulus*, gives a clue to their untamed nature. The genus name *lupulus* means "small wolf," referring to the Romans' observation that the plants are quite capable of swallowing up their garden neighbors. Give hops plenty of sun, enough water, and the slightest excuse, and they will run wild across the fields and menace passers-by with stems covered in tiny, flesh-grabbing hooks.

For gardeners who admire ambition in their plants and know better than to rub against the bristly bines, hops are a beautiful, useful addition to the garden. The bines will sprawl if unsupported and are best grown vertically. When trained up trellises, poles, or stringed supports, they can stretch to 20 feet (6 m) or more. In summer, the handsome three-lobed leaves are joined on female plants by papery, cone-like flowers properly termed *strobili*.

Within these flowers lies the essence of modern beer. Small glands between the scale-like bracts of the female hops flowers produce a yellow powder called *lupulin*. This resinous substance contains alpha and beta acids that give beer its distinctive flavor and acts as a preservative. Hops are dioecious—each plant either male or female. Only females produce cones. In hopyards, male strays are removed. The males are easily unmasked; upon blooming, the male flowers are merely flowers, very different from the papery inflorescences of the female.

Fortunately for the backyard grower, female plants are the only sex commonly sold. Hops plants are also easily shared, and a piece of female hops rhizome donated by a fellow gardener will yield another female plant. Male plants are not necessary to female flowering; in fact, if the females are fertilized, the resulting seeds make the cones useless for beer production. The flowers of hops make beer, not the fruit.

HOPS BY CLIMATE

While hops are extremely accommodating garden plants in regions where they grow well, they do not grow equally well in all regions. Hops plants are cold hardy and can be grown from Canada to northern Mexico. However, survival and production are two different things. These plants appreciate as many hours of sunlight as they can get. Hops require a minimum of 15 hours of daylight for optimum flowering, which puts them at their best at or above 35 degrees latitude. This range excludes much of the lower third of the United States, although intrepid hop growers report success in such lower Zone 8 states as Florida, North Carolina, Texas, and New Mexico. In hot regions, hops will need less direct sun and more water. Recommended hops varieties for hot regions include Cascade, Centennial, Chinook Clusters, Crystal, Galena, Horizon, Magnum, Newport, Nugget, and Summit.

In states with high humidity, including North Carolina, Florida, and much of New England and the Midwest, hops may suffer from powdery and downy mildew. Varieties often grown in these areas are Cascade, Centennial, Columbus, Chinook, Glacier, Golding, Hallertau, Magnum, Mount Hood, Northern Brewer, Nugget, Perle, Saaz, Summit, Tettnang, and Williamette. Hops handle cold well, but they do require a minimum of 120 frost-free days to produce cones. Growers in the frigid Midwest have good results with Cascade, Centennial, Chinook, Columbus, Galena, Glacier, Mt. Hood, Northern Brewer, Nugget, Sterling, Willamette, and Zeus. The best advice when growing hops in the home garden is this: keep what performs well, produces wantonly, and tastes good; replace the rest.

HOPS

Botanical name: *Humulus lupulus*

Plant type: perennial vine

USDA zones: 3 to 8

Height: 20 feet (6 m) or more with trellising

Soil: well-drained loam

Light: full sun

Water: regular

Growth habit: vining bines. The plants should be trellised.

Propogate by: rhizomes. Plant the rhizomes vertically with the buds facing up, or horizontally 1 to 2 inches (2.5 to 5 cm) deep after the threat of frost is past.

Spacing: 3 feet (1 m) between plants of the same cultivar or 5 feet (1.5 m) between different varieties

Years to bearing: one to three. The first year's crop is usually weak. Generally, hops plants take 3 years to produce a brew-worthy harvest. Yields continue to increase over the next several years.

Pruning: Failure to prune results in badly tangled bines and difficulty in harvesting. Train three to four main bines up strings on a hops trellis. As the season progresses, cut out any bines that scramble along the ground. At the end of the growing season, prune the vines to 2 to 3 feet (61 to 91 cm).

Harvest: From midsummer on, check the cones regularly for ripeness. Indicators are a pleasant aroma, papery feel, and—in some varieties—a change in color from green to yellow-green. Ripe cones feel dry and will leave behind a slightly sticky lupulin residue upon handling. Begin picking at the top of the plants where the cones are likely to be ready soonest. On a single plant, the cones mature at different rates, so be prepared to harvest every few days until the cropping is complete, usually by the end of September.

Notes: A single well-grown hops plant can yield up to 6 pounds (2.7 kg) of fresh cones—plenty for most homebrewers. Fertilize first-year plants once a month with a balanced fertilizer such as 10-10-10. For established plants, apply the same fertilizer twice a month from emergence of the cones until flowering. A mulch of compost or manure applied once a year is helpful.

TALK HOPS LIKE A PRO

Bine: a plant with climbing shoots that circle around an object to climb. In the case of some bines, including hops, backward-facing bristles help the stems cling. They are distinct from vines that ascend via suckers or tendrils. Hops (and many other bining plants) twine clockwise, as opposed to the counterclockwise direction of most vines.

Crown: where the upper structures of a plant meet the roots at or just above the ground. In the case of hops, which die to the ground each winter, the crown is where new growth emerges in the spring.

Dioecious: plant species that have male and female flowers on separate plants. Examples of dioecious plants are hops, holly, cannabis, kiwi, ginkgo, and yew.

Lupulin: a resinous, yellow powder produced by female hops flowers and used by humans to preserve and flavor beer.

Oast: a structure ranging in size from a barn to a box used to dry hops via circulated heat or air.

Rhizome: underground stems with the appearance of swollen roots. Hops rhizomes can be dug up and divided to propagate new plants.

Strobilus: female hops flower. Strobili are cone-like inflorescences.

ORNAMENTAL HOPS

If you have the space for yet another hops plant, consider the lovely golden hops, *Humulus lupulus* 'Aureus'. Its name refers to the color of its leaves, which are more of a bright acid green than gold. Like its green-leaved relatives, this vigorous climber produces decorative, papery cones in the summer. The cones are not usually used in brewing, but since golden hops is a genetic mutation of beer hops, their use is at least a possibility.

If you live in the Pacific Northwest, rejoice! Washington, Oregon, and Idaho are the big three of hops-producing states. Home growers in these states and other areas with mild temperatures and low humidity can choose from such favorites as Cascade, Centennial, Newport, Sterling, and Nugget or can experiment with any other hop variety that tickles their fancy. The choices are head spinning: There are more than 100 varieties of hops from across the globe. Europe, Asia, the Czech Republic, New Zealand, and Australia have all added to the gene pool. The key ancestor for today's bittering cultivars came from Manitoba, Canada. And new selections keep coming. Hops hybridizers delight in introducing new varieties. If the botanists have their way, the next decade will see hops that are daylight-neutral, mildew resistant, early maturing, and even higher yielding.

Fortunately, among the dozens of varieties available to the homeowner, there are already varieties of hops that fare well against heat, mildew, pests, and diseases. At the top of most lists is aromatic, all-purpose Cascade, which has been performing reliably in a wide range of climates for 60 years.

HOPS FOR FLAVOR

Let's not lose sight of the fact that choosing hops is about more than horticulture; it's about taste. Brewers know that different hops impart different characteristics. For example, hops can be used for bitterness, aroma, or both. Which hops are best suited for each purpose relates to the alpha and beta acids contained in hops flowers that are integral to the brewing process. Alpha acids are so important that hops varieties are rated according to how much they produce: The higher the percentage, the higher the potential bitterness. Be aware, though—the alpha acid percentages of homegrown hops can vary from year to year. For this reason, many homebrewers use their homegrown hops for aroma purposes only and use commercial hops for bittering.

The most overt result of these alpha acids is the bitter flavor they bring to beer. This quality adds to the distinctive flavor of beer and offsets the yeasty overtones of the malt. Alpha acids are released through boiling. Longer boil times free up more alpha acids, resulting in increasingly bitter brews. Hops that are used for bittering are usually added at the start of a boil that will last for at least 60 minutes. All hops release different levels of bitterness, aromas, and flavors depending on when they are added during the boil.

In addition, alpha acids have antibacterial properties that act to preserve beer. This antiseptic additive was a breakthrough for early brewers who knew the heartbreak of a spoiled cask. Before hops, beer was made with whatever herbs the brewmaster had on hand. Then one happy day, hops came to hand, and beer was redefined. Flavor was a big piece of the epiphany, but equally important were the microbe-killing capabilities of hops, which elevated the act of tapping a keg from potential disappointment to predicable joy.

In days past, hops with high levels of alpha acids were classed as bittering hops, while those with alpha acid ratios closer to those of its beta acids were termed aroma hops. This is no longer true. Breeding breakthroughs in the United States have simplified brewing with the development of dual-purpose hops, such as Simcoe, Amarillo, and Citra, which have high alpha acid levels but are also used for aroma. Adding hops after fermentation, also known as "dry hopping," is widely considered the most effective way to extract the delicate hop aroma. They also can be extracted during the boil, but if added too early, the aromatic properties are reduced. During fermentation and storage, the alpha acids gradually mellow and beta acids increase by oxidation. This process lies behind the distinctive taste and quality of lagers and aged beers. It's also why hoppy beers like India Pale Ales are best consumed fresh.

HOP VARIETIES

In the United States, hops are best adapted to Washington, Idaho, Oregon, California, and other regions with mild temperatures and low humidity. This does not, however, rule out homegrown hops in other parts of the country. At one time or another, hops have been grown in every state in the nation. In ultra-chilly New England and the Midwest, the sticky southeast, and the baking southwest, hops can be produced with a bit of extra planning and preparation.

Hops are hardy in USDA Zones 5 to 9, but winter hardiness is just one consideration. Know your region and the challenges hops plants may face. Does high humidity encourage diseases such as powdery mildew that can kill some varieties to their crowns? Do harsh, prolonged winters mean seeking out particularly hardy hops? Recommendations from local growers can go a long way toward your success. In the end, trial and error is your surest means to a productive hop yard.

TETTNANG HOPS ON THE BINE

The most challenging conditions for hops are hot, dry locales below the 35th parallel. (Yes, Phoenix, I'm talking about you.) But dedication can win the day. If you prepare a deep planting bed with lots of compost, are willing to experiment, and give your hops lots of shade and water (especially in July and August), you have a chance of overcoming your climate. In these punishing regions, bittering hops may be a better bet than aromatics. In this case, you (the hobby grower) actually have an advantage over commercial growers in that you can afford to coddle your few plants.

HOPS VARIETIES

BREWER'S GOLD: bittering (high alpha) hop. Black currant, citrus. Vigorous. High yield. Susceptible to all hop diseases. Midseason harvest. OK for Midwest.

BULLION: bittering (high alpha) hop. Blackberry. Vigorous. High yield. Somewhat disease resistant. Late season harvest.

CASCADE: aroma hop. Spicy, floral, citrus. Gives flavor and aroma to American light lagers, American-style pale ales, and many other brews. Vigorous. High yield. Tolerant of verticillium wilt and downy mildew but susceptible to aphids. Midseason harvest. OK for Midwest and New England. A good choice for the Southeast.

CENTENNIAL: bittering (alpha acid) hop. Floral, citrus. Good in pale ales. Vigorous. Moderate yield. Moderately resistant to downy mildew and verticillium wilt. Midseason harvest. OK for Midwest and New England.

CHINOOK: bittering (high alpha) hop. Very bitter. Grapefruit, pine. High yield. Good storage stability. Midseason harvest. OK for Midwest. Somewhat tolerant of downy mildew and highly tolerant of insects, so a good choice for the Southeast. Also a good try for the Southwest.

CRYSTAL: aroma hop. Mild, slightly spicy. Citrus. Vigorous. High yield. Cone tolerance to downy mildew.

EAST KENT GOLDINGS: aroma hop. Spicy, floral, honey. Low yield. Susceptible to downy and powdery mildew and wilt. OK for Midwest.

EROICA: bittering (high alpha) hop. Vigorous. High yields. Resistant to insects and disease. Midseason harvest.

FUGGLE(S): aroma hop. Mild, grass, flowers. Traditional English ale hop. Low to moderate yield. Susceptible to verticillium wilt. Early harvest. OK for Midwest.

GALENA: bittering (high alpha) hop. Black currant, grapefruit. Very bitter. Vigorous. High yield. Midseason harvest.

GLACIER: dual-purpose (bittering and aroma) hop. Citrus, fruit. High yield. Susceptible to mildew. Midseason harvest. OK for Midwest and New England.

GOLDING: English ale aroma hop. Honey, earthy. Moderate yield. Susceptible to powdery and downy mildew. Early to midseason harvest. OK for New England.

LIBERTY: aroma hop. Spicy, citrus. Good for finishing German-style lagers. Moderate yield. Midseason harvest.

MAGNUM: bittering (alpha acid) hop. A clean bittering hop for ales and lagers. High yield. Tolerant of downy mildew and wilt; susceptible to powdery mildew. Good storage stability. Late harvest. Good option for the Southwest.

MOUNT HOOD: aroma hop. Grapefruit, herbal. Vigorous. Moderate to high yield. Moderately disease resistant. Midseason harvest. OK for Midwest.

NEWPORT: bittering (alpha acid) hop. Herbal, cedar. High yield. Resistant to powdery mildew, susceptible to downy mildew. OK for Midwest. Good for Pacific Northwest.

NORTHERN BREWER: dual-purpose (bittering and aroma) hop. Spicy, resinous. Low to moderate yield. Tolerant of verticillium wilt, susceptible to powdery mildew. Midseason harvest. OK for Midwest and New England.

NUGGET: bittering (high alpha) hop. Spicy, fruit. Good for light lagers. Vigorous. High yield. Disease resistant. Good storage stability. Midseason harvest. Popular in the Pacific Northwest. OK for Midwest and New England. A good choice for the Southeast.

PERLE: bittering (alpha acid) hop. German lager hop. Citrus, cedar. Moderate yield. Early season harvest. OK for Midwest and New England.

SAAZ: high-quality aroma hop. Earthy, herbal, mildly floral. Weak grower. Low yield. Susceptible to downy mildew. Early season harvest. OK for New England.

SPALT SELECT: aroma hop. Herbal, floral. German lager and ale hop. Moderate yield. Tolerant of verticillium wilt, downy mildew. Late harvest. OK for Midwest. Good in Pacific Northwest.

TETTNANG: aroma hop. Mild, spicy, herbal. Good for finishing German lagers. Moderately vigorous. Low yield. Tolerant of verticillium wilt. Early season harvest. Good for New England. Also a good try for the southwest.

WILLAMETTE: aroma hop. Mild spicy, grassy, black currant. American ale hop. Moderate yield. Tolerant of downy mildew, resistant to viruses. Midseason harvest. Grown almost exclusively in the Pacific Northwest. OK for Midwest and New England.

ZEUS: bittering (alpha acid) hop. Black pepper, licorice. Vigorous. Hardy. High yield. Susceptible to downy and powdery mildew as well as aphids and mites. Mid- to late-season harvest. OK for Midwest and New England. Closely related to Columbus and Tomahawk.

CASCADE HOPS ON
THE BINE

HOPS IN THE GARDEN

At last, it's time to stop researching and start ordering your plants. Grab a cold one and find a source of hops plants that specializes in your region, often a local homebrew supplier. As you peruse their offerings keep this in mind: If your goal is to brew, start with at least three or four varieties. This not only helps ensure against crop failure but also gives you a range of flavors and alpha acid levels with which to experiment. Consider starting small with only a few plants. Four plants grown well will yield more and better hops than a whole row of neglected plants. A single well-grown hops plant can yield up to 6 pounds (2.7 kg) of fresh cones—plenty for most homebrewers. Although the initial crop may be disappointing, the harvest will increase in subsequent years.

Hops are sold as dormant rhizomes or potted plants. Hops in pots can be planted any time the soil can be worked, but may be hard to find in all seasons. Freshly dug rhizomes are offered only in early spring. If the rhizomes cannot be planted immediately upon arrival, wrap them in damp newspaper or damp sawdust and store in a cool place. The refrigerator works well if you have room in your crisper for large, lumpy roots.

When the time comes to plant your hops, siting is critical. For best production, hops want a site with full sun, good air circulation, soil that neither bakes nor bogs, and room for some form of trellising. Although a southern exposure is not absolutely necessary, less optimal exposures will result in smaller cones. Home growers should place one plant per hill with a manageable 3-foot (1 m) spacing for plants of the same cultivar or 5 feet (1.5 m) between different varieties. The difference in spacing between like and unlike cultivars is one of order and identification: The closer the plants are, the more prone they are to hopeless tangling, in which case you'll never know which flowers you're picking. Tight spacing also lowers yields as the plants compete for light. Plant the rhizomes vertically with the buds facing up, or horizontally 1 to 2 inches (2.5 to 5 cm) deep after the threat of frost is past. Then, stand back. At the peak of growth, the plants can climb as much as a foot (30 cm) per day to a height of 20 feet (6 m) or more. Bloom time is from mid- to late summer. The plants should have at least 10 to 12 productive years ahead.

YOU CAN USE A PLASTIC PIPE TO SUPPORT YOUR HOPS.

Hops are climbers. Period. If not provided with support, they will find their own. Fences, trees, telephone poles, the neighbor's garage—nothing within 10 feet (3 m) that can't run away is immune to their hoppy hug. That said, the bines' tiny, clinging hooks do not seem to damage the host, especially if the bines are removed each winter when they die back to the crown. To be safe, use caution in allowing hops to climb on porch supports or thin-barked trees.

Although hops will grow up practically anything they can wrap themselves around, for ease of picking consider growing your plants on strings or poles attached at the top to a strong horizontal wire. This system can be designed so that the wire can be unfastened and lowered for easy harvesting. Once the hops raise their heads a foot (30 cm) above the ground, coax them clockwise around their supports. As they grow, continue to steer them in the right direction as needed.

Fertilize first-year plants once a month with a balanced fertilizer such as 10-10-10. Follow the manufacturer's directions and apply to new plants from the first sight of new growth until early July. For established plants, apply the same fertilizer twice a month from emergence until flowering. A mulch of compost or manure applied once a year also helps the plants along. Water well during the growing season, especially for the first two years after your hops are planted, but don't let them sit in soggy soil.

In swampy ground, plant the rhizomes in mounds raised 6 to 8 inches (15 to 20 cm) above ground level. If the site drains well, regular watering will fuel the bines' rocket-like growth and boost flower production.

SUPPORTING YOUR HOPS

A hops structure must, above all else, be sturdy. Forget lacy lattice; you need support that's up to the job. Although hops can be grown on a fence or other horizontal structure, the bines are equally adept at climbing straight up. Professional hops growers take advantage of this upstanding nature with vertical trellis systems that allow maximum sun exposure to the plants as well as easier access to the cones. Hop yards are forests of 18-foot (5 m) poles spaced 3 to 4 feet (~1 m) in rows 14 feet (4 m) apart. Guy wires are attached at the top of the poles down each row. Upright wires are then placed along the row in Vs, starting at the ground and angling up to each side.

A system like this is certainly useful to a home hops growers; however, other supports can be considered. An old flagpole can be pressed into service, with three or more support lines spaced evenly around the base, beginning several feet (approximately 2 m) away and attaching to the top. Even better, attach them to the pulley system so that the lines can be lowered at harvest time. If no flagpole is available, a similar system can be devised with a pole or 4x4 post. To avoid posts altogether, three or four support wires can be run from the ground and angled up to meet at the peak of the eaves of a building with a southern exposure; once again, a pulley makes bringing the bines down a simple job.

For most hops supports, poles or posts and some form of line is standard. Wire rope, aircraft cable, or heavy twine can be used. Hops bines will also happily scramble directly up the posts themselves or the narrow columns of a porch or pergola. Avoid lattice or chain-link fencing. The bines will tangle hopelessly in anything they can, which will make the job of winter removal a bigger chore than it needs to be.

HARVESTING YOUR HOPS

You've been patient, sitting in the shade of your hops bower dreaming of worts and sparging. It's finally time to harvest those hops. How do you know? Beginning in August—as early as June in some regions—the cones should be checked regularly for ripeness. Indicators are a pleasant aroma, papery feel, and in some varieties, a change in color from green to yellow-green. Ripe cones feel dry and will leave behind a slightly sticky lupulin residue upon handling. The base of the bracts should be heavy with lupulin. To check the readiness of your crop, pull open a cone and look for this dark gold powder. Cones that are deep green, vaguely damp, and smell of hay are unripe; if these cones are pressed between the fingers they remain flattened while a ripe cone will spring back. If, on the other hand, cones are beginning to brown or smell unpleasantly strong, they have passed their prime.

Begin picking at the top of the plants where the cones are likely to be ready first. On a single plant the cones mature at different rates, so be prepared to harvest every few days until the cropping is complete, usually by the end of September. Wear long sleeves and gloves when harvesting to guard against the skin-raking bine spines. Remove the cones gently, with two hands, to avoid losing any of the precious lupulin. Use a picking basket or bag that can be slung over your shoulder or attached to your belt to keep your hands free. Once picked, the hops should never again be in direct sunlight—unless you prefer beer that has overtones of scared skunk.

The hops may be used immediately as green hops in a wet-hopped ale to commemorate the harvest, or dried for future use. In wet-hopped brews, hops fresh off the plant are added during the boil. This gives the resulting beer a fresh, springy flavor. The downside to this is the difficultly of knowing how much of the fresh hops to add. When fresh, hops have a much higher and more unpredictable moisture ratio than dried hops, and this makes it a bit tricky to judge the amount of green hops to be used in any recipe.

DEVELOPING NEW HOPS

Not all hops cultivars are available to the homegrowing public. Many newly developed hops are protected by public and private breeders. Until the 1990s, most new varieties were released directly to the public. Now, however, it's common for private companies to keep their plants proprietary. That's not to say homegrowers will never have access to these varieties. Public breeders eventually bring their best creations to market, and the patents on privately held hops ultimately expire. And we have plenty to keep us busy in the meantime; while we wait for the new and novel, there are more than two dozen good and commonly available cultivars from which we can choose today.

Many modern hops cultivars have arisen, in part, from three key parents. Brewer's Gold (bittering), Fuggle (English aroma), and Hallertauer mittelfrueh (German aroma) are ancestors of most of the hops available today. Until recently, breeding programs focused on improved hops strains to replace existing ones. For example, a new variety may have improved resistance to spider mites, aphids, or powdery and downy mildew, or produce higher yields, but otherwise match the acid and alpha ratios of the plant it was designed to replace. This kind of linear breeding is purely practical; large brewers don't want to change their recipes, but hop growers benefit from productive plants that require minimal pest control.

The recent rise of the craft beer industry has led to a widening of some breeding programs to develop cultivars with unique chemical and aroma profiles. For professional hops breeders, the road from pollination to production is a long and expensive one. New releases can be in development for fourteen or more years. As the new varieties mature, hops breeders compile data on traits such as disease resistance, yield, age of maturity, coning habit, and many different chemical characteristics such as bittering acids and essential oil content. Hops take years to come to full fruition.

DRYING HOPS

Most brews rely on dried hops. Dried hops allow more precise control over lupulin amounts and, thus, the final result. For best quality, the hops must be properly dried as soon after harvest as possible to preserve their flavor and aroma. Hops can be dried via old-fashioned air drying or with mechanically assisted methods such as a fan, food dehydrator, oven, microwave, or even a homemade hop drier. Low and slow should be your mantra when drying hops. Heat drives off some of the aromatic complexity of the cones; too much heat will ruin them completely.

Two preservation methods, air and fan drying, avoid heat altogether. Air drying can be done in any warm, dark, dry room with good air circulation and enough space for the hops to be laid out in a single layer on anything from open paper bags to clean window screens. Fluff the cones every day or two and cover them with cheesecloth if dust is a concern. Your hops should be ready in 3 days to 1 week. When the lupulin is falling away and the stems snap when bent, the cones are sufficiently dry. If not thoroughly dried, the hops will mold and be unfit for brewing.

If you recognize the benefits of air drying, but crave a more dynamic and faster method than that of passive screen drying, put a fan beneath the screen. For air-dried hops in 24 hours, attach two screens together with a layer of hops in between. Bungee cord the result to a box fan. Keep watch over the hops in the final hours to keep them from becoming overly dry. If they dry too much, your lupulin can be gone with the wind.

Food dehydrators should be turned to the lowest temperature, around 95°F (35°C), to dry hops. At this setting, the cones may take up to three days to dry. To avoid having the house smell like a Bourbon Street bar on a Sunday morning, move the dehydrator to a garage or outbuilding. Ovens pose an even greater aroma risk, since the temperature may be higher and portability is impossible. Never dry hops at a temperature higher than 140°F (60°C).

As with all heat-drying methods, microwaves can reduce the delicate aromatic essence of hops. On the plus side, microwaves can dry small batches of hops in only a few minutes. Dry the cones at fifty percent power. Stir every 30 seconds. When the hops are partially dried, remove them and give them time to finish drying. If they seem at all damp once they have cooled, return them to the microwave and continue the process. Once again, be prepared for a strong and potentially unpleasant smell.

Die-hard brewmasters can follow in the footsteps of the professionals by constructing a hops dryer, known as an oast. Oasts, or hop kilns, are derived from traditional English oast houses, which are the size of barns. Oasts rely on heated, circulating air for desiccation. A homemade, beehive-sized oast may not be as imposing as a three-story, furnace-heated architectural behemoth, but it is more appropriate to a backyard harvest. The best reason for considering an oast is to deal with a very large home harvest consisting of pounds (kilograms) of hops.

STORING HOPS

Dried cones should be sealed in airtight plastic bags. Pack the bags tightly and squeeze out all the air or, better yet, vacuum seal them. The hops can be refrigerated to be brewed within 1 week, or frozen for up to a year. When you're ready to fire up the kettle, the hops can be used directly from the freezer. Remove only the hops you need as thawing and refreezing can degrade the essential oils.

CANNABACEAE

Hops, *Humulus lupulus*, is a member of the family Cannabaceae. Sound familiar? Cannabaceae, as is cannabis, as in marijuana. The two genera, *Humulus* and *Cannabis*, may not be instantly recognizable as relatives, but their flowering gives a clue to their kinship: both have resinous, imperfect flowers with male flowers on one plant, female flowers on another.

BARLEY

If hops are the heart of beer, barley is its backbone. And for good reason: Barley is an alcohol alchemist. No other cereal grain contains as much of the fermentation-friendly enzymes that break down grains' stored starches into the sugars required for turning seeds into beer, whiskey, and other spirits. Barley's effect is so powerful that it acts as a catalyst to ferment other, less endowed, grains such as wheat, rice, rye, corn, oats, and millet.

Growing your own backyard barley may sound hardcore, but it's actually surprisingly easy. Barley, *Hordeum vulgare*, is a forgiving crop in northern climates. In addition, it is high yielding, matures early, and is widely adapted to all but the hottest and driest conditions. But growing barley is only half the battle. Once you've gone through all the trouble of growing and harvesting a crop of barley, it needs to be dried and then malted, which can be a timely process that requires a learning curve. If you are really committed to making a farm-to-table beer, growing and malting your own barley could be a fun project if you have the time and growing space. However, practically speaking, it is much easier to purchase malt from a homebrew supplier and get right to making beer. Commercially produced malts will have much more consistent results, and you can exercise your green thumb by growing some hops and herbs to include in your brews.

GRUIT PLANTS

If making medieval-style beer intrigues you enough to want to grow and brew an herb or three, the good news is that most of them grow with ease in a wide variety of gardens. Provided there is enough sunshine on the space, even an apartment balcony garden using large pots can grow many of the herbs you need to brew a batch of Gruitbier.

YARROW

Yarrow is the most widely used medicinal herb species from Europe, and the plant has naturalized in the northern temperate regions around the globe. So perhaps it's not surprising that it also ended up as an ingredient in ales! Historically speaking, the herb has a long association with *Homo sapiens* and our distant and extinct relatives. A story about yarrow pollen found in 60,000-year-old Neanderthal burial caves makes for an interesting topic of conversation while sitting around a backyard fire with friends sipping a brew made from this herb. Its botanical name, *Achillea*, refers to a 3,000-year-old story from the Trojan War, in which Achilles used yarrow on wounds to stop the bleeding.

Brewers frequently used the highly aromatic flowers and leaves of the common yarrow plant (*Achillea millefolium*) as a substitute for hops to give beer a satisfying floral and herbal quality.

Linnaeus, the father of botany, originally gave yarrow the name *Galentara*, which meant "causing madness," perhaps in reference to its role in alcoholic beverages. You'll find the herb grows with ease in the garden; actually, it grows with wild abandon. For a brewer's first foray into grow your own, this would be a great starter plant. However, choose a white flowering strain for your beer and leave the colorful flowering strains for the ornamental garden. Yarrow can be grown in pots or in the ground, as the herb can handle a variety of growing conditions. Wet or dry, shade or sun, open or deep woods, meadows, prairies, or your lawn, you'll find yarrow is a plant that adapts. However, the optimum conditions for harvesting are full sun and moist, fertile, well-drained soil. The plant likes to romp beyond its bounds, so either grow the herb in a container or somewhere between a foundation and a sidewalk. In 2 years, for example, yarrow spaced 4 feet (1.2 m) apart will be one solid mass of plant!

After a few growing seasons, yarrow will need rejuvenating. The herb will continue to live and grow, but it settles in with a thick mat of leaves and doesn't flower as prolifically as it does when invading new land. You can smother an old plot of yarrow by covering with a thick layer of newspaper, covered in thick mulch. Leave a few plants on the edge and let it invade a new area or divide the plants and start over in another plot. You can also alternate where you allow it to invade, so it is always on the move conquering new ground and happily flowering in the process.

The first harvest of the leaves and flowers begins when the flowers first start to show in late spring to early summer. Adjust the timing of your harvest accordingly to accommodate your climate and weather patterns. You can usually get two to three harvests in a growing season. When harvesting leaves, choose only those that are fresh and green; discard any shaded out yellow to black leaves underneath. After the first and second harvests, cut the yarrow all the way down to encourage new green growth. After the third harvest, let the herb grow on its merry way.

Time your brew schedule with the harvest of the flowers and leaves to use them fresh. For later use, cut the stems and flowers in the morning; tie the stems together and hang upside down in a well-ventilated, dark, dry space; and let them dry at temperatures that don't exceed 95°F (35°C). Store your dried herbs in airtight containers.

Because of yarrow's antiseptic, antimicrobial, and antibacterial properties, it acts as a preservative in ales—much like hops. The strong, astringent-tasting flowers or leaves should be used sparingly in the brewing process or the plant will overpower the beer. One ounce of dried yarrow or up to 2 ounces (55 g) of fresh flower tops is a good starting point, or start with some tried-and-true recipes before you venture out with your own creative concoctions.

YARROW

Botanical name: *Achillea millefolium*

Plant type: perennial herb

USDA zones: 3 to 10

Height: 2 to 3 feet (61 to 91 cm)

Soil: well-drained to moist; tolerates poor, dry soil

Light: full sun

Water: low to moderate

Growth habit: clumps spread 18 to 36 inches (45 to 91 cm) by underground runners.

Propagate by: division

Spacing: 2 to 4 feet (0.6 to 1.2 m)

Years to bearing: 1 year

Pruning: Cut old stems to ground during dormant season. After a few growing seasons, yarrow needs rejuvenating. By the third year, the herb becomes a thick mat of leaves with reduced flowering. Divide and replant or smother the old plot with a layer of four sheets or more of newspaper, covered in thick mulch. A few plants left on the edge will take over with fresh, new growth and lots of flowers.

Harvest: The first of two to three harvests is taken when the leaves and flowers first show in late spring. Pick flowers and only healthy green leaves. After the first and second harvests, cut the yarrow all the way down to encourage new growth. After the third harvest, let the herb grow. Use the flowers and leaves fresh when possible. To dry, cut the stems and flowers in the morning, tie the stems together, and hang upside down in a well-ventilated, dark, dry space.

Notes: Choose a white-flowered strain for beer. Yarrow can be invasive in the garden. It's good for container culture.

BUNDLES OF
LAVENDER READY
FOR DRYING

ENGLISH LAVENDER

The English lavenders (*Lavandula angustifolia*) are used for complex bitterness in beer, much like heathers (*Calluna vulgaris*). Also used in gin and liqueurs, English lavender imparts a milder taste than other species of lavender. In a Mediterranean-style garden, these shrub-like herbs are stunning with their silver-gray leaves and purple-blue flowers. *Lavandula angustifolia* 'Tucker's Early', 'Munstead', or 'Hidcote' are good choices to grow for your brew. *L.* 'Tucker's Early' is a compact erect plant that is one of the earliest blooming English lavenders, yet other cultivars work as well.

English lavenders prefer the Mediterranean-like, dry summers of the West Coast. However, if you live in an area with steamy, hot summers, you can substitute *L.* x *intermedia* cultivars that can handle more humidity such as *L.* 'Grosso' or 'Gros Bleu' that impart a sharper flavor. Other lavender species outside of *L. angustifolia* or x *intermedia* cultivars are not suitable for consumption as they are mildly toxic.

You don't need to fertilize lavenders. After the initial flower harvest when the flowers begin to fade, shear your plants back to keep them compact and tidy. Prune above the wood where there are leaves. The stems won't regrow if you cut into the wood. Lavender plants will grow woody and gangly over time, so many people replace their lavender plants after five years. You can propagate your plants by taking softwood cuttings in summer. Harvest the flowers when the blooms are just opening up. Tie the stems together and hang upside down in a well-ventilated, dark, dry space and let them dry at temperatures that don't exceed 95°F (35°C). Store your dried herbs in airtight containers.

A good starting point is about 0.25 ounce (7 g) of fresh or dried flowers added towards the end of the boil. You can also use the flowers as you would hops for dry hopping.

ENGLISH LAVENDER

Botanical name: *Lavandula angustifolia*

Plan type: shrubby evergreen herb

USDA zones: 5 to 8

Height: 2 to 3 feet (61 to 91 cm) with a spread equal to or twice that, depending on cultivar

Soil: well-drained, neutral pH

Light: full sun

Water: low

Growth habit: low, shrubby perennial

Propagate by: softwood cuttings in summer

Spacing: 1 to 2 feet (30 to 61 cm), depending on cultivar

Years to bearing: 2 years until harvest

Pruning: Shear down half of new growth each year after bloom or the following year before growth begins. The stems won't regrow if you cut into the old wood. Lavender plants grow woody and gangly over time; replace them when they become unsightly.

Harvest: Pick the flowers when the blooms are just opening up. Tie stems together and hang upside down to dry in a cool, dry location.

Notes: English lavender lends a milder taste to beverages than other lavender species. *L. angustifolia* 'Tucker's Early', 'Munstead', or 'Hidcote' are good choices for brewing, yet other cultivars work as well.

HEATHER

In the nineteenth century, Robert Louis Stevenson wrote a poem about the Scottish version of the legend of heather ale. It's a gruesome tale of a battle set in pre-Roman times, where a Pict (thought to be pre-Celtic people) gave up his life and that of his son, rather than reveal the secret of a heather ale recipe to the Scots. As many legends go, the truth is bent or stretched beyond repair. There was no genocide of the Picts; many of their descendants live in parts of Scotland today.

The Irish have their own version of the legend, only the last man was a Viking in the last clash with the Irish. Rather than give up the recipe for *bheóir Lochlannach* (which translates as Viking beer), the Viking chooses death. Still, even without the recipe, Viking beer most likely was a heather-flavored mead or cider. The idea of brewing a tasty, legendary ale is intriguing. With many heather ale recipes readily available, you won't need to threaten anyone for a secret one!

If you wish to grow *Calluna vulgaris* for such a purpose, a dozen or more plants will be necessary to harvest enough for your brew. It takes up to 3 quarts (3.3 L) of fresh-picked flowering heather tips for a 5-gallon (19 L) batch of beer. Fortunately, the plants are small enough that you can easily grow many of them in your garden. Some homebrew supply stores carry dried heather, too, but heather is beautiful in the garden and easily harvested, so why not grow your own?

Your best bet is to grow plants in full sun, in well-drained, slightly acidic soil. However, heather grows well in rock gardens, too. The plants can tolerate dry soil, but will need irrigation during a prolonged summer drought. Shear lightly after flowers fade to keep the plant from becoming straggly. Also, avoid pruning into woody barren branches or the stem won't regrow. Propagate by semiripe cuttings in midsummer or sow seed as soon as ripe and place in a cold frame for the winter. It is preferable to pick the fresh flowers in late summer; however, you can dry the stems by bundling and hanging them upside down in a cool, dry, dark place. The heather tips can be added to the boil. Some recipes also suggest dropping sprigs in beer after primary fermentation (similar to dry hopping).

HEATHER

Botanical name: *Calluna vulgaris*

Plant type: low evergreen shrubs

USDA zones: 5 to 7

Height: 8 to 24 inches (20 to 60 cm)

Soil: well-drained, slightly acidic

Light: full sun

Water: low, but best with summer irrigation

Growth habit: low-growing mounds or spreading mats

Propagate by: semiripe cuttings in midsummer, or sow seed as soon as ripe and place in a cold frame for the winter

Spacing: Heathers vary widely in spread, so space the plants about as far apart as the plant's mature width as listed on the nursery tag.

Years to bearing: once plants are large enough to provide ample tips

Pruning: If heather is used for brewing, harvest by shearing when the flowers are fresh in late summer, which will double as the plants' yearly pruning. Otherwise, shear lightly after flowers fade to keep the plant from becoming straggly. Avoid pruning into woody barren branches, which won't produce new growth.

Harvest: Shear fresh flowers in late summer.

Notes: At least a dozen plants are required to harvest enough heather tips for brewing. It's a good rock garden or raised bed plant. The heather tips are added to the boil and sometimes the sprigs are dry-hopped in some recipes.

SWEET GALE

Sweet gale literally gets around, growing circumpolar in the northern latitudes throughout the world. In North America, its native haunts are throughout Canada and Alaska but it is equally at home in Oregon, Washington, the Great Lakes states, New England states, and even dips down into North Carolina and Tennessee.

Before hops appeared, sweet gale may have been the most prominent gruit ingredient in Britain. Beer enthusiasts have a difference of opinion on the claim that both sweet gale and marsh rosemary are brewed in the same historic gruit recipes since the shrubs grow in different regions in Europe. It may be that the flavoring that went into a regional gruit would have used the shrub native to where the brew was developed, not both as some claim. Considered the true gale, sweet gale appears to be the preferred flavoring of the two as evidenced by some of the common names of the time for marsh rosemary—false gale and pig's gale. There are many common names for *Myrica gale* such as bog myrtle, Dutch myrtle, meadow fern, and English myrtle, yet sweet gale is neither a myrtle nor a fern!

The shrubs are dioecious, meaning they are either male or female; however, some individuals can change from male to female and back again. If you wish to propagate your plants from seed, you will need at least one male and one female plant, and hope they are not fickle enough to change to the same gender in any given year. The male catkins emit pollen that is carried by the wind to pollinate the female catkins. (If you have pollen allergies you won't want to aggravate the problem by growing this in your garden.)

Sweet gale is a bushy, 2- to 4-foot (0.6 to 1.2 m) deciduous shrub. The nitrogen-fixing abilities of nodules in the sweet gale's roots and its symbiotic relationship with a fungus called *Frankia* mean it can grow in nitrogen-poor soil. As with marsh rosemary, do not use any fungicides near the shrubs. In its native habitat, sweet gale grows in perpetually wet conditions next to lakes and streams and in fens, bogs, and swamps.

Covered in glands, the glossy, blue-green leaves emit a pleasing, sweet-smelling, resinous fragrance. Harvest the leaves and dry them on a drying rack in well-ventilated, dark, dry space; and let them dry at temperatures that don't exceed 95°F (35°C). Store your dried herbs in airtight containers.

To make a gale ale use 0.25 ounce (7 g) of dried sweet gale leaves and mix with other herbs such as lavender and rosemary.

Warning: The plant is an abortifacient; if you are pregnant do not consume beer made with this ingredient.

SWEET GALE

Botanical name: *Myrica gale*

Plant type: low, deciduous shrub

USDA zones: 2 to 9

Height: 4 to 6 feet (1.2 to 1.8 m)

Soil: damp, peaty, acidic

Light: full sun to light shade

Water: constant; suitable for bogs

Growth habit: shrubby

Propagate by: softwood cuttings, layering, seed

Spacing: 4 to 6 feet (1.2 to 1.8 m)

Years to bearing: when large enough to give up the required number of leaves

Pruning: Pinch to keep dense; use harvesting as pruning.

Harvest: At the time of flowering, harvest only new leaves growing on new stems. Don't over harvest an individual plant. Dry the leaves using a drying rack in a ventilated area.

Notes: Sweet gale is a soil-improving nitrogen fixer.

PURPLE HEATHER PLANTS ARE AS BEAUTIFUL AS THEY ARE FUNCTIONAL IN A MULTI-PURPOSE GARDEN.

JUNIPER

Common juniper is a low-growing, or upright, evergreen bush native to high northern latitudes around the entire globe. Here in North America it grows in alpine meadows, the plains, and as an understory plant for wooded areas of native conifers and quaking aspen trees (*Populus tremuloides*). Historically, Native Americans used juniper medicinally as a tonic for an assortment of ailments and used the branches as a smudge to repel insects. They believed that the branches brought good luck, protected you from disease, kept evil spirits away, and protected you from lightning and thunder.

The berries are still used today in potpourris, but more importantly as an ingredient for beer! (After brewing, feel free to toss any of your unused berries into the potpourri dish.) Both berries and boughs have been used during the brewing process and for filtering out grains and hops in the bottom of brew vessels, and juniper can be found in recipes for porters, stouts, and doppelbocks. Common juniper goes by other names such as dwarf juniper, prostrate juniper, mountain common juniper, old-field common juniper, and ground juniper. Some good selections for the garden and for brewing include *Juniperus communis* var. *charlottensis*, *J. communis* var. *megistocarpa*, *J. communis* var. *depressa*, and *J. communis* var. *montana*. The last two varieties rarely grow taller than 1 to 3 feet (0.3 to 0.9 m).

The low-growing conifer is a popular groundcover for the garden because it grows on a variety of soils including stony or sandy soils. Junipers will grow in acidic to alkaline pH soil, but in the garden, you want maximum growth potential; it will grow its best in a sandy-loam to loamy soil in full sun.

J. communis is not recommended for homes located in dangerous fire zones, where fire-resistant landscapes are a necessity. The plant is highly flammable with resinous foliage that burns more intensely than many other herbaceous plants.

These plants rarely need to be pruned, unless they're placed where their width overcomes a sidewalk. Site your plants carefully in the first place and you won't have deal with plants outgrowing their space. When harvesting or pruning boughs, it is important not to cut below the green needles. Prune only where needles appear along the stem; otherwise, the branch will not regrow.

A small amount of potent juniper berries goes a long way, if you don't want your beer to end up tasting like gin. One ounce (28 g) of berries per 5 gallons (19 L) added the last 10 to 15 minutes of the boil is a commonly advised starting point.

Warning: Women who are pregnant or anyone with kidney disease should not ingest juniper berries or anything made with them. Because gin (also called mother's ruin) is flavored with juniper berries, it has the ability to cause miscarriage, so any juniper berry brew should be avoided by mothers to be.

JUNIPER

Botanical name: *Juniperus communis*

Plant type: coniferous evergreen shrub

USDA zones: 3 to 8

Height: shrubs, 1 to 13 feet (0.3 to 4 m); trees to 30 feet (9 m)

Soil: tolerates poor soil, but best in a sandy loam

Light: full sun to shade

Water: dry to moist; can tolerate drought

Growth habit: low-growing or upright shrub or small columnar tree. Common juniper has many cultivars with a wide variety of growth habits.

Propagate by: cuttings

Spacing: dependent on cultivar

Years to bearing: once plants are large enough to harvest foliage. Cones, three years.

Pruning: rarely needs pruning. Snip back individual stems to shape. When harvesting or pruning boughs, don't cut below the green needles or the branch won't regrow.

Harvest: Ripe, plump berries should be gathered in autumn and dried slowly in the shade to retain the oil

Notes: Any juniper berry brew should be avoided by mothers to be.

THE CUCURBITS

Cucumber saison, pumpkin ale, and watermelon wheat are just some of the beers that are possible, thanks to the cucurbits family of plants.

Melons can be problematic, but pumpkins, squash, and cucumbers are not hard to grow in most climates, except for the shorter-season ones. The biggest complaint we hear about growing cucurbits is the powdery mildew they can get later in the season. The fungus is unruly once the weather turns cool and humid. When the mildew sets in, the plant's ripening process halts permanently. However, researchers in South America found that a foliar spray of milk controls powdery mildew on squash, cucumber, melon, and pumpkin plants. Just mix a spray of one part nonfat milk to nine parts water and spray weekly to reduce the disease-causing organisms *Sphaerotheca fuliginea*. Not only does the spray keep the fungus in check, it fertilizes the plants at the same time. This is an inexpensive, organic, and easy way to protect and grow healthy cucurbits. Cucumber beetles and squash borers can also attack the plants. The best line of defense is using a row cover on the plants until they start flowering. Take the covers off at that point or the bees won't be able to pollinate the plants.

Cucurbit vines produce male and female flowers. Plenty of beginner gardeners ask why their flowers don't produce fruit early in the season. It's because the first flowers to open are typically the male ones. (You can tell the difference between the male and the female, as the female flowers have a swollen ovary at their base that looks like a baby fruit.)

Once the female flowers open, if you are not seeing any fruit develop, you may need to channel your inner bee and do some hand pollinating. Cut a male flower off the vine and pull off the petals. You will see the pollen on the stamens. Simply touch the pollen to the female flower's sticky pistil. Also, if you don't have enough pollinators in your garden, you may want to learn how to attract them to your plot of land. If you are spraying with pesticides, you may be killing off the beneficial insects who pollinate plants, keep pests at bay, or both.

PUMPKIN AND SQUASH

When fall moves in, we love pumpkin flavor in almost everything. Of course, beer is no exception! The best edible pumpkins are actually squashes, though. In fact, canned pumpkin—the kind you might use for cooking or for brewing—isn't really pumpkin, but squash. Why they call it pumpkin is a mystery. Perhaps canned squash doesn't sound as appetizing, even if the fruit is sweeter and purées into a beautiful consistency for pie. Still, fresh is always best, for baking and for brewing! Squash is not a tough vine to grow and

harvest, but it does take up a lot of room in the garden. One solution is to plant a "three sisters" combination in your allotted space, which is an ingenious, ancient Native American way to grow corn, squash, and pole beans in the same plot. The beans are a legume that fixes nitrogen into the soil, while the corn stands tall and feels entitled to steal all the nutrients. The beans wind their way up the corn, while the pumpkins and squash wander around at the base, effectively covering the bare ground and shading out the weeds. Or, you can plant just pumpkin and just grow some vines to cover ground. The large leaves are actually quite handsome in a tropical-looking way. Try to give your vines full sun, although a little bit of shade won't harm them. Give them a lot of room to grow—overcrowding them reduces fruit yield. Space hills 4 to 5 feet (1.2 to 1.5 m) apart and plant four to six seeds per hill. After the seedlings emerge, thin the sprouts to the most vigorous plant in each mound. Don't pull the weaker ones out; cut them to ground level with your pruners to prevent disturbing the roots of the chosen one. When sowing the seeds or transplanting, add 1 cup (240 ml) of a complete organic fertilizer to each hill and fertilize every 2 to 3 weeks after that. Harvest your squash after the first light frost when the vine wilts and before a hard frost. When you cut the squash from the wilted vine, leave 2 inches (5 cm) of stem on the fruit. Leave the fruit out in the sun to cure for a few days. Protect your fruit from a hard frost during the curing time.

Botanical name: *Cucurbita* spp

Plant type: vining annual vegetables

USDA zones: 3 to 9

Height: 2.5 feet (76 cm) trailing, or 6 to 8 feet (1.8 to 2.4 m) if trellised

Soil: rich and well-drained, amended with compost

Light: full sun

Water: regular; at least 1 inch (2.5 cm) of water a week

Growth habit: trailing vines

Propagate by: seed planted directly in the ground. If the growing season is short, seed can be started in peat pots and planted out when the soil is warm.

Spacing: 18 to 36 inches (46 to 91 cm). Plant several seeds in one spot—or hill—and thin to the best seedling.

Months to bearing: four to five

Pruning: none

Harvest: A pumpkin or squash is ripe when its skin turns the solid color of its type (typically orange) and the rind resists puncture when pressed with a thumbnail. Harvest after the first light frost when the vine wilts, but before a hard frost. Leave a 2-inch (5 cm) stem on the fruit. Leave your squash in the sun to cure for a few days.

Notes: Pumpkins and squash are heavy feeders. Apply fish emulsion every month, beginning when plants are 8 inches (20 cm) tall. The first flowers are male, and so will not become fruit. The best pumpkin for eating is squash; even commercially canned pumpkin is actually a mix of winter squash. Be warned that pumpkins can cause a difficult brew, especially for all-grain brewers, but the flavor of the ale is worth the effort. The best flavor comes from putting the cooked fruit in the mash, rather than in the boil. The trade-off for good flavor is the amount of time it takes to run-off the wort to the kettle.

The amount of pumpkin or squash you'll use in a pumpkin beer recipe varies, but you'll want to think in pounds (kg) rather than ounces (g) if you want any flavor to come through. If you want your beer to really smack of pumpkin, there are two tips. First, consider using some pumpkin pie spices in your beer recipe as well—while they will mask the gourd flavor somewhat, they also remind the drinker of pumpkin desserts when they smell or taste the beer. The second tip is to chop up and bake your squash on a cookie sheet before brewing with it. Some caramelized (but not burnt) pieces are optional but can provide additional depth of flavor. When the fruit cools, mash well by hand or purée the fruit in a blender. If you plan to freeze your squash, divide it up in amounts called for in your recipes to brew at a later date or to steal for homegrown pumpkin pies.

Flavor-wise, there are many excellent cultivars to consider. The first is Rouge vif d'Etampes (cucurbita maxima). Commonly called the Cinderella pumpkin, this plant is actually a squash. Average weight per pumpkin is 15 pounds (6.8 kg) and yield is two pumpkins per plant. 'Sunshine Kabocha' is a beautiful and delicious winter squash with space-saving, 6- to 8-foot (1.8 to 2.4 m) vines. 'Waltham' butternut squash is a classic, culinary favorite that is an important part of the "pumpkin" in canned pumpkin. Any type of acorn squash will have bright,

creamy flesh and a nutty-sweet flavor, but a compact early such as 'Early Acorn Hybrid' produces four to six large fruits that have a chance of ripening even in short-summer areas; they are also good for container culture.

Atlantic Dill, Big Moon, or Prizewinner (*Cucurbita maxima*): These are the most likely contenders for the Great Pumpkin that poor Linus van Pelt, of the Peanuts gang, patiently waits for in the pumpkin patch every Halloween. These squashes are the ones that most avid growers cultivate as giants to enter into the biggest pumpkin contests. However, you don't want to grow one to its maximum size for your pumpkin ale. Let these vines set many pumpkins to keep the size from becoming too large to move or fit in the oven come roasting time.

Butternut or acorn squash (*Cucurbita moschata*): While definitely not a pumpkin, butternut and acorn squash are delicious and some of the easiest winter squashes to bring from harvest to puree. These provide great flavoring for pies and have a smooth flesh, so grow some for Thanksgiving deserts and put the rest into your favorite beer recipe.

Botanical name: *Cucumis sativus*

Plant type: vining annual vegetable

USDA zones: 4 to 11

Height: 2 feet (61 cm) trailing, or can be trellised to 6 to 8 feet (1.8 to 2.4 m)

Soil: rich and well-drained, amended with compost

Light: full sun

Water: regular; apply 1 gallon (3.8 L) per week once the fruit sets.

Growth habit: trailing vines

Propagate by: seed. Sow seeds in the ground 2 weeks after the average date of last frost. To get an earlier start, seed indoors about 3 weeks before you will transplant them in the ground. They like bottom heat from a heat mat.

Spacing: 18 to 36 inches (46 to 91 cm). Plant several seeds in one spot and thin to the best seedling.

Months to bearing: two to three

Pruning: none

Harvest: Harvest slicing cucumbers when they about 6 to 8 inches (15 to 20 cm), picklers at 4 to 6 inches (10 to 15 cm). Pick when they are uniformly green and before they begin to yellow. Keep the fruit picked or the vines will stop producing.

Notes: Bush-type cucumbers can be grown in containers. Cucumbers are heavy feeders. Apply fish emulsion every month, beginning when plants are 8 inches (20 cm) tall. Add cucumber to beer as a secondary to help retain the fresh, crisp flavor. Put it in sooner and you lose the flavor.

CUCUMBERS

This popular warm-season crop has about the same cultivation requirements as pumpkins and squash. Unlike their cousins, cucumbers don't need the same amount of real estate to grow in the garden, and you can grow the vine up a trellis system or grow the bush types on the ground or in a 5-gallon (19 L) container if you are short on space. If you trellis your cucumber plants, you can space them closer together at 6 inches (15 cm) apart. Growing them on the ground, you will need to space your plants 18 to 36 inches (46 to 91 cm) apart depending on the variety. The seed packet will tell you the best spacing for a particular variety.

LEMON CUCUMBER

The day before sowing cucumber seeds, presoak the seeds in water overnight. Sow two to three seeds per hill. When they germinate, choose the best seedling and prune or pinch out (don't pull) the other plants to the ground. Cucumbers grow quickly and are heavy feeders, so throw in a handful of a complete organic fertilizer at planting time and give them monthly feedings after they sprout. Plants grown in containers will need a weekly feeding. Keep the plants consistently watered or you will end up with hollow, bitter fruit. When hot weather arrives, containers can dry out quickly and you may need to water daily. If you grow your vines vertically, keep training them up their trellis.

You might want to try the somewhat sweeter tasting lemon cucumber as an alternative to the green one for your beer. Either way, cucumber is an ingredient you will want to add after primary fermentation, as the flavor is quite delicate.

MELONS

For the amount of space they need, melons have slow-growing vines and yields are not very high. You must be a serious gardener and brewer to want to grow melons to put in your brew. However, you will earn the bragging rights for this crop.

Keep your melon patch weeded so the vines won't have to compete for nutrients. Consistent watering is a must for best flavor. You want your soil to be humus rich because when the melons begin to ripen you will need to cut back on the amount of water you add to the soil. The humus in the soil retains moisture while keeping the soil from becoming too soggy, which in turn will give you better tasting melons.

Muskmelons (cantaloupe being one of them) can be trellised if you are short on space. Presoak your seeds to aid in germinating. The seeds will not germinate if soil temperatures are below 65°F (18°C). You can prewarm the soil by putting a plastic tunnel over it. Plant seeds 2 weeks after the average last frost date for your area in hills 1 foot (30 cm) apart if you grow them vertically, or plant them 3 to 4 feet (0.9 to 1.2 m) apart and let them

wander around on the ground. To harvest your melons, hold the stem in one hand and give the fruit a twist with your other hand. When the melon is ripe, it slips off the stem easily. If the melon doesn't slip off, leave it for a few more days and try again. Watermelon is another beer-friendly melon. Two incurable diseases that are prevalent in watermelon are fusarium and bacterial wilt, so choose disease-resistant varieties. As with other summer melons, watermelons need warm soil to germinate and warm weather to ripen. Plant seeds 2 weeks after the average last frost date for your area. Alternatively, you can transplant starts that were sown 6 weeks earlier and grown in a greenhouse or under lights. The starts resent transplanting, so plant them carefully with little disturbance of their roots. Space planting hills about 6 feet (1.8 m) apart and sow four to six seeds per hill. Thin seedlings down to the healthiest three. You can also grow in rows with one plant every 2 to 4 feet (0.6 to 1.2 m). Cover with plastic tunnels to keep the soil warm if the weather is still on the cool side or nighttime temperatures are dipping down below 50°F (10°C).

It is important to give your watermelon plants regular deep watering the first month. After the vine starts to set fruit, cut back on watering so as not to dilute the fruit sugars and make the fruit less flavorful. You can tell the watermelon is ripe when the curly tendril closest to the fruit turns brown.

Botanical name: *Cucumis melo* (muskmelon varieties); *Citrullus lanatus* (watermelon)

Plant type: vining annual vegetable

USDA zones: 4 to 11

Height: 1 to 2 feet (30 to 61 cm) trailing. Trellised muskmelons can reach 6 to 8 feet (1.8 to 2.4 m).

Soil: rich and well-drained, amended with compost

Light: full sun, three months of heat

Water: consistent; cut back on water as the fruit begins to ripen. Use soaker hoses or drip irrigation to keep water off the leaves.

Growth habit: trailing vines

Propagate by: seed. Plant when the ground temperature is above 70°F (21°C). Presoak seed to increase germination. Plant seeds 2 weeks after average last frost date. Or, transplant from starts sown 6 weeks earlier in peat pots and grown in a greenhouse or under lights. Don't disturb the roots at planting out.

Spacing: 1 foot (30 cm) apart if grown on a trellis, or 3 to 4 feet (0.9 to 1.2 m) apart if allowed to sprawl. Sow several seeds per spot and thin to the best two to three seedlings.

Months to bearing: three

Pruning: none

Harvest: For muskmelons, hold the stem in one hand and give the fruit a twist with your other hand. When the melon is ripe, it slips off the stem easily. If the melon doesn't slip off, leave it for a few more days and try again. For watermelon, pick when the curly tendril closest to the fruit turns brown.

Notes: Muskmelons can be trellised. Amend the planting area with 4 to 6 inches (10 to 15 cm) of compost or well-rotted manure. Like other cucurbits, they are heavy feeders and need room to grow. Apply fish emulsion every month, beginning when plants are 8 inches (20 cm) tall. Choose watermelon varieties that are fusarium and bacterial wilt resistant.

A FEW FINAL IDEAS

You've seen the range of plants that made gruit ale popular for centuries, thought about watermelons, and maybe even planted your squash or cucumber. What else could there possibly be for your beer? Well, there are plenty of other options.

SPRUCE

Spruce needle beer is a spring tradition that dates back centuries, mainly because making the beer with fresh spring needles brings a refreshing, unsweetened cola-like taste to beer. (If you harvest the needles later in the season, your beer will smell more as though it's made for thinning paint!)

SPRUCE

Botanical name: *Picea* species

Plant type: coniferous evergreen trees

USDA zones: 2 to 8 depending on species; prefer cool, mild summers

Height: 4 to 150 feet (1.2 to 46 m) depending on species and type. Dwarf varieties are available, which can be grown in a container on the deck or as part of the landscape.

Soil: moderately moist, sandy, acidic, well-drained soil

Light: full sun to part shade

Water: low to moderate

Growth habit: pyramidal to conical, dwarf varieties available

Propagate by: cuttings, grafting

Spacing: dependent on cultivar

Years to bearing: 1 to 2 years

Pruning: little needed; light pinching or shearing to maintain tidy shape

Harvest: You don't need to harvest many needles for the brew, but keep in mind to always use the freshest new needles.

Notes: Spruces are low-maintenance landscape plants. They do not perform well in areas of high heat and humidity. Fresh, young, spring needles are used to give beer a refreshing, unsweetened cola flavor. Mature needles are not used because they taste like turpentine. Spruce essence is available in brew shops, but doesn't compare to the taste of fresh needles. Many species of spruce can be used for flavoring.

The new shoots of many spruces are a great source of vitamin C, which helps stabilize the finished beer. Historically, the British Royal Navy added the needles to their ship-brewed beer to treat scurvy.

Harvesting fresh needles from the wild can mean climbing towering trees, but it can also be as simple as hunting down young trees. In fact, if you're looking for a small tree to plant, your yard can easily accommodate a dwarf version of a recommended spruce in a container on the deck, or as part of the landscape—and you can use the first growth of fresh, new needles.

If you live in an area where you can grow a spruce, they are wonderful conifer trees for the home landscape. For the Pacific Northwest, a dwarf spruce such as Sitka spruce (*Picea* 'Papoose') would be the best choice. The conical Alberta spruce (*Picea glauca* 'Conica') or blue spruce (*Picea pungens*) would be better suited for many colder regions. The Colorado blue spruce, *Picea pungens*, 'Fat Albert,' is worth growing for the name alone but is also an outstanding garden specimen.

Choose the best-recommended variety for the region you live in. The trees will reward you as a beautiful specimen in your landscape and provide some fresh needles for your spring brew.

Most recipes use a very small quantity of needles—not more than 4 or 5 ounces (115 or 140 g). Even though you don't need to harvest many needles for the brew, keep in mind to always use the freshest new ones. Even a small amount of old spruce can ruin a beer. Also, if you've ever bought spruce essence in homebrew shops, keep in mind that fresh spruce is very different. While the bottled stuff can come off like a pine-cleaning product, fresh spruce in small amounts can make a light bodied beer with a cola-like taste—and it could become a new favorite spring brew.

CITRUS

Unless you are living in Arizona, Florida, or parts of California—or equally warm areas of your continent where you can grow them in the ground—citrus will not grow well in your region, and growing your citrus in a container will be necessary.

To grow citrus successfully in pots, choose varieties grafted onto dwarf rootstock, which are suitable for confinement in a container. Some cultivars will do well growing outside in cold climates when brought into a greenhouse for the colder months. Other varieties can transition to houseplant status when the weather turns cold outside. Even a balcony garden can accommodate a dwarf citrus tree as long as it is growing in full sun.

Botanical name: *Citrus × limon* (lemon), *C. latifolia* and *C. aurantifolia* (lime), *C. × sinensis* (orange), *C. × paradis* (grapefruit)

Plant type: broadleaf evergreen trees

USDA zones: 9 to 11 in the ground. Farther north in a greenhouse or sunroom.

Height: up to 50 feet (15 m) depending on variety; dwarf 3 to 10 feet (0.9 to 3 m)

Soil: Citrus is adaptable to a range of soil types. It does poorly in salty soil.

Light: full sun. The bark of citrus is thin and must be protected from intense sun.

Water: regular. Citrus trees have relatively shallow root systems. Water well over the entire root zone. Established trees will tolerate some drought but won't produce high-quality fruit.

Growth habit: dense

Propagate by: grafting, budding, cuttings

Spacing: dependent on type and variety

Years to bearing: 3 to 5 years

Pruning: Remove suckers coming from below the graft. Remove any shoots that extend beyond the general shape of the tree. Thin overly dense foliage to promote air circulation and light penetration. Citrus can be trained as shrubs or hedges, or limbed up into a tree. If the trunk is exposed, it will need protection from sunburn. Many citrus types have formidable thorns.

Harvest: Oranges, lemons, and grapefruit should all be completely free of green coloration. Limes don't change color, so judge ripeness by size and season.

Notes: Where you live determines which types and varieties of citrus you can grow. Gardeners out of citrus-friendly climates can grow containerized Improved Meyer lemons, bringing them into the house or greenhouse for the winter. In fact, the farther you live from the equator, the better the quality of your citrus fruit—until you hit frost. In order from least- to most-resilient to frost: lime, lemon, grapefruit, orange, Meyer lemon. Fertilize trees in January through March. Citrus in containers should be fed January through June. A fertilizer with micronutrients is important, especially for container-grown trees.

LEMON FLOWERS

As in any other gardening endeavor, choose the best varieties for your specific region to increase your chances of success. Often a plant does not grow well because it was the wrong variety for the climate, soil type, and so on. In warm zones where you can grow your trees and shrubs in the ground, check with your County Extension agent to find out the best varieties suitable for your county. Another source for information on good cultivars for the home garden is a local citrus garden club. Some clubs may even have local plant sales or exhibits of the best cultivars to grow. The big box stores may sell citrus, but the plants may be more suitable for another region and not yours, so buy your stock plants from reputable, locally owned garden nurseries that choose the best varieties for your area. Invest in good quality stock that will give you fruit for many years to come.

HOT PEPPERS

Peppers—no matter if they are hot, sweet, or bland tasting—like growing in the heat. If the climate where you live doesn't give you hot summers, grow your pepper plants against a south-facing wall or in a hoop house to increase the warmth around your plants. You can harvest your fruit at almost any stage of their growth. The heat of your peppers will be considerably greater the more mature they are at the time of picking. Once the pepper has turned its final color, pick it; waiting any longer causes the peppers to decline quickly. If you aren't sure when they are mature, the rule of thumb is to begin harvesting the first peppers 75 to 90 days after transplanting them. However, the hotter the climate, the sooner the peppers are ready. The easiest way to harvest most peppers is to use pruners to cut the fruit off the plant.

Generally, serrano peppers are picked while they are still green, and the cayennes and tabasco peppers are picked when they are red and a bit soft and come off the plant easily. Jalapeños should be their full size of around 3 inches (7.6 cm), depending on the variety, and dark green when you begin harvesting them. Later, when they display corking (tan streaking), they are good for pickling. Red is their final mature stage and that is when the flavor turns both hot and sweet. Habaneros' ripe color will vary according to variety, but are picked at their final stage color.

Same cautions apply when you are harvesting your hot fruit and want to rub your eyes. Don't! Wear gloves and keep those away from your eyes, too.

Caution also applies to how many peppers to add to your batch of beer. Do you like just a touch of pepper heat and good flavor or would you prefer more of a jalapeño twist? Maybe you prefer a breathe-through-your-ears sensation from the hottest, spiciest beer your mouth can handle. For your first venture into spicing up your brew, start with a recipe with good reviews. Some recipes call for adding peppers to the boil; others call for using them in the secondary; and some call for both. Adjust and experiment until you design your own recipe that matches your heat tolerance. If you find a batch is too hot, let the bottles age to mellow the heat. Still too hot? Use the beer in a chili recipe! If you can't use your peppers right away, store them in a paper bag with their stems still attached and place in the refrigerator where they will store up to 1 week.

Botanical name: *Capsicum annuum* (jalapeños, wax, cayenne, paprika, and bell peppers), *Capsicum chinense* (habanero)

Plant type: herbaceous perennials, grown as annuals in cooler zones

USDA zones: 4 to 13, hardy in Zone 11 and above

Height: 1 to 4 feet (0.3 to 1.2 m)

Soil: sandy loam amended with compost

Light: full sun

Water: regular

Growth habit: low, shrubby

Propagate by: seed

Spacing: 18 to 24 inches (46 to 61 cm)

Months to harvest: 2 to 5 months from planting out

Pruning: none

Harvest: Most peppers reach peak flavor once they turn their mature color of red, orange, yellow, or purple.

Notes: Peppers need at least 70°F (21°C) to grow and set flowers. However, if the temperature is higher than 90°F (32°C) or lower than 60°F (16°C), the plants drop their blossoms. Peppers are only direct-seeded in the very warmest zones. Most gardeners buy starts or sow pepper seed indoors 10 to 12 weeks before the last expected frost. Transplants are set out when nights are consistently at or above 55°F (13°C), approximately 2 to 3 weeks after the last expected date of frost. Peppers make good container plants. In the ground or in containers, peppers benefit from a complete organic fertilizer worked into the soil before transplanting, which should be enough to see the plants through the season.

ANAHEIM CHILI

PEPPER PLANTS

RESOURCES

BOOKS

BREWING PUBLICATIONS

Calagione, Sam
Brewing Up a Business: Adventures in Beer from the Founder of Dogfish Head Craft Brewery. Hoboken, NJ: John Wiley and Sons Inc, 2005

Calagione, Sam
Extreme Brewing: An Enthusiast's Guide to Brewing Craft Beer at Home. Beverly, MA: Quarry Books, 2006

Daniels, Ray
Designing Great Beers: The Ultimate Guide to Brewing Classic Beer Styles. Boulder, CO: Brewers Publications, 2000

Hieronymus, Stan
Brew Like a Monk: Trappist, Abbey, and Strong Belgian Ales and How to Brew Them. Boulder, CO: Brewers Publications, 2005

Higgins, Patrick
The Homebrewers' Recipe Guide. New York, NY: Fireside, 1996

Mosher, Randy
Radical Brewing: Recipes, Tales and World-Altering Meditations in a Glass. Boulder, CO: Brewers Publications, 2004

Noonan, Gregory J
New Brewing Lager Beer: The Most Comprehensive Book for Home and Microbrewers. Boulder, CO: Brewers Publications, 2003

Palmer, John J
How to Brew: Everything You Need to Know to Brew Beer Right the First Time. Boulder, CO: Brewers Publications, 2006

Papazian, Charlie
The Complete Joy of Homebrewing. New York, NY: HarperResource, 2003

Schramm, Ken
The Complete Meadmaker: Home Production of Honey Wine from Your First Batch to Award-winning Fruit and Herb Variations. Boulder, CO: Brewers Publications, 2003

Sparrow, Jeff
Wild Brews: Beer Beyond the Influence of Brewer's Yeast. Boulder, CO: Brewers Publications, 2005

Watson, Ben
Cider, Hard and Sweet: History, Traditions, and Making Your Own. Woodstock, VT: Countryman Press, 2008

Wheeler, Graham
Brew Your Own British Real Ale. St Albans, England: CAMRA Books, 2009

White, Chris and Jamil Zainasheff
Yeast: The Practical Guide to Beer Fermentation. Boulder, CO: Brewers Publications, 2010

Brew Your Own
Battenkill Communications.
www.byo.com

The New Brewer
https://www.brewersassociation.org/resources/the-new-brewer/current-issue/

Zymurgy
https://www.homebrewersassociation.org/magazine/ezymurgy/

ONLINE RESOURCES

BeerAdvocate
Beer ratings and forums.
www.beeradvocate.com

Brewing Network Forum
Brewing forums and radio.
www.thebrewingnetwork.com/
forum

Cicerone
Cicerone Certification Program.
www.cicerone.org

CraftBeer.com
Beer guide from the Brewers
Association.
www.craftbeer.com

HomeBrewTalk
Homebrewing community and
forums.
www.homebrewtalk.com

**Northern Brewer Homebrew
Forum**
Popular forums connected to
the homebrew retailer.
forum.northernbrewer.com

RateBeer
Beer ratings and forums.
www.ratebeer.com

ONLINE HOMEBREW SHOPS

Austin Homebrew Supply
Austin, TX
www.austinhomebrew.com

Brooklyn Homebrew
Brooklyn, NY
www.brooklyn-homebrew.com

Home Brew Mart
San Diego, CA
www.homebrewmart.com

Keystone Homebrew Supply
Montgomeryville, PA
www.keystonehomebrew.com

Midwest Supplies
Minneapolis, MN
www.midwestsupplies.com

More Beer!
Concord, CA
www.morebeer.com

Northern Brewer
St. Paul, MN
www.northernbrewer.com

William's Brewing
San Leandro, CA
www.williamsbrewing.com

PHOTO CREDITS

Chapter 1
Belgian Tourist Office: page 36

BillBl, flickr.com/photos/
billbliss: page 31

John Bollwitt (johnbollwitt.
com): page 35

Jonathan Castner
Photography: page 32

Lorena Cupcake, flickr.com/
photos/juliet-banana: page 30
(left)

@epicbeer: page 27 (bottom)
Firestone Walker Brewing Co.:
page 34

Joe Hakim/thehungrydudes.
com: page 29

Hameisterphoto.com: page 39

Logan Ingalls: page 13

k4dordy: page 25

Bernt Rostad, flickr.com/
photos/brostad: pages 24 and
30 (right)

Russian River Brewing
Company: pages 22 and 23

DJ Spiess: page 33

Hans Splinter: page 10

shutterstock.com: page 7

Stone Brewing Co.: 19 (bottom)

Urban Knaves of Grain:
page 38

Gail Williams: page 21

Ralph Woodall, courtesy of
Hopunion, LLC: pages 19
(top) and 27 (top)

Chapter 2
All photos provided by
shutterstock.com

Chapter 3
All photography by Kevin
Fleming, except page 67,
provided by shutterstock.
com

Chapter 4
Historical Images:
Jonny Thompson/www.
jonnythompson.co.uk
shutterstock.com: pages
113 and 116

Studio photography:
© 2013 Glenn Scott
Photography/www.
glennscottphotography.
com

Chapter 5
All photos provided by
Wendy Tweton and Debbie
Teashon, except for pages
177, 179, 180, 182, 187,
189, 191, 198, 202, 205,
and 206, provided by
shutterstock.com

Other
Photos on pages 5 and 177
provided by shutterstock.
com

GLOSSARY

ABV: alcohol percentage by volume.

Aerate: the process of dissolving air into wort at the beginning of fermentation to promote yeast cell growth.

Airlock: the device used to allow gas to escape but prevent air from entering the neck of the carboy of fermenting beer.

Ale yeast: a top fermenting yeast that ferments best at warmer temperatures. This yeast is anaerobic and will settle to the bottom of the carboy after fermentation.

Alpha acids: the amount of bitterness in hops. Low alpha hops are in the 2 to 5 percent range; high alpha hops are in the 9 percent and over range. Brewers also calibrate hopping volumes in IBUS (International Bittering Units), which tell how bitter the beer is, whereas alpha acids indicate how bitter the hops themselves are.

Attemperator: a network of pipes inside a fermenting vessel through which cold water is passed to cool fermenting wort.

Attenuation: the degree to which the sugars in a wort have been fermented. Apparent attenuation is calculated by subtracting the final gravity from the original gravity and dividing the result by the original gravity.

Barley: the grain that provides the most common source of fermentable sugar in beer.

Beta acid: a chemical found in the lupulin gland of hops.

Brettanomyces: a type of yeast responsible for the secondary conditioning of stock ales. It was first discovered in a sample of British beer analyzed in 1904 by N. Hjelte Claussen at the Carlsberg brewery.

Brewpot: a pot, preferably stainless steel, in which beer is brewed.

Carboy: the preferred fermenting and aging vessel used in homebrewing. Usually this glass container is either 5 or 6.5 gallons (19 L or 25 L) and has a thin neck at the top into which you can insert a rubber stopper and fermentation lock.

Cleansing: removing yeast from fermenting wort.

Coke: a type of smokeless fuel produced by heating coal to very high temperatures.

Conical fermenters: large, closed cylindrical fermentation vessels, usually made from stainless steel, with a cone at the bottom.

Copper: the vessel in which the wort is boiled with the hops.

Demerara sugar: a brown sugar that is commonly used in brewing.

Diastatic malt: malt in which sufficient enzymes remain to convert the starches in the grains into fermentable sugars. Most modern colored malts, such as amber, black, and brown, have been kilned in such a way that the enzymes are destroyed. These malts cannot be used by themselves and require a diastatic malt such as pale malt to provide the necessary enzymes for mashing.

Dry hopping: the addition of whole leaf or palletized hops during or after primary fermentation.

Ester: a fermentation byproduct that contributes fruity characteristics to the aroma and flavor of the beer.

Export: the name given in Scotland to a strong pale ale.

Fermentation: the natural process by which yeast converts sugar to alcohol and the byproduct in carbon dioxide.

Fermentation lock: the plastic device that fits into the top of your fermenting bucket or carboy. It allows carbon dioxide to escape but prevents unsterile air from getting into beer.

Fermenter: the vessel to which you add the wort and yeast to ferment into beer.

Final gravity (FG): the specific gravity of the wort before fermentation.

Fined: beer that has been cleared using finings.

Fining: a clarifying procedure used in the brewing process. Usually these gelatinous products (isinglass and Irish moss are most common) are added to brighten and clarify the beer.

Finish hops: also called aroma hops, Pelletized or whole-leaf hops used toward the end of the boil. The late addition of these hops will contribute more hop aroma in the smell of the beer than hop flavor in the taste.

Free Mash Tun Act: an 1880 act of Parliament that removed restrictions on brewing ingredients, allowing brewers to use whatever they chose. Between 1816 and 1880, only malt, hops, water, and yeast (after 1847, also sugar) had been allowed.

Gantry: a metal frame used to hold together the casks in a Burton union set.

Gravity: this term is used three ways in homebrewing—specific, original, and final. Specific gravity is the measure of the density of beer compared to the density of water. If a reading is higher than 1,000 than the liquid is more dense than water. The higher the concentrations of sugar in a beer the higher the gravity. Original gravity is the density of the beer before it starts to ferment. Final gravity is the density of the beer after it has finished fermenting.

Grup up: dig up plants and destroy them.

Gyle: the same as wort.

Hop pellets: Hop buds that have been processed and compressed.

Hop tea: a solution of hops and hot water.

Hops: a perennial flowering vine; the female buds are used in flavoring, bittering, and preserving beer.

Hot break: the settling of protein and hop solids that condense and collect in the bottom of your kettle after the beer has been boiled.

Hydrometer: a glass, calibrated, measuring device that reveals the specific gravity of a liquid.

Initial heat: the heat of the mash after the water and grains have been mixed.

Invert sugar: a mixture of fructose and glucose that is made by breaking apart sucrose (table sugar).

Keeping beer: beer that was aged, in the case of porter and stout in enormous vats, before sale.

Kiln: the equipment used to reduce moisture during the malt and hop manufacturing processes.

Krausen: the fluffy foam that grows on the top of wort as it begins to ferment.

Lactose: or milk sugar, a type of sugar found in milk that cannot be fermented by normal yeast. It is used to add sweetness.

Lager (verb): derived from the German term for storage; to age or condition the beer for extended periods of time at cool temperatures.

Lager yeast: a family of brewing yeasts that work best at cooler temperatures; considered a bottom-fermenting yeast because it doesn't form a head and ferments within, and not on top of, the beer.

Lambic: Belgian-style beers fermented via wild yeast and bacteria present in the air and aged in wood barrels.

Lovibond: a measurement scale that calibrates the level of color in barley.

Maillard reaction: a form of browning caused by a chemical reaction between sugar and an amino acid under the influence of heat.

Malt: any cereal grain that has gone through the malting process.

Malt extract (or wort concentrate): a syrup or powder that has been created by condensing wort or prefermented beer. The most common form of barley sugars in novice homebrewing.

Malted barley: the form of barley used by brewers, it has been partially germinated and then quickly dried so that sugars, starches, and enzymes can be accessed through the brewing process.

Maltose: malt sugar.

Maltster: a person who works in a malting facility.

Mash tun: the vessel used for mashing.

Mashing: hydrating the milled malted barley to convert the grain starches into sugars. The process of conversion occurs between 140°F and 160°F (60°C and 70°C).

Multiroom pub: where the middle classes drank or men accompanied by their wives.

Parti-gyling: blending the worts produced from mashing and sparging to make several beers of different strengths.

Pitching: the adding of yeast to the wort after it has come down to a desired temperature. The pitching rate of a beer is determined by calculating how many yeast cells are required to ferment a certain volume of beer.

Ponto: a large barrel used for cleansing.

Priming: a high-gravity sugar solution added at racking time to provide fermentable material for cask conditioning.

Proprietary sugar: a blend of different sugars sold as a proprietary brand.

Public bar: the cheapest room in a multiroom pub; often men only

Racking: the term for transferring wort or beer from one vessel to another. A siphon and hose are commonly used in racking beer that has finished fermenting so as to leave the unwanted yeast solids behind.

Round: a round vessel used for primary fermentation.

Running beer: beer sold almost immediately after the end of primary fermentation, without being aged.

Saccharomyces cerevisiae: the Latin name for any ale or lager yeast.

Saloon bar: a more expensive room in a multiroom pub.

Sanitize: the process of cleaning and sterilizing any surface that comes into contact with beer or brewing materials. Yeast is highly susceptible to mutation and poor fermentation in a poorly sanitized environment.

Secondary conditioning or secondary fermentation: a long, slow fermentation that takes place during the aging process usually as a result of the activity of Brettanomyces.

Settling square: used in the dropping system of fermentation, a broad, shallow vessel into which the wort is dropped after one or two days of fermenting in a taller, narrower vessel.

Sparging: the process of rinsing the grains with hot water to optimize the collection of sugars.

Square: a square vessel used for primary fermentation.

SRM (standard reference method): a scale used to describe the color of beer.

Steep: adding grains or hops to hot, but not boiling, wort.

Stillion: a metal frame used for holding barrels during the cleansing process.

Strike heat: the heat of mashing water before being mixed with the grains.

Top-fermenting beer: beer brewed with yeast that rises to the top during fermentation and that also prefers relatively warm temperatures, 60°F to 70°F (15.6°C to 21.1°C).

Tun: a cask with a capacity of 108 imperial gallons (408 L).

Underletting: adding water to the mash tun via the underlet, i.e., from the bottom of the mash tun

Whole-leaf hops: hops leaves that have been dried but not compressed into pellets and are ready to be used in their natural state

Wort: the sugary liquid produced by mashing or sparging

Yeast: the living organism that coverts sugar into alcohol. In addition to driving the fermentation process, certain yeast strains will contribute different flavors and aromas to different beers. The fermentation process is anaerobic and, at a certain concentration, alcohol becomes toxic to the yeast and breaks down its cell wall. That is why no naturally fermented beer can be as strong as a distilled spirit.

INDEX

ALSO AVAILABLE FROM THE QUARTO GROUP

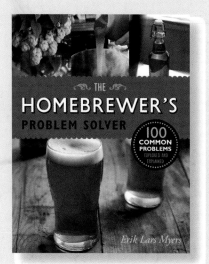

The Homebrewer's
Problem Solver
978-1-63159-308-6

Apples to Cider
978-1-59253-918-5

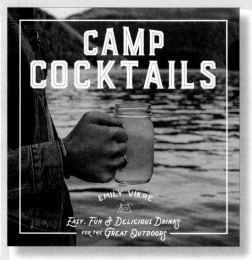

Camp Cocktails
978-0-76036-253-2

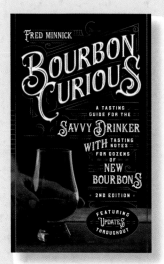

Bourbon Curious
978-0-76036-490-1

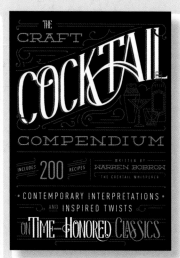

The Craft Cocktail
Compendium
978-1-59233-762-0

DIY Bitters
978-1-59233-704-0